Dissent and the Failure of Leadership

NEW HORIZONS IN LEADERSHIP STUDIES

Series Editor: Joanne B. Ciulla
Professor and Coston Family Chair in Leadership and Ethics,
Jepson School of Leadership Studies, University of Richmond, USA

This important series is designed to make a significant contribution to the development of leadership studies. This field has expanded dramatically in recent years and the series provides an invaluable forum for the publication of high quality works of scholarship and shows the diversity of leadership issues and practices around the world.

The main emphasis of the series is on the development and application of new and original ideas in leadership studies. It pays particular attention to leadership in business, economics and public policy and incorporates the wide range of disciplines which are now part of the field. Global in its approach, it includes some of the best theoretical and empirical work with contributions to fundamental principles, rigorous evaluations and existing concepts and competing theories, historical surveys and future visions.

Titles in the series include:

The Moral Capital of Leaders
Why Virtue Matters
Alejo José G. Sison

The Leadership Dilemma in Modern Democracy
Kenneth P. Ruscio

The New Russian Business Leaders
Manfred F.R. Kets de Vries, Stanislav Shekshnia, Konstantin Korotov and Elizabeth Florent-Treacy

Lessons on Leadership by Terror
Finding Shaka Zulu in the Attic
Manfred F.R. Kets de Vries

Leadership in Context
The Four Faces of Capitalism
Mark N. Wexler

The Quest for Moral Leaders
Essays on Leadership Ethics
Edited by Joanne B. Ciulla, Terry L. Price and Susan E. Murphy

The Quest for a General Theory of Leadership
Edited by George R. Goethals and Georgia L.J. Sorenson

Inventing Leadership
The Challenge of Democracy
J. Thomas Wren

Dissent and the Failure of Leadership
Edited by Stephen P. Banks

Dissent and the Failure of Leadership

Edited by

Stephen P. Banks

University of Idaho, USA

NEW HORIZONS IN LEADERSHIP STUDIES

Edward Elgar

Cheltenham, UK • Northampton, MA, USA

Published by
Edward Elgar Publishing Limited
Glensanda House
Montpellier Parade
Cheltenham
Glos GL50 1UA
UK

Edward Elgar Publishing, Inc.
William Pratt House
9 Dewey Court
Northampton
Massachusetts 01060
USA

A catalogue record for this book
is available from the British Library

Library of Congress Control Number: 2008927700

ISBN 978 1 84720 575 9

Printed and bound in Great Britain by MPG Books Ltd, Bodmin, Cornwall

Contents

v

Contributors

David S. Allen PhD is Professor and Chair of the Department of Communication at the University of Wisconsin, USA.

Stephen P. Banks PhD is Professor and Head of the Communication Studies Program at the University of Idaho, USA.

Patrice M. Buzzanell PhD is Professor of Communication at Purdue University, USA.

George Cheney PhD is Professor of Communication and Director of Peace and Conflict Studies, University of Utah, USA.

Gail T. Fairhurst PhD is Professor of Communication and Director of the Center for the Study of Environmental Communication at the University of Cincinnati, USA.

Ruth Guzley PhD is Professor, Chair of the Department of Communication and Coordinator of the Leadership Studies Program at California State University, Chico, USA.

Stephanie Hamel PhD is Assistant Professor of Communication at California State University, Chico, USA.

Daniel J. Lair PhD is Assistant Professor of Communication at the University of Denver, USA.

Jean Lipman-Blumen PhD is Thornton Bradshaw Professor of Public Policy and co-founding Director of the Institute for Advanced Studies in Leadership at the Claremont Graduate School, USA.

Brian Martin PhD is Professor of Social Sciences in the School of Social Sciences, Media and Communication at the University of Wollongong, Australia.

Rebecca Meisenbach PhD is Assistant Professor of Communication at the University of Missouri-Columbia, USA.

Robyn Penman PhD is an independent scholar and Affiliate Professor at the University of Canberra, Australia.

Robyn Remke PhD is Assistant Professor of Communication at Southern Illinois University, USA.

Howard F. Stein PhD is Professor of Organizational Psychology at the University of Oklahoma School of Medicine, USA.

Paul Toscano JD is an attorney in private practice in Salt Lake City, Utah, USA.

Heather Zoller PhD is Associate Professor of Communication at the University of Cincinnati, USA.

Preface

The contributors to this volume were moved to write about leadership and dissent because of the persistence and growth of leadership failures. Over the past two decades, as research studies and popular books on leadership effectiveness multiplied exponentially, instances of leaders who have ruined business organizations, led religious institutions to cover up illegal and immoral behavior, initiated pre-emptive war and failed to prevent whole-sale slaughter of civilian populations – that is, instances of leadership failure – have mushroomed to the point where we no longer are shocked by scandals and institutional catastrophes. Lee Iacocca's strenuous demand to know 'what the hell has happened to our leaders?' (Iacocca, 2007: 7), seems almost quaintly atavistic.

Yet Iacocca's polemic has merit. We agree that there are unprecedented failings among leaders of democratic institutions and purportedly merit-driven systems. We agree that much of the trend is attributable to personal greed, careerism, hubris and arrogance – and passivity among the elec-torate and consumer public. What is missing from Iacocca's analysis, however, and from most scholarly work on leadership, is a focus on the crit-ically important role of dissent.

Leaders face the influence of dissent in two main ways. First, one of the central tasks undertaken by all position-leaders is to deal with resistance to their leadership. That is, what leaders do fundamentally is to overcome con-trarian challenges to their vision of problems and opportunities, to their direction-giving and to their meanings. In short, leaders manage dissent. Of course managing dissent isn't all that leaders do. But if they don't do *something* about contrarian visions, contested power and diverse understand-ings, they aren't leading or in a leadership situation. They're merely occupying a position.

The second way leaders and dissent are related is found in the resources dissent brings to leadership. Dissent is the contrast medium by which we recognize leadership. More importantly, dissenters bring to decision-making fresh information, unpopular or non-normative perspectives and agendas, challenges to accepted ways of thinking and acting, opportunities to test and improve understandings. In the highly dynamic environment faced by governments, work organizations and other institutions in the early twenty-first century, vigorous and open engagement of leaders and dissenters is essential for successful anticipation and response to increasingly rapid social and technological change.

For these reasons, we offer in this collection of essays a focused exploration of dissent and leadership failures. By examining how the subversion or denial of dissent contributes to leadership failure, we aim to provide a diagnosis that will head us toward some tentative remedies. In the first chapter I analyze shortcomings in our language of leadership and our understanding of its foundational assumptions. Brian Martin describes in Chapter 2 the wide variety of forms dissent takes, along with their contexts and their typical consequences. The social and psychological aspects of dissent when the going is tense or dangerous because of perceived crises is the topic of Jean Lipman-Blumen's Chapter 3. In Chapter 4 Stephanie Hamel and Ruth Guzley examine the potential for effective dissent across generations, with special concern for the 'Millennial' generation.

Following these foundational chapters are essays that focus on ways dissent is expressed and managed in various settings. In Chapter 5 Howard F. Stein explores the language of dissent management in work organizations and presents vivid cases to illustrate the human consequences of suppressed dissent. Chapter 6 presents an examination of leaders' uses of public relations for engaging dissenters; there I also show how public relations can be a force for dissenting from misguided leadership. In Chapter 7 Patrice M. Buzzanell, Rebecca Meisenbach and Robyn Remke illustrate how women in work and community organizations become channeled into dissenting roles; more pivotally, they show how women use dissent productively, both for improving institutional processes and for balancing women's power in groups by engaging in dissent leadership. Chapter 8, by Gail T. Fairhurst and Heather Zoller, takes leadership in dissenting groups as its central concern; through analysis of resistance within team-based participative management systems, they highlight five key lessons for leadership generated by understanding dissent. In David S. Allen's Chapter 9, the professionalization and rationalization of journalism are shown to exert contraining forces on dissent among journalists and, by extension, to manage dissent among citizens. Paul Toscano argues in Chapter 10 that to dissent is a sacred act, and he shows how dissent in religious life is necessary for the spiritual well-being of believers and religious institutions. Chapter 11 engages one of the most profound concerns of dissent and leadership – their interrelation in cultures of fear during war and in people's work lives. Considering both political discourse and work discourse to be our new public sphere, George Cheney and Daniel J. Lair argue that fear and fearfulness are behind the paradoxes and parallels of dissent in the public spheres of politics, particularly during times of war, and the workplace.

In the penultimate chapter, Chapter 12, Robyn Penman offers fresh thinking on the problems of dissent management by leaders. Linking dissent to the Enlightenment quest for certainty and the denial of diversity, Penman demonstrates how a new approach to communicating and a post-modern view of social relations and practice can create the necessary space for effective dissent. In the concluding chapter I ask (and offer provisional answers to the questions) how does dissent benefit leaders, and what steps can leaders take to engage dissenters in collaborations for change?

In preparing this volume I have been uncommonly lucky to enjoy the collaboration and guidance of many fine colleagues. My first and largest debt is to the contributing authors, whose diligence and enthusiasm for this project were unwavering. I also am grateful for the encouragement of my advisory team, Warren Bennis, George Cheney, Ruth Guzley, Gail T. Fairhurst, Jean Lipman-Blumen, Jeff Schmidt and Meg Wheatley. We all owe a special thank-you to Ruth Guzley, whose idea originated the project at the 2003 meeting of the International Leadership Association in Guadalajara, Mexico. My thanks also go to the Edward Elgar editorial staff. Alan Sturmer has been of inestimable help in the early stages of the work. Bob Pickens and the production staff have made the process a truly enjoyable collaboration. I am grateful to Joanne Ciulla, New Horizons in Leadership Series editor, who has inspired and informed many of us by her innovative thinking and writings about moral leadership.

Last, first and most heartfelt is my gratitude to Anna Banks.

Stephen P. Banks

REFERENCE

Iacocca, Lee (2007), *Where Have All the Leaders Gone?*, with Catherine Whitney, New York: Scribner.

1. The troubles with leadership

Stephen P. Banks

INTRODUCTION

During the summer of 2005 tragedy struck the Boy Scouts of America, not once but several times. On Monday, 25 July, at the National Boy Scout Jamboree held at Camp Hill Army Base in Virginia, four Boy Scout leaders were electrocuted when they tried to erect a mess tent under power lines. Later the same week seven Boy Scouts and five adult Scout leaders set out to hike the John Muir Trail in California's High Sierra. The troop encountered a severe thunderstorm on Thursday, 28 July at Sandy Meadow in Sequoia National Park, and they set up two tarp shelters and a tent in a high meadow to protect themselves from the storm's fury. Lightning made a direct strike on one of the tarps, killing Assistant Scoutmaster Steve McCullagh and one 13-year-old Boy Scout.

On 3 August, 2005, after the deaths at Sandy Meadow had been featured prominently in the national media, Boy Scouts of Troop 56 from Salt Lake City were hiking in the Uinta Mountains near Camp Steiner – at 10 400 ft (3170 m) the highest elevation Boy Scout camp in the US – when a thunderstorm arose. A group of six Scouts and two leaders from the troop had hiked to a spot above Camp Steiner and had taken shelter in a three-sided log structure the Scouts call an Adirondack. There they lay in sleeping bags to wait out the storm. Lightning struck either the Adirondack or a tree touching it, instantly killing a 15-year-old Eagle Scout and injuring three others.

Experts' assessments afterward generally concluded that several basic rules of mountaineering had not been followed at the Camp Steiner site. Contrary to some newspaper accounts, the log hut provided no protection from a lightning strike, especially located as it was on a ridge; moreover, the trees in contact with the hut made the structure a lightning attraction, rather than a shelter from lightning. The standard position for a person to take in an electrical storm is squatting down while on the balls of the feet, placing as little area in contact with the ground as possible. The Scouts, however, were allowed to – or were instructed to – lie flat in sleeping bags on the ground and on cots, maximizing their contact points with the ground. More fundamentally, the first rule of mountaineering in a gathering lightning storm is to retreat to a lower elevation, something the members of Troop 56 easily could have done but failed to do (see Kithill, 2003).

It is unclear whether the Troop 56 leaders knew about the two earlier fatal accidents that summer involving Boy Scouts, but almost certainly they did. Both incidents were widely reported in print and television news. One would expect executives of the National Council of the Boy Scouts of America to send bulletins with cautions and instructions for responding to encounters with lightning. They would have had extensive experience with such emergency situations. Between 1995 and 2005 three other deaths and 44 injuries involving the Boy Scouts occurred in 15 separate incidents involving lightning. Even if the leaders were uninformed about the earlier events, they were supposed to be trained in mountaineering and were responsible for the Scouts in their care at Camp Steiner.[1]

These Boy Scout cases bring to mind at least three sorts of troubles with contemporary leadership. The first sort of trouble is about the label 'leader' and naming what a person or class of persons does as 'leadership'. In these instances persons called 'leader' in fact did not guide their followers through change to realize a vision of improved conditions for their follow-ers or others, nor did the purported leaders even deliver them from danger. Instead, they amplified the danger of the situations they encountered, both to their charges and to themselves. There seems to have been, in retrospect, a fundamental confusion about what sort of person can be called and deserves to be called leader and what can be expected of leadership. I will call this the 'definition trouble' with leadership. A highly ambiguous or polymorphous terminology of leadership easily can produce practices that in fact are antithetical to what we nomally desire of leaders. It also calls into question just what our subject is when we study and theorize about leadership.

The second trouble is closely related to the first. It seems fitting to wonder if the persons who were placed in charge of these fatal encounters were competent to take up the duties of their authorization or whether they even recognized their duty. In reality every person placed 'in charge' or who takes charge makes a mistake now and then. These lethal mistakes, however, occurred at the pivotal moments of activating their responsibility, just when duty most critically called upon them to serve. A remarkably similar confusion can be found in allegations about the failure of Michael Brown, then-head of the Federal Emergency Management Agency, to execute his duties when most needed at the time of Hurricane Katrina. The key is not that these so-called leaders were acting recklessly or wantonly; more likely it is a confusion about when accountability can be associated with the terms leader and leadership. I will call this the 'performance trouble' with leadership. It is mainly concerned about the fundamental nature of the relationship between the designation of leaders and the attribution of leadership, on the one hand, and how their activities and duties are connected to accountability. This trouble invites us to ask, 'Are failed leaders nonetheless still leaders?'

The third trouble goes to the underlying conceptual foundation of what is meant when we say 'leadership'. In many situations, possibly including all three Boy Scout debacles described above, some of those identified as followers challenge the directions of leaders. Yet, the very casting of persons into leader and follower positions suggests a relationship of obedience and compliance. As Thomas Cronin pointed out, there is a fundamental tension between leadership and democracy (Cronin, 1998: 388). The compelling force of leadership can be generated by organizational structures, personal power, persuasive competence and many other sources.

The Boy Scouts organization, for example, is structured as a steeply rigid authority and information hierarchy, closely modeled on the military. Its central practice of directing boys to learn progressively more challenging and intricate lore from adult men is marked with the accumulation of badges and ranks. The adults also are arranged in rank order of authority and specialized knowledge, both within troops and across troops into councils and from there into a national umbrella organization, where overall mission, policy and control are maintained. The stated vision of the organization is to produce leaders of the future. 'The Boy Scouts of America is the nation's foremost youth program of character development and values-based leadership training', says the official mission statement (see http://www.scouting.org/nav/enter. jsp?s=mc&c=mv).

Implicit in this design is the aim of producing leadership in every Boy Scout: Leadership appears to be understood as something every boy – more accurately, anybody – can do or have. Indeed, among the many trends in recent leadership studies is the invention and advocacy of 'shared leadership', 'servant leadership', 'empowered leadership', 'self-leadership', 'followers who lead themselves', 'superleadership' and 'democratic leadership' (for example, Gastil, 1997; Greenleaf and Spears,1998; Kelley, 1992; Manz and Sims, 1989; Pearce and Conger, 2003; Senge, 1990). Here is an apparent confusion about the relationship among leaders, followers and social position. I will call this the 'relationship trouble' with leadership. It is mainly concerned about who is a leader, who is a follower, and, most importantly, what quality connects them in a relationship. It asks: How and why do followers follow and leaders lead, when in fact they do so at all? More fundamentally, the relationship trouble directs us to take a stand on the diverse and mutually contradictory views held about the underlying principle of leadership.

In the rest of this chapter I will examine these three interrelated troubles more or less in order, returning occasionally to instances of leadership failure, where it seems helpful to clarify my analysis. I aim to show that understanding these troubles, taken together, can open up new thinking about how groups and organizations can more effectively respond to challenges, imagine and create change, and improve themselves. I will argue that the troubles with leadership are grounded most crucially in two misunderstandings. First is a misunderstanding of the fundamental nature of group relationships, and second is the misunderstanding of how difference and dissent should be conceived and treated by persons 'in charge'. In citing examples of failed leadership my purpose is not to jeer at the actions of people who have failed but to illustrate the dysfunctional assumptions, systemic problems and unwillingness to think boldly about the often maladapative, all-too-frequently unproductive and occasionally catastrophic practices of people who get situated, by one means or another, in charge of others.

A CONFUSION OF LEADERS

In his 2006 State of the Union Address, President Bush used the terms 'leader', 'lead' and 'leadership' on 19 separate occasions (Bush, 2006). Not counting instances of naming the United States of America, Mr Bush uttered the leadership word-family more frequently than any other term except the 'terror/terrorist/terrorism' group, which appeared in 22 instances. Following in third place was the 'free/freedom' group. From this evidence alone it is clear that the lead/leader/leadership language is important to the President – perhaps because he and his advisors believe it is persuasive in moving audiences – and is a word-family almost as salient to his purposes as terrorism and arguably somewhat more salient than freedom.

It's nonetheless instructive to note how Mr Bush used the leadership terms, because he illustrates some of the ways it can be deployed with distinctively different but ambiguously framed meanings.[2] To identify the various meanings that can be associated with lead/leader/leadership, I will label each with a subscript number. Two meanings were more prominently displayed than the rest: (a) Leadership$_1$ prompts the sense of being in the forefront, in a vague sense standing ahead of everyone else in a narrative about change or progress; and (b) leadership$_2$ means control, directing and reorienting others toward correct action. An example of leadership$_1$ occurred when, speaking of American competitiveness, Bush said, 'we must continue to lead the world in human talent and creativity'. Here, to lead is to stand ahead of others, to have more, better or more advanced qualities or resources. Clearly, America is not leading in the sense of showing the rest of the world how to equal the US in talent and creativity; otherwise, he would have said '. . . lead the world in developing talent and creativity'. Leadership$_2$ as control is revealed in Bush's statement, 'The only alternative to American leadership is a dramatically more dangerous and anxious world. Yet we also choose to lead, because it is a privilege to serve the values that gave us birth.' Aside from the smug metaphors of genetic superiority and inherited power over the planet, this quote demonstrates the comforting sense of leadership as controlling destiny by showing others the way.

But these two senses of leadership also amplify one another. A blend of these categories is evident in the following example. Early in the speech Bush contrasted acting confidently versus the false alternative of retreating 'in the hope of an easier life'. He followed that utterance with: 'We will choose to build our prosperity by leading the world economy, or shut ourselves off from trade and opportunity'. To lead the world economy could mean to remain the most powerful player, or it could mean to control the direction of the world economy, or both. Appending 'or shut ourselves off from trade and opportunity' signals that the idea of controlling the world economy is meant to be heard in a mitigated way, as if to say that to lead the world economy is to perpetuate and strengthen our already-established values and practices of expanded trade – a rhetorically effective deployment of ambiguity and indirection. Part of the purpose of his either/or construction of the nation's choices, of course, is to foreclose on the possibility of other actions or directions the US might take, including improved regional economic collaboration, participation in cooperative international initiatives or reallocation of economic prosperity globally.

This example simultaneously hints at striking off ahead independently, which is a third possible meaning of leadership. In leadership$_3$, the sense of moving ahead of the crowd, the term is ramified by what immediately follows in Bush's speech, an even more indirect and ambiguous declaration that 'The only way to protect our people, the only way to secure the peace, the only way to control our destiny is by our leadership. So the United States of America will continue to lead.' Controlling our destiny means to control all possible influences, and it is a worthy ambition because it is the way to protect our people and secure the peace. There is only one peace, yet it is unspecified, floating as an assumptive state we all will recognize once it is achieved. Leadership$_3$ thus carries a suggestion of going it alone as the initiating and controlling power for one's own purposes, regardless of others' destinies or desire for protection, as in being the leader in a race.

Briefly, the remaining meanings of leadership that are interpretable in Mr Bush's State of the Union Address are: Leadership$_3$, to strike off ahead of others; leadership$_4$ as the top positions or people in the top positions; leadership$_5$, to take initiative and responsibility; leadership$_6$, a status as controlling faction or predominator; leadership$_7$, to head toward a destination; and leadership$_8$, to represent, speak for and personify. These eight sorts of meaning for leading/lead/leadership and their blends are only the beginning of possibilities. Others can be added to these by consulting any good English dictionary: Examples include leadership$_9$, having the ability to anticipate a target's position and intercept it by being ahead of it; leadership$_{10}$, to have the starting position or central melodic role in music; leadership$_{11}$, conducting and guiding, as an orchestra; leadership$_{12}$, to mark the way toward a destination.

Because these words were uttered by Mr Bush in a major speech, however, his usages might evoke the most politically consequential meanings for this set of terms. The President's demonstration of leadership's multiple meanings points up the richly ambiguous nature of the leadership word-family and the rhetorically strategic value in exploiting its ambiguity. In each instance of its use, leadership's many meanings converge, so that the sense of top rank and position, controller, innovator, guide, predominator and so forth are sedimented into our understanding without refined distinctions of meaning readily coming under scrutiny.

It also is instructive to note the similarities among terrorism, leadership and freedom as highly ambiguous words that invite hearers to interpret them in ways that fit with their own needs and perceptions. Communication scholar Eric Eisenberg points out that strategically ambiguous expression has the advantages of giving speakers deniability while at the same time giving hearers a vague sense of agreement, even when they otherwise would understand the expression in diverse ways (Eisenberg, 1984). The political advantages are that such ambiguity-laden words sound appealing to hearers and resist interrogation; strategic ambiguity was known to Henry Kissinger as 'constructive ambiguity', but also is the principle underlying the CIA's deceptive 'plausible deniability'. Howard Stein, whose chapter on the language of totalitarian leadership is included in this volume, has demonstrated in an earlier work how euphemism and indirection can be a balm to those in control of organizations. In his book *Euphemism, Spin and the Crisis in Organizational Life* (Stein, 1998), Stein argues that euphemistic language like 'downsize' and 'reengineer' not only smooths over the adverse consequences of executive decisions but also deflects criticism and helps executives avoid accountability and guilt for the human consequences of their leadership.

The definition trouble in leadership is deeper than George W. Bush's exploitation of ambiguous language, though. Scholars entertain widely divergent views of what leadership is, and they persist in pointing out the difficulty in studying and creating theories about an elusive set of ideas and behaviors that seems to mean many different things to different observers and practitioners. In a recent book review, for example, management researcher Kevin Lowe notes that 'the lack of an agreed upon definition [for leadership] is endemic to the leadership field in general' (Lowe, 2006: 106). His essay cites 13 definitions for leadership in the single volume under review – Craig Pearce and Jay Conger's *Shared Leadership: Reframing the Hows and Whys of Leadership*. Similarly, in the inaugural issue of the scholarly journal *Leadership* (January 2005), editors David Collinson and Keith Grint note, 'there is little consensus on what counts as leadership, whether it can be taught, or even how effective it might be'. The first Harvard Center for Public Leadership roundtable concluded that there is a semantic problem with leadership. In his summary of that 2000 roundtable, Phillip Heymann identified four different fundamental concepts for leadership and argued that the phenomenon – and implicitly, the term – can only be understood in relation to the contexts in which leaders operate. In other words, we'll know it when we see it in action. Despite, or perhaps because of, the obvious tautology in using the term 'leaders' in this construction, Heymann's conclusion sets up a nearly impossible agenda for leadership scholars – to find a way to retain the vocabulary of leadership and generate consensus on what it means while at the same time to preserve the generality and ambiguity of the actual use of the vocabulary. Rather than studying behavior of people in group activities, influential scholars and popularizers have been commited to, and persist in, preserving something called leadership, even though they can't say what it is. The confusion is not limited to scholars who study leadership. Research has shown that managers hold conflicting and self-contradictory views as well (Alvesson and Sveningsson, 2003).

Why am I so focused on meanings attached to this family of labels? As Kenneth Burke cautioned, we know the world and understand how to act only in virtue of the names we give to phenomena. Our naming practices are communal and make our actions comprehensible only when definitions circulate that we can use in common. This applies to making theories as well as to performing ordinary actions. In his essay 'Antinomies of Definition', Burke showed that the act of defining demands that we bring together a name and the context of the named, the thing to be defined and that which it is not (Burke, 1969). Focusing on 'substance' and using insights from Locke and Spinoza, Burke argued that our definitions – our creating labels for this on the basis of labels for that, the 'that' being what 'this' is not – inevitably encounter the paradox of what today we might call a 'slippage of meaning'. Since there is no absolute and final substance on which to base a definition, no ultimate 'that' we can regress to, every name carries ambiguity: 'The ambiguity of substance affords, as one might expect, a major source of rhetoric', he quipped (Burke, 1969: 51). In the case of leadership, however, we seem to agree on neither what the 'this' is nor what the 'that' is.

POSITIONAL LEADERS AND ACCOUNTABILITY

Confusion about the naming of leadership (and related terms) and bamboozlements from the rhetorical strategies that such confusion enables aren't the whole story of the troubles. A more obvious sort of trouble involves failures of groups to prosper or in some cases even to survive, in part as a consequence of our habit of being vague or ambiguous about not just the name but the function and efficacy of leadership. This section is inspired in part by the confusion my students express when I ask them to explain how it can be that Hitler and Stalin were important leaders at the same time as Gandhi and Churchill were important leaders. They inevitably respond by drawing a distinction between good leaders and bad leaders, which tells us something about the imprecise distinctions inherent in leadership terminology. This impoverished vocabulary is reflected in recent books that attempt to partition off 'toxic' leaders (Lipman-Blumen, 2004), 'counterfeit' leaders (Williams, 2005) and 'bad' leaders (Kellerman, 2004) from effective, real, and good leaders.

At the time of writing, a massive migration of refugees were crossing the border from Sudan's Darfur region into Chad, where an incipient civil war had been raging. Despite a series of tentative cease-fire agreements among most of the 'leaders' involved, the tragedy continued: horrendous infant mortality, murders and rapes of mothers by Sudanese *Janjui* rebels and other guerilla groups, wholesale theft of emergency relief supplies, and other atrocities occurred not for weeks, but years. How can we reconcile the attribution of leadership by any definition with those persons who have failed to staunch the flow of blood, prevent or reverse the flow of refugees, protect the vulnerable from the victimizers? It is not difficult to find other tragedies and instances of failed projects and responsibilities unfulfilled; the other chapters in this volume provide ample examples of failure occasioned by leadership that doesn't lead. But why does it happen?

In his charming book *The Contrarian's Guide to Leadership*, University of Southern California President Steven Sample tells a story about a colleague who, when learning of Sample's ambition to apprentice for executive positions early in his career, pointed out the difference between *being* president and *doing* president. Related to my original example of failed leadership, we might say there's a difference between being Boy Scout leader and doing Boy Scout leader. Indeed, leadership in contemporary affairs seems to be more about an individual's professional and institutional status or position than the actual behaviors that enhance a group, project or program. I say 'individual' because, as Pearce and Conger observe in their groundbreaking book, 'historically, leadership has been conceived around a single individual – the leader – and the relationship of that individual to subordinates or followers' (Pearce and Conger, 2003: 4). Examine any popular trade or text book on leadership and it soon becomes obvious that the authors equate leader with executive, manager, or, in the ungraceful language of George W. Bush, 'the decider'. The exceptions might seem to be instances of applying the label 'leader' to individuals who exert self-control (see for example Manz and Neck, 2003; Sims and Lorenzi, 1991). Even in those cases, however, what is meant is self-managing and independent deciding.

There might be a hint of an explanation to the performance trouble with leadership in Sample's anecdote. It points out the common error of linking leadership to position, status or echelon, rather than to action. One convenient quality of leadership-as-position is that followership is preordained. Followers in this view are compelled to bend to leaders' control, because authority is built into the structure of a relationship based on hierarchy. If there were no hierarchy, there would be no asymmetry of influence in the relationship. The truth of this claim is evident in the coincidence of the common usage of the language of leadership with the rise of democratic forms of organizing, starting with sovereign nations and in industrialism with the rise of a labor class. As hierarchy became rationalized in democratic governments and the factory system, authority became rationalized in parallel, vesting legitimate control in positions, instead of in individuals by inheritance.[3] Some analysts theorize that hierarchy is not natural in life-systems, and the way to reconstruct leadership is to do away with hierarchical relationships entirely (for example, Wheatley, 2005). While such an approach is an admirable prescription for an ideal future state of affairs, the current observable state of affairs is that most institutions of consequence are vested in hierarchical relationships. Moreover, Joanne Ciulla's recent research finds that hierarchy and heterarchy are not only ubiquitous in most natural systems but that they are generally functional in higher mammalian groups (Ciulla, 2004, 2005).

A related but more consequential quality of leadership-as-position involves accountability. If leading is an aspect of taking up a position and assuming a title, then the consequences of actions conveniently can be accounted to the position-role but not necessarily to the person. In the summer of 2006 a US Department of Veterans Affairs (VA) analyst compromised the personal information of some 26 million veterans when he took records home in his laptop computer without authorization and the laptop subsequently was stolen. Not only were those veterans suddenly exposed to identity theft, but the security of records throughout the federal government was called into question. The Secretary of Veterans Affairs, R. James (Jim) Nicholson, apologized. It was, he said, his responsibility, and he alone was accountable to those 26 million veterans for possible damages. Note, however, that leader accountability here is a formality but is nothing personal: no restitution for damages will come from the Secretary's bank accounts, no disciplinary action befell the Secretary, and in fact the major news stories in the weeks that followed disclosure of the stolen laptop focused on the Secretary's chagrin over the two-week delay before he learned of the incident from subordinates. Similarly, no official above the military rank of Staff Sergeant paid a penalty of jail time or fine for the atrocities committed at Abu Ghraib prison in Iraq (Who's Who, 2005), and only Brigadier General Janis Karpinski, the prison commander, was reduced in rank as a consequence. Nonetheless, on 7 May, 2004, Secretary of Defense Donald Rumsfeld said before the US Senate Armed Services Committee, 'these events occurred on my watch as secretary of defense. I am account-able for them. I take full responsibility' (Danner, 2004).

These examples represent a form of bureaucratic accountability, as opposed to personal accountability. A well-run organization has clearly specified expectations for successful performance built into positions – incumbents come and go, and some fulfill those expectations better than others. A positional leader can deflect charges of failure by pointing out the subordinates' poor position-person match, inadequate training or resources for the enterprise, low follower performance, resistance to leadership, system glitches, sabotage or political intrigue. But the person who authenti-cally takes charge, enrolls others to accept her or his vision for change and changes the group's direction, purpose or ways of doing things irrespective of position authority, the one whose focus is on the doing rather than the being of a title – that is, the person who genuinely takes action and respon-sibility – can only have personal accountability.

BETWEEN LEADERS AND FOLLOWERS: THE CORE TROUBLE

Earlier I argued, following Kenneth Burke, that we need to know what lead-ership is not, so that we can have a useful sense of what it is. A recent and growing interest in effective followership – beginning no earlier than Chester Barnard's '*The nature of leadership*' (1948) – indicates it is becom-ing more widely recognized that leaders inevitably are associated with followers (even if conceived as dwelling within the same person), and that we need to know something about followers (the 'that') to understand leaders (the 'this') (Atchison, 2003; Chaleff, 2003). For my purposes, the two key questions that seem to escape most theorists' and practitioners' scrutiny are: What is the underlying principle on which the relationship of leader and followers operates? And: What is the commonality that links followership to the differences between failed leadership and successful leadership or between good and bad leaders? When asking the second question, it is important to recognize that the attributions 'good' leadership and 'bad' or 'failed' leadership can only be made in retrospect, after the consequences of the actions of those in charge and followers are known, and are not properly attributes of leaders and followers before or during their actions. Just as history is written by those who are victorious or who remain in office, so the quality of leadership is known only as a consequence of actions. At the same time, we also must examine whether position leaders are acting ethically and compassionately in the course of their acting (see Ciulla *et al.*, 2006). If we fail to do so, legal but unethical practices like Hewlett Packard's pretexting-for-hire might be overlooked in a Machiavellian concern for outcomes.

Conventionally, leaders show the way, are positioned in the vanguard, guide and direct, innovate, and have a vision for change and make it come to actuality. Followers on the other hand conventionally track the leader from behind, obey and report, implement innovations and accept leaders' vision for change. Yet the followership literature portrays effective followers as being very similar to leaders. In fact, one followership scholar, Robert Kelley, has been severely criticized for failing to distinguish effective followers from effective leaders. Such criticism seems to miss the point. But for their positional designations, followers and leaders share a crucial quality in group relationships – they mutually manage and distribute influence. The more effective a follower is, this line of reasoning says, the more control over herself she has and the less she is under the influence of the leader. In this sense, the perfect follower needs no leader.

Thus influence is central to what leaders actually do. Every major theorist recognizes that leaders influence and followers are influenced. Management scholar Gary Yukl asserts that 'influence is the essence of leadership' (Yukl, 2005: 2). In their authoritative collection, *The Nature of Leadership*, John Antonakis, Anna Cianciolo and Robert Sternberg confirm this view. 'Most leadership scholars', they write, 'probably would agree, in principle, that leadership can be defined as the nature of the influencing process – and its resultant outcomes – that occurs between a leader and followers and how this influencing process is explained by [various contingent factors]' (Antonakis *et al.*, 2004: 5). In his plainspoken critique of contemporary views of leadership, Dean Williams says, 'basically, the goal is to get people to do what you want them to do' (Williams, 2005: 4).

But that's not so very different from what each of us does every day – getting others to do what we want and doing what others want us to do, or resisting them. For the idea of leadership to have any distinctive utility, it must carry more meaning than mere influence. Indeed, the usual view of leaders is that they influence in a group context and are accountable for group outcomes. Ironically, it is an essential task of leaders, conceived in this way, to persuade followers that the leader will be accountable. In a sort of devil's bargain, the exchange offered is: Follow my lead, do what I want you to do, and I will be out in front no matter what the consequences turn out to be.

Gilbert Fairholm sees the influence relationship as a special case of the more general one in which leaders and followers use and redistribute power. 'Power', he writes, 'is the essence of leadership' (1993: 18). Further, 'personal influence . . . is a form power takes. Influence is a form of power, often subtle and indirect, by which we impact the situations and behaviors of others' (p. 20). Fairholm takes leadership as a euphemism for power use, arguing that we use leadership euphemisms because we are ambivalent about the moral status of power relationships (p. 192 et seq.). In calling leadership 'the exercise of power', Manfred Kets de Vries agrees that we are ambivalent about power and we hold 'contradictory feelings of unease and suspicion about the way power is directed toward us or, indeed, the way we handle it ourselves' (1993, p. 22).

If leadership is about the exercise of power in group contexts, a couple of further questions arise: First, how, specifically, is power exercised as leadership? Williams makes a distinction between 'real leadership' and 'counterfeit leadership'. Real leadership deals with 'real problems', while counterfeit leadership creates false solutions that allow the group to bypass 'reality'. It is not much help simply to invalidate leadership that isn't effective by calling it counterfeit; however, the idea of bypassing reality is a handy lens for understanding leadership as the exercise of power. Williams never asks, but it is most relevant to wonder, whose reality is the one that counts? The point of influence is to bring followers to a sufficiently shared version of reality, including a vision of a future reality, so that coordinated action can go forward effectively. The aim of leaders, then, is to foster the coconstruction of a jointly validated reality. For such a sharing to take hold, people must see themselves as being in the vision and must buy-in, or identify with, the reality being constructed. This involves becoming 'one of us', when 'us' is the group comprised of leader and followers.

Recent research on leadership and identity argues that leadership depends on influencing group members' identities and transforming their sense of social realities. Indeed, Stephen Reicher and his colleagues have identified three factors that are critical to coconstructing identities and realities (Reicher *et al.*, 2005; also see van Knippenberg and Hogg, 2003). The first factor is the leader's ability to mobilize people and establish a compelling vision of social identity. This basically rhetorical act taps into cultural knowledge, individual and group psychology, language and metaphor, and the power of social position. Of course followers do not automatically fall in line; they might, for a variety of reasons, resist mobilization efforts and the selling of a social reality and identity. Yet for the process to work without coersion, members must take up identities and visions of social reality more or less voluntarily.

Resistance is central to the second factor, the leader's ability to organize group development based on an assessment of dissent (seen in the researchers' scheme as outgroup resistance). As 'entrepreneurs of identity' leaders manage group allegiances and identities to isolate and marginalize those who resist transformation or hold alternate views of reality, visions of the future and self-constructions. The third factor is the effectiveness and power of countermobilizations. In other words, success is measured by the degree to which group dynamics can suppress dissenting views. This model provides a useful principle. Followers are active participants, not only in the cocreation of individual and group identities and therefore of a vision for transformation, but also in the management of dissent. As Reicher and his colleagues point out, for group members not to actively participate in the process is to invite tyranny: 'If one presupposes that leadership takes away the agency of followers then one fails to address the conditions under which tyrannical leadership thrives' (Reicher *et al.*, 2005: 562).

True enough. The reality of everyday life, though, is that leaders either turn to their position of power as the instrument of persuasion, rather than employ eloquence, rationality and identity work; or they hold position power as a potent instrument-in-reserve. Followers, in institutional settings, always know of the power differences between themselves and position-leaders and are constantly reminded of those differences by myriad cultural cues. More to the point, even if members succeed in managing outgroup resistance, there is no assurance the vision championed by the leader will become an authentically improved future state of affairs. There is no assurance the group's actions will be ethical or wise or will add value. In the end, the identity model helps us understand how leaders – and followers – exercise power, but it fails to answer a further question about leadership as the exercise of power. That question is: How can a useful distinction be made between leadership (power use) that succeeds and leadership (power use) that fails – fails in the sense of not producing outcomes that are morally supportable, socially beneficial and life-affirming, instead of their opposites – or being merely what the leader wants to happen? Another way of asking this question is: Other than observing failures, how can we differentiate leadership that is likely to succeed from leadership that is likely to fail?

A key point here is the proposition that all tyrannical leadership will fail. This is a fundamental position of the US Constitution and of most scholars of leadership in the modern era. In taking up leadership roles, tyrants manage the relationship with followers by insisting on assent. The tools of this management are familiar and explored in detail in later chapters of this book: Direct coercion, fear-induction, dissembling and manipulation, creating dependencies of other sorts. But in all cases, tyranny needs to suppress dissent. The heart of democratic process is the impulse to open up a system to challenge from diverse viewpoints and arguments; once challenged, the leader must either defend her vision or negate the challenge. Thus, encouraging dissent is key to avoiding tyranny and fostering democratic process. On this point Constitutional theorist Cass Sunstein argues 'organizations and nations are far more likely to prosper if they welcome dissent and promote openness' (Sunstein, 2003: 210–11).

But it is not just to enhance democracy and avoid tyrranical relationships that dissent must be embraced by leadership. It is essential for the very adaptability and sustainability of any institution or ongoing social group. Social systems theory, since the time of Ross Ashby's 1952 essay on requisite variety in self-organizing systems, has recognized that for human groups to be self-sustaining they must adapt to changes occurring among influences outside their own group. The basic idea, greatly simplified, is that social units must be as informationally complex and as diverse in other resources as are the surrounding influences that impinge on those social units. In Ashby's terms, '[f]or appropriate regulation the variety in the regulator must be equal to or greater than the variety in the system being regulated' (Ashby, 1952).

Organizational psychologist Karl Weick, following Ashby's theory, observes that not all changes and influences can be detected, and not all are seen as relevant. He argues that organizations and social groups act only in awareness of those environmental aspects they detect and direct attention toward. This he calls the 'enacted environment', and he argues that responsibility for defining a world that must be responded to belongs to the social group or organization itself (Weick, 1979). For this reason, acquiring information about the relevant influences from outside the group is a necessary activity for sustainability. Weick points out that information obtainable from a narrow cluster of close-knit followers (called strong ties) tends itself to be narrow and prone to redundancies, while information from weak ties (a larger number of network connections with less in common) tends to provide diverse and less redundant portrayals of the enacted environment. This information richness that helps groups obtain portrayals of the relevant world and its challenges is what Weick means by 'the strength of weak ties'. Weick recently has argued that in the twenty-first century leaders must learn to say 'I don't know' and live with their doubt (Weick, 2001). This is so, he argues, because in an increasingly dynamic, unpredictable world leaders must pursue contingent sensemaking for ongoing action rather than knowledge for decision making, and rely on plausibility instead of certainty.

Yet to optimize weak ties, self-organizing social systems – such as business organizations, governments, community associations, possibly even families – must shift power from leaders and their closely known and trusted members to the less familiar, perhaps even different, deviant and less trusted members. Those identified as outsiders or marginal characters must be legitimated and engaged, as a way of learning what they see and breaking with the status quo. This is why Weick uses the phrase 'leadership as the legitimation of doubt'. Bengt Gustavsson argues that leaders must balance the necessity for defining reality for followers with the need to 'unlearn' previous definitions of reality so as to remain responsive to change and develop business. He notes that unlearning has a liberating consequence that transfers control over the definition of self and reality to participating members: 'She cannot be controlled by meanings that have been based on institutional self-interest, rather than human values. She retains intrinsic power over meaning in work and life' (Gustavsson, 2001, p. 358).

The key purveyors of different viewpoints, identities and visions often, however, are labeled as dissenters. The very labeling of persons with different viewpoints, identities and visions as dissenters is to resist shifting power by refusing to legitimate their participation in the social group. The denial of power to dissenters is further enacted by characterizing them as disloyal, subversive or, worse, as the enemy of the group. For example, in another Boy Scout leadership failure, in which nine Scouts were treated for hypothermia following a winter camp at high elevation in Idaho, the boys who argued that the troop should retreat were called 'babies' by their leaders and characterized as behaving 'not like Scouts'.[4] Opponents of World Trade Organization policies are transformed and simplified when lumped together as 'demonstrators', and they are further neutralized when sequestered in 'free speech zones' behind chain-link fences blocks away from WTO meetings.

A successfully led organization, every bit as much as a sustainable democratic society, therefore depends on embracing highly complex ideas of identity, membership and relevance. If leadership means the deployment of power in service to a vision of change, then the vision must reflect an enacted environment that contains relevant information about challenges and contextual features, such as new technologies and concepts, changes in markets, new social tastes and trends and similar potential influences on change. It also must embrace alternative views of present and future realities and engage their advocates' reasons and methods. If rationality is to be trusted over raw command, dissent must be welcomed into the system. If doubt and sensemaking are to be hallmarks of sustainability of social groups, dissenters must be reconceived as necessary, if not sufficient, contributors. Merely to tolerate or acknowledge dissent suboptimizes leading, because mere tolerance cannot extract the optimal benefits of dissent to enhance the system. Dissenters must have equal standing and trust, as well as equal access to power to persuade. From this perspective, leaders have a core responsibility of inviting and facilitating dissent and expanding the dispersal of power.

CONCLUSION

I have described three main troubles associated with our notions of leadership. The definition trouble is unavoidable, given the nature of language and discourse. 'Leadership', 'leader', 'to lead' and related terms are rhetorical conveniences and seductions, emergent in a historical period when hierarchies of power have become flatter as principles of equality, fairness and diversity have been written into the social, cultural and legal frameworks of sovereign nations. The emergence of leadership also is coincident with an increasing complexity of societies, driven by exponential increases of information, which in turn is produced by technological changes. The transformation of the essential power distributing relationship from one of feudal lord and servant (where lord is inherited and absolute) to one of leader and follower (where almost anybody can become a leader and indeed the roles might be exchanged for one another) means that as long as there is positional hierarchy in organizations a vocabulary for the varieties of the core relationship will be needed, whether it be called leadership or something else. A way to help minimize the definition problem is to mindfully transform the abstraction inherent in the noun-forms into the action form inherent in the verb, and then, when needed, to connect one or more modifiers to 'leading', as a mechanism for specifying what domain of meaning is legitimately intended. To say 'task leading' or 'developmental leading' or 'innovation leading' and so forth both clarifies the term and reduces the opportunities for manipulation by exploiting its strategic ambiguity. A more specific naming practice recognizes that leading has not one domain or theory but many.[5] Such a practice also takes a stand against command through rhetoric and covert reversion to lordship. A model for this move from the noun forms of leadership to the verb forms of leading can be found in Robyn Penman's theory of communicating, which she applies in her chapter of this volume. Similarly, specifiers can be added to the noun forms: position-leader, consensual leader, assumed leadership, team leadership, and so on. Hearing the term leader or leadership as nouns without a clarifying modifier should signal that it is being said mindlessly or perhaps with strategic ambiguity in mind.

The performance trouble with leadership is grounded in the capacity for leaders to evade accountability as they continue to harvest the benefits of leadership positions. Organizational systems that explicitly require inclusion of dissenting voices in their quotidian deliberations and transform groups into sensemakers and action-takers not only are more effectively responsive to change, but they also set the stage for shared accountability for actions' consequences. Explicitly celebrating dissent as a vital element in deliberation and acting also profoundly improves the conceptual trouble with leadership – the inherent struggle over power between leaders and followers. Exclusion or marginalization of dissenters fosters fragmented identities; inclusion fosters coalescing and clarifies identities and a more richly conceived universe of practical action.

Keying on dissent as a vital and positive principle of organizational leading also produces progressive results. This is not just a theoretical claim; I will conclude with the example of Brazil's transnational firm Semco. Ricardo Semler, chief executive of Semco has demonstrated how a highly open social system, shared trust and the celebration of dissent generate a powerful capacity for creating change. As of 2004, Semco had experienced 15 straight years of more than 30 percent annual increases in value and profitability. Yet Semler will not and cannot say what business Semco is in. He argues that to say what you do today is to foreclose on what you might find more interesting or useful to do tomorrow. Instead of dictating Semco's identity, he says:

> I let our employees shape it with their individual efforts, interests, and initiatives . . . Instead of explaining what Semco does, I'll take a run at what it doesn't do. Semco has no official structure. It has no organizational chart. There's no business plan or company strategy, no two-year or five-year plan, no goal or mission statement, no long-term budget. The company often does not have a fixed CEO. There are no vice presidents or chief officers for information technology or operations. There are no standards or practices. There's no human resources department. There are no career plans, no job descriptions or employee contracts. No one approves reports or expense accounts. Supervision or monitoring of workers is rare indeed. Most important, success is not measured only in profit and growth . . . Our 'architecture' is really the sum of all the conventional business practices we avoid. It's our lack of formal structure, our

willingness to let workers follow their interests and their instincts when choosing jobs or projects. It's our insistence that workers seek personal challenges and satisfaction before trying to meet the company's goals. It's our commitment to encouraging employees to ramble through their day or week so that they will meander into new ideas and new business opportunities. It's our philosophy of embracing democracy and open communication, and inciting questions and dissent in the workplace. On-the-job democracy isn't just a lofty concept but a better, more profitable way to do things. (Semler, 2004: 2–4)

Semco holds as a core value the democratic diffusion of power across the organization. Semler describes it as a fundamental 'need – the absolute necessity – to give up control in order to cope with changes that are transforming the way we live and work. As counterintuitive as that sounds', he says, 'it does not contradict the experience and values at the core of free market, democratic capitalism' (2004: 2).

Two qualities mark Semco's experience as rare. One is the degree of success in all facets of work life Semco people have enjoyed, even through the worst of economic times in Brazil. The other is the honored place of dissent in the set of underlying operational principles that have produced that success. As Semler describes it, 'until these [conventional] organizations face reality, give up the futile quest for control and begin to respect such concepts as workplace democracy, the need to question everything, and the search for a more balanced existence, even the most modest goals will be beyond reach' (2004: 234).

NOTES

1. For news accounts of the Boy Scout accidents, see, for example, http://www. cbsnews.com/stories/2005/08/03/national/main713809.shtml and http://www.usatoday. com/news/nation/2005-07-29-scouts-lightning_x.htm. The Boy Scouts of America website shows no mention of these incidents or of the agency's responses, nor is there mention of the accidents on the regional Boy Scout Councils' websites. For descriptions of earlier Boy Scout encounters with lightning, see http://www.usatoday.com/news/ nation/2005-07-29-scouts-lightning_x.htm and http://findarticles.com/p/articles/mi_ qn4188/is_20060108/ai_n15993500).
2. A critical language analysis examines how the terms can be interpreted, in part by examining the linguistic context of the terms – the material that precedes it and follows it in the text – and partly by examining the social and historical contexts in which the terms are deployed – that is, by considering the setting in which the speech is performed and the practical conditions that provide the political, economic or historical backdrop for interpretation.
3. For a full discussion of the relationships among democratic forms of organizing, positional authority and leadership, see Pearce and Conger, 2003; Williams, 2005; also see Vilfredo Pareto's essay, 'The treatise on general sociology', in Grint (1997), pp. 70–81.
4. The case was contributed by a student in my advanced organizational communication course in the fall of 2006. The student wished to remain anonymous. A similar case can be accessed at http://americasroof.com/wp/archives/2005/01/24/11-boy-scouts-and-3-searchers-hospitalized-with-frostbite-at-grayson-highlands/.

5. This conclusion is supported by the long-term General Theory of Leadership Project, in which it was demonstrated that the foremost scholars on leadership can not agree on an integrating theory for the field (see Goethals and Sorenson, 2006).

REFERENCES

Alvesson, Mats and Stefan Sveningsson (2003), 'The great disappearing act: difficulties in doing "leadership"', *The Leadership Quarterly*, **14** (3), 359–81.

Antonakis, J., Cianciolo, A. T. and Sternberg, R. J. (2004), *The Nature of Leadership*, Thousand Oaks, CA: Sage.

Ashby, Ross (1952), 'General theories in system science', accessed 13 September 2006 at www.gwu.edu/~umpleby/recent_papers/2001_two_general_theories_ insystem_science.htm.

Atchison, T. A. (2003), *Followership: A Practical Guide to Aligning Leaders and Followers*, Chicago, IL: Health Administration Press.

Barnard, C. (1948), 'The nature of leadership', in C. Barnard, *Organization and Management: Selected Papers*, Cambridge, MA: Harvard University Press.

Burke, Kenneth (1969), *A Grammar of Motives*, Berkeley, CA: University of California Press.

Bush, George H. (2006), 'We strive to be a compassionate, decent, hopeful society', *The New York Times*, 31 January, national edn, A18.

Bush, G. W. (2006), *State of the Union Address by the President*, www:// whitehouse.gov/stateoftheunion/2006/.

Chaleff, I. (2003), *The Courageous Follower: Standing Up To and For Our Leaders*, San Francisco, CA: Berrett-Koehler.

Ciulla, Joanne B. (2004), 'The biological and ethical challenges to leadership', in *Proceedings of the International Leadership Association*, University Park, MD: University of Maryland, James McGregor Burns Academy of Leadership.

Ciulla, Joanne B. (2005), 'Integrating leadership with ethics: is good leadership contrary to human nature?' in J. Doh and F. Strumpf (eds), *Handbook of Responsible Leadership and Governance in Global Business*, Cheltenham, UK and Northampton, MA: Edward Elgar, Chapter 9.

Ciulla, Joanne B., T. L. Price and S. E. Murphy (eds) (2006), *The Quest for Moral Leaders*, Cheltenham, UK and Northampton, MA: Edward Elgar.

Cronin, Thomas E. (1998), 'Leadership and democracy', in J. Thomas Wren (ed.), *The Leader's Companion: Insights on Leadership Through the Ages*, New York: The Free Press, pp. 303–9.

Danner, M. (2004), *Torture and Truth: America, Abu Ghraib, and the War on Terror*, New York: The New York Review of Books.

Eisenberg, Eric M. (1984), 'Ambiguity as strategy in organizational communication', *Communication Monographs*, **51**, 227–42.

Fairholm, Gilbert W. (1993), *Organizational Power Politics: Tactics in Organizational Leadership*, Westport, CT: Praeger.

Gastil, John (1997), 'A definition and illustration of democratic leadership', in Keith Grint (ed.), *Leadership: Classical, Contemporary and Critical Approaches*, Oxford: Oxford University Press, pp. 155–78.

Goethals, G. R. and G. L. J. Sorenson (eds) (2006), *The Quest for a General Theory of Leadership*, Cheltenham, UK and Northampton, US: Edward Elgar.

Greenleaf, R. K. and L. C. Spears (1998), *The Power of Servant Leadership: Essays*, San Francisco, CA: Berrett-Koehler.

Grint, Keith (ed.) (1997), *Leadership: Classical, Contemporary, and Critical Approaches*, New York: Oxford University Press.

Gustavsson, Bengt (2001), 'Managerial power over meaning: whither human values?' in S. K. Chakraborty and Pradip Bhattacharya (eds), *Leadership and Power: Ethical Explorations*, Oxford: Oxford University Press, pp. 339–58.

Kellerman, Barbara (2004), *Bad Leadership: What it is, How it Happens, Why it Matters*, Cambridge, MA: Harvard Business School Press.

Kelley, Robert E. (1992), *The Power of Followership*, New York: Doubleday Currency.

Kets de Vries, Manfred (1993), *Leaders, Fools, and Imposters: Essays on the Psychology of Leadership*, San Francisco, CA: Jossey-Bass.

Kithill, Richard (2003), 'Lightning safety for campers, hikers, & backpackers', accessed 15 November 2006 at www.sierrapacktrip.com/lightning_safety.html.

Lipman-Blumen, Jean (2004), *The Allure of Toxic Leaders: Why We Follow Destructive Bosses and Corrupt Politicians – and How We Can Survive Them*, New York: Oxford University Press.

Lowe, K. B. (2006), 'Shared leadership: reframing the hows and whys of leadership', book review, *The Leadership Quarterly*, **17** (1), 105–8.

Manz, C. C. and C. Neck (2003), *Mastering Self Leadership*, 3rd edn, New York: Prentice Hall.

Manz, C. C. and H. P. Sims Jr. (1989), *SuperLeadership: Leading Others to Lead Themselves*, New York: Prentice-Hall.

Pearce, C. L. and Jay A. Conger (eds) (2003), *Shared Leadership: Reframing the Hows and Whys of Leadership*, Thousand Oaks, CA: Sage.

Reicher, Stephen, S. Alexander Haslam and Nick Hopkins (2005), 'Social identity and the dynamics of leadership: leaders and followers as collaborative agents in the transformation of social reality', *The Leadership Quarterly*, **16** (4), 547–68.

Sample, S. B. (2002), *The Contrarian's Guide to Leaderships* San Francisco, CA: Jossey-Bass.

Semler, Ricardo (2004), *The Seven Day Weekend: Changing the Way Work Works*, New York: Portfolio/Penguin.

Senge, Peter (1990), *The Fifth Discipline: The Art and Practice of the Learning Organization*, New York: Doubleday.

Sims, Jr., H. P. and P. Lorenzi (1991), *The New Leadership Paradigm: Social Learning and Cognition in Organizations*. Newbury Park, CA: Sage.

Stein, H. F. (1998), *Euphemism, Spin, and the Crisis in Organizational Life*, Westport, CT: Quorum Books.

Sunstein, Cass (2003), *Why Societies Need Dissent*, Cambridge, MA: Harvard University Press.

van Knippenberg, Daan and M. A. Hogg (eds) (2003), *Identity, Leadership, and Power*, Thousand Oaks, CA: Sage.

Weick, Karl E. (1979), *The Social Psychology of Organizing*, Reading, MA: Addison-Wesley.

Weick, Karl E. (2001), 'Leadership as the legitimation of doubt', in Warren Bennis, Gretchen M. Spreitzer and Thomas G. Cummings (eds), *The Future of Leadership: Today's Top Leadership Thinkers Speak to Tomorrow's Leaders*, San Francisco, CA: Jossey-Bass, pp. 91–102.

Wheatley, Margaret (2005), *Finding Our Way: Leadership for an Uncertain Time*, San Francisco, CA: Berrett-Koehler Publishers, Inc.

Who's Who (2005), 'Who's who on Abu Ghraib', 4 May, Associated Press, accessed 26 May, 2006 at www.msnbc.msn.com/id/7709487/.

Williams, D. (2005), *Real Leadership: Helping People and Organizations Face Their Toughest Challenges*, San Francisco, CA: Berrett-Koehler Publishers.

Yukl, Gary A. (2005), *Leadership in Organizations*, 5th edn, New York: Prentice Hall.

2. Varieties of dissent

Brian Martin

INTRODUCTION

- A scientist publishes a research paper questioning the dominant view on global warming.
- A minister gives a sermon suggesting the Holy Ghost is irrelevant to Christian belief.
- A company accountant meets with the boss to query the boss's favored tax write-off scheme.
- Protesters join rallies against corporate globalization.
- A doctor in China sends e-mails alleging corruption in the Communist Party.

Each of these scenarios might be considered an expression of dissent. What they have in common is questioning or challenging a dominant belief system, dominant either via widespread acceptance or via the power of those in charge.

Dissent depends on your perspective: It is both lauded and loathed. It is lauded when it is in the glorious, unthreatening past. Famous dissenters include Socrates, Galileo and Martin Luther. Dissent is especially lauded when dissenters emerge victorious, such as the signers of the Declaration of Independence. It is also more easily lauded when it is geographically distant. Aung San Suu Kyi, the charismatic leader of the opposition to Burma's repressive regime, is an example.

But closer to home dissent is less attractive – at least to those whose power or position is threatened by it. Whistleblowers, for example, are individuals who speak out in the public interest. The classic whistleblower is a loyal, trusting employee who reports either internally or to outside audiences on a problem in the organization, such as corruption or a danger to the public. For their trouble, whistleblowers are routinely ostracized, threatened, harassed, reprimanded, referred to psychiatrists, demoted, dismissed and blacklisted (De Maria, 1999). They commonly suffer damage to their careers and large financial losses; often their health and relationships suffer as well. There are two main types of leakers. First are the politicians and senior officials who leak information to journalists as a means of manipulating public opinion. Second are the public-interest leakers, usually junior employees, who seek to expose wrongdoing. The second sort, when identified, are treated just like whistleblowers. When there's a furious investigation into the source of a leak, you can be sure it was a public interest issue.

Whistleblowers usually suffer reprisals, but does that mean reprisals are a necessary part of dissent? Dissent assumes a challenge to some system of power or belief – what can be called an establishment – but how the system responds to a challenge arguably is a separate matter. Ten-year-old Brett tells his father Frank they shouldn't watch football on television as usual on Sunday – in fact they shouldn't watch sport on television ever again! Frank has several options. He can simply ignore young Brett, or laugh off his comment as a silly idea. Or he can earnestly explain the importance of Sunday football and give Brett guidance on understanding its subtleties. He might try to bribe Brett by offering to play with him outside afterwards, or by giving Brett some money. If Frank is an authoritarian, he may punish Brett, perhaps with a beating. On the other hand, Frank might try to co-opt Brett's dissent by offering to make one day per year 'No TV Day'. Finally, it is possible Frank might capitulate to Brett's demand. Maybe he was under pressure to cut his TV watching and Brett's plaintive request was enough to tip the balance.

Frank's options are pretty much the same options every establishment has for responding to dissent – repress the challenge, ignore it, communicate with and attempt to educate the dissenters, incorporate the challenge and the challengers into the system, or capitulate. We tend to hear much more about the response of repression, but the other responses can and do occur. In 1989, when the ruling Communist parties in Eastern Europe were faced with escalating popular protest, most of them capitulated without a fight.

DISAGREEMENT, DISSENT, REBELLION AND HERESY

In analyzing challenges within professions, social scientist Paul Root Wolpe (1994) makes useful distinctions among dissent, rebellion and heresy. Suppose some medical researchers challenge the current knowledge about the cause of a disease but remain committed to conventional scientific methods for assessing the knowledge. Wolpe calls this 'dissent'. An example is the idea that HIV does not cause AIDS. The idea that bacteria cause ulcers was dissent just a few decades ago, but has now become orthodoxy. In both cases the challengers were committed to conventional scientific methods.

A different sort of challenge is to the authority structure of the profession, such as women entering medical domains previously dominated by men or barefoot doctors carrying out procedures that professionals claim as their exclusive domain. Wolpe calls this 'rebellion'.

Another category is 'heresy', which for Wolpe is a challenge to central values of the orthodoxy, including how claims should be evaluated. An example is homeopathy, in which very tiny doses of substances are used to treat diseases, with some doses so diluted that not one molecule of the active ingredient might be expected to remain, in apparent contradiction to pharmacological principles.

To this classification can be added 'disagreement', denoting a milder form of challenge than dissent. Disagreement might occur over which antidepressant drug is more effective. Dissent concerning antidepressants would be a deeper form of challenge, such as questioning the value of drug treatment altogether – and providing clinical evidence to support this skepticism. If a new non-clinical group claimed the right to make interventions against depression, that would be rebellion. To claim depression does not exist would be heresy. This classification can easily be transposed into other domains. In a business, questioning when to hold a sale would be a disagreement. Questioning a well-established policy on hiring would be dissent. Pushing for a maverick group of directors would be rebellion. Advocating pulling out of the main line of business or paying everyone equally would be heresy.

When a disagreement – a mild challenge – succeeds, a typical outcome is a changed practical decision or evaluative judgment. For successful dissent a typical outcome is a changed policy or practice, which can be called reform, because basic operating principles are unchanged. For a successful rebellion a typical outcome is a new set of leaders and perhaps a new power structure. A successful heresy brings about an entirely different conception of what is going on – it is revolutionary, in that guiding principles are changed.

At the scale of national political systems, a disagreement might be over how to implement an agreed policy, for example a disagreement over which military helicopters to buy, or how many. Dissent might be a challenge over something more fundamental, such as whether defense alliances should be changed. Rebellion might be over who controls defense decision-making, with a challenge made by civilians to take over from military figures or vice versa. A possible heresy would be to get rid of the army altogether, such as was put to the Swiss electorate in a 1989 referendum.

A military coup is a type of rebellion, as the label suggests: it changes the decision makers but does not necessarily change the system, at least if it was already authoritarian. More far-reaching is revolution, in which the operating principles of the political and economic system are dramatically altered: the French Revolution introduced republicanism and the Russian Revolution introduced state socialism. What was previously heresy became orthodoxy. Revolutions usually involve a changing of the ruling group; in other words, successful heresies usually are linked to successful rebellions. But not always. Mao Zedong, as head of the Chinese Communist Party, launched the Cultural Revolution, with revolutionary changes in social relationships, in a way that cemented his own power.

The distinction between dissent, rebellion and heresy can be useful at times, but there are continuities between them as well. Dissenters, in order to gain a hearing for their ideas, often band together and take concerted action, thereby becoming rebels, as in religious dissent that becomes the foundation for a new denomination. The reaction of powerholders can turn dissenters into heretics, as when defenders of religious orthodoxy excommunicate someone for actions that might otherwise be treated as a trivial difference. On the other side of the fence, rebels may latch onto a heretical doctrine as a way of fostering internal unity. So, for convenience, when I use the word dissent, it sometimes also covers rebellion and heresy.

Reasons for Dissenting

Given the likelihood of reprisals, why would anyone want to dissent? One reason is they didn't realize there would be reprisals for expressing a difference of opinion. Many whistleblowers did not set out to challenge the organization. From their point of view, they were just doing their job, reporting a financial anomaly, pointing out that rules hadn't been followed, or putting in a grievance using the standard procedure. They were naive: They didn't realize the official rhetoric was not the actual way people were expected to behave. These inadvertent whistleblowers are particularly tragic. They suffer reprisals for doing their job according to the organization's espoused ideals and, as a result, their whole conception of the world is turned upside down.

Many dissenters, though, know exactly what they are doing: They know the risks but they proceed anyway. Why? Sometimes it is pure ambition and self-interest. In some fields of science, the surest way to fame is to challenge and overthrow the ruling paradigm. To be sure, some paradigm-busting scientists like Einstein conform to the gentle image of being interested only in ideas. But others are more calculating. James Watson, codiscoverer of the structure of DNA, revealed the ruthless side of research in his book *The Double Helix* (Watson, 2001).

There are some dissenters who are driven by malice, for example by envy of those who have power and prestige. Before the 1917 Russian Revolution, some anarchists presciently warned that Marxists seeking power in the name of the workers might become new oppressors. A writer named Max Nomad in the 1930s wrote a book titled *Rebels and Renegades* in which he attributed base motives to all manner of left-wing intellectuals and revolutionary leaders (Nomad, 1932). One need not tar every left-wing figure with the same brush to recognize that some may be driven by self-interest. Of course the same could be said of the radical right.

Psychologist David Kipnis has carried out ingenious experiments supporting Lord Acton's famous aphorism that 'power tends to corrupt and absolute power corrupts absolutely'. For example he showed that when powerful people used strong tactics to influence others, this made the powerholders believe that the others did not control their own behavior. This belief in turn led the powerholders to devalue those over whom they held power (Kipnis, 1981). To this sequence we need only add that the possibility of having power also can be corrupting.

On the other hand, many dissenters seem to have no ambitions aside from bringing about a better world, whether in the family, the workplace, or the political system. Many altruists operate behind the scenes, taking risks without seeking glory. For example, during the 1968 massacre of Vietnamese civilians by US troops at My Lai, a few US soldiers intervened against the killings and reported their concerns to superiors, later suffering in their army careers as a consequence. Only decades later were their honorable actions widely recognized. And for each such dissenter who is eventually seen as a hero, there are many others who never receive public validation.

It's also possible for dissent to be a role learned through experience. In his path-breaking book *Born to Rebel* Frank Sulloway (1996) argues that first-born children are more likely to conform to their parents' career and beliefs because this is effective in winning their parents' attention, whereas later-born children – Charles Darwin is an example – often innovate to gain parental attention, and thus are more likely to become dissenters. In Sulloway's picture, dissent becomes an acquired behavior, almost a reflex action.

To enhance understanding of dissenters and their reasons, it is illuminating to consider conformists. Psychiatrist Arthur Deikman (1990) argues that everyone as a child has the experience of being dependent and, as an adult, may long to return to a state of 'oneness'. This can lead to cult-like dynamics in which leaders are idolized – like parents – and hierarchy dominates over truth. Outsiders and opponents are devalued, with the conformist's own anger and resentment projected onto them. In Deikman's picture, suppression of dissent is the most characteristic feature of cult life. He argues that many conventional organizations, including businesses and governments, have cult-like features.

TACTICS OF DISSENT

The engagement of dissenters and the ruling establishment can be called the 'dance of dissent'. Dissenters choose the music – the subject for the engagement – and usually choose how to begin the dance. They choose the dance floor, namely the arena for the engagement. And they choose the dance style, or how to express their dissent. These choices by dissenters comprise the tactics of dissent. As already illustrated, establishments can respond in a variety of ways. They can ignore it, refusing to dance. They can communicate with the dissenter, joining the dance but attempting to convince their partner to retire from the floor or change the steps. They can attempt to repress the challenge, turning the dance into a duel. They can divert the dissenter through tortuous formal procedures, pretending to dance while sabotaging the steps. They can incorporate the challenge, making the dance part of the establishment's ritual. Or they can capitulate, leaving the dissenters to run the dance hall.

Methods for Dissenting – the Dance Style

Dissent is most readily recognized in the form of words or symbols, such as speeches, petitions, slogans, pictures, films, clothes, and the like. Soviet dissidents typed their seditious thoughts and circulated the original and carbon copies for others to reproduce, creating a genre of dissident writing called *samizdat*. But it's also possible to dissent through one's actions. Of course, all actions have communicative dimensions, but they need not be symbolic in obvious ways. Many of those who sheltered Jews during the Nazi occupation of Europe did so at great risk and without any fanfare afterward. They dissented from Nazi policies without any distinctive verbal or other symbolic accompaniment. Because dissent-through-action is less familiar, it's worth examining more closely.

If actions can constitute dissent, then why not violent actions, including terrorism? Indeed, insurgent (non-state) terrorism has been called, by scholars Alex Schmid and Janny de Graaf, communication activated and amplified by violence (Schmid and de Graaf, 1982). Conceived as a communication strategy, terrorists are the senders, their victims are the message generators, the western mass media carry the message, and the public or the enemy are the receivers of the message. If terrorism can be a taken as a method of dissent, then it argues that dissent is not necessarily a good thing – it depends on how the dissent is carried out.

Another behavioral way of expressing dissent is via what is called non-violent action. Pioneer nonviolence scholar Gene Sharp (2005) divides nonviolent action into three main types. The first is protest and persuasion, such as speeches, petitions, slogans, rallies, mock elections, prayer and rude gestures. To count as nonviolent action, an action needs to be something beyond conventional politics: lobbying and voting do not count as non-violent action because they are institutionalized and routine. Likewise, when a method becomes conventional, such as petitions used to support increased hospital funding or to designate a new public holiday, the challenge to dominant beliefs may be minimal. In an authoritarian society, though, a petition can be deeply subversive. What counts as nonviolent action depends on the context as much as the category, and similarly for dissent.

The second main type of nonviolent action is noncooperation, which includes social ostracism, protest emigration, consumer boycotts, withdrawal of bank deposits, embargoes, judicial noncooperation and a huge variety of strikes. Noncooperation can certainly be a way of expressing dissent. Canadian auto workers shut down General Motors factories during 1984 contract negotiations as an expression of dissent from the deal made earlier between GM and the International Auto Workers Union to change the principle for calculating pay increases.

The third main type of nonviolent action is intervention, which includes methods such as fasts, sit-ins, alternative media and setting up alternative political institutions. These also can be forms of dissent. When members of a neighborhood join together to clean up a vacant lot, plant flowers and shrubs and install outdoor furniture, they are engaging in nonviolent action and dissenting from conventional views about ownership and responsibility. Like many other dissenters, they and their efforts may well come under attack.

At the other end of the spectrum of methods is dissent through thought. A subversive thought need not manifest itself in any communication or action – the point is it could. That is why totalitarian governments and cults attempt to crush autonomous thinking, as George Orwell portrayed so frighteningly in *Nineteen Eighty-four* (Orwell, 1949).

More on Methods

Often it is assumed that dissent is expressed in words, and furthermore as particular types of words: polite, rational, intellectual discourse. This is the way most writers about dissent – such as contributors to this book, including me – operate. But dissent in practice often goes beyond these stereotypes. Instead of being polite, rational, intellectual discourse, it can be rude, absurd and action-oriented.

Civility, namely being polite according to the norms of a situation, is characteristic of much discourse, including dissent. It includes behaviors like using moderate language, being respectful of opponents, and paying deference to cultural icons. We need only think of carefully crafted articles or eloquent talks expounding radical ideas. Op-ed pieces in the *New York Times* opposing government policies are representative. But there is another style: a talk filled with shouting and swearing or an article with strong language and **ALARMING *DEPARTURES* from** CIVILIZED FORMATTING!!!

The civil style has advantages. It is less likely to polarize the situation and allows the reader or listener to concentrate on the content without the distraction of unconventionality. It is more likely to fit into an ongoing dialogue. But at the same time, dissent in a civil style is far easier to ignore or to dismiss with spurious arguments. Rudeness and other convention violations break through business as usual and put a spotlight on dissent, though at the risk of diverting attention from substance to style and from dissent to the dissenter.

Defenders of the status quo can be rude too. In fact, rudeness can be their standard style, as in the case of bullying bosses or abusive radio talk-show hosts. This attitude sometimes leads to the curious phenomenon of challengers behaving more politely and according to the ostensible norms of civility than those they are challenging. In some rare circumstances, polite dissent can be highly effective, winning sympathy through a graceful style. But polite behavior can easily be ignored, by contemptuous higher-ups and especially by media seeking conflict and drama. If orthodoxy is bound up in elaborate rituals to which dissenters have no easy access, then norm violations can be effective in breaking through the orthodoxy. Think of Martin Luther nailing his challenges to the church door.

Sometimes a movement benefits from a dual-track approach, with challengers on the outside using rude techniques to bring dissent to attention and allies on the inside calmly making a sensible case. For example, opposition to genetic engineering includes both direct activists who destroy crops and policy advisers who argue the case for organic farming.

Next consider rationality, which includes having a logical line of argument based on clear premises and appropriate use of evidence. Much civil dissent is couched in rational form, from detailed mathematical arguments that quantum theory is false to highly documented criminological arguments that longer sentences do not reduce the crime rate. In many cases, dissent is formulated more rigorously than orthodoxy, for example when establishment views are founded on unexamined premises. The scientific establishment mostly relegates paranormal phenomena – such as precognition and psychokinesis – to the fringe, not taking them seriously. In response to claims about weaknesses in their evidence and research methods, parapsychologists have developed research protocols, such as double blinding, far more rigorous than those used in most research in physics and other conventional scientific disciplines.

The alternative to rationality can be called absurdity, which includes paradox and humor. Strategic uses of absurdity can sometimes trigger a change in perspective in a more profound and rapid way than rationality. Consider the elaborate strategic justifications for nuclear weapons based on deterrence theory. If having nuclear weapons helps prevent nuclear war through deterrence, then wouldn't it be better for more countries to have nuclear weapons – indeed for every town to have some? The level of deterrence would be enormously greater! This sort of satirical challenge exposes an unexamined double standard underlying deterrence theory: it is good for the US government to have nuclear weapons but not for the governments of Iraq, Iran or North Korea.

There is a long tradition of humor used for dissent. The court jester was allowed to express home truths to the sovereign that were impermissible for others to voice. Today, cartoonists can question policy in more profound ways than normally expressed in print: Garry Trudeau arguably is far more biting than any conventional columnist.

Intellectuals are very good at developing rationales for any action they care to defend. Indeed, most people are quite competent at this. Evidence from brain imaging reveals that people make decisions slightly before their conscious minds prepare rational explanations. If subjects are presented with an unexpected object in a room, they will come up with a plausible reason for why it is there. The entire status quo benefits from an assumption of rationality: If this is the way things are done, people assume there must be a good reason for doing it, and come up with plausible explanations. If someone is arrested, many people assume the arrested person must have done something wrong.

Yet many customs have lost any rationale they might once have had. There is no obvious rational case for putting the fork on the left side of the plate; it is simply a convention. Putting the fork on the right could be a form of dissent – or eating with fingers, as is conventional in some cultures. Similarly, business meetings, financial statements, news broadcasts and much else operate according to convention, often with little rational basis. Humor and absurdity can be used to expose and challenge such conventions.

Finally, return to the assumption that dissent is intellectual, expressed in words. As discussed previously, dissent can also be expressed through action, including violence as well as nonviolent methods such as rallies, strikes, boycotts and sit-ins. The more drastic or confrontational measures are not necessarily more effective. Blowing the whistle polarizes the situation; it might be better to work quietly on the inside. Likewise, violence, even in support of a good cause, can be counterproductive, because people react against the violence itself, especially when it is used against those seen as innocent or defenseless. Using violence reduces the moral advantage of the attacker, which is why terrorism alienates observers. It is far better for dissenters to be the ones attacked. Think of the Indian protesters in 1930 being brutally beaten at the behest of the British colonial rulers, as portrayed in the 1982 film *Gandhi*, an event that galvanized support for Indian independence within India and internationally. In practical terms, nonviolent action often can be more effective than violence, even against ruthless leaders. So it is best to be wary about any generalizations about the effectiveness of tactics of dissent. Sometimes rational, civil discourse works best. Sometimes absurd and rude direct action is more effective.

Arenas for Dissenting – the Dance Floor

Dissent can occur in the most private and confidential circumstances and in huge, public arenas. Consider the accountant who queries the boss's tax write-off scheme. She could arrange a private meeting to discuss the issue. Or she could send a letter or a report just for the boss. A slightly more open method would be to send a circular to a select group pointing out that certain types of tax write-offs raise difficulties. This approach wouldn't single out the boss but at the same time might alert others to possible irregularities in the boss's actions. Another option is to report the matter to the company auditor, to the boss's boss, or to someone else who might take action. These choices of arena restrict the number of people who know about the matter but differ in exactly who is told about it.

A different approach is to raise the matter with larger numbers of people. One possibility is to raise it at a staff meeting. Another is to circulate a report on a company e-mail list. Taking the matter to an outside body, such as a government audit department or oversight agency, is yet another alternative. Others include giving information to the media or setting up a website and alerting a wide range of e-mail recipients.

These examples show there can be a variety of arenas through which dissent can be expressed. In many cases, private arenas are safer, but not always. Many people believe organizational dissenters should start internally and try all possible internal channels before going public. That is exactly the path pursued by many of those who end up being called whistle-blowers. They begin with an informal report to a colleague or the boss. When that doesn't work, they might go to a higher boss or to members of the governing board. Often by this time reprisals have begun, becoming an additional source of grievance, with relief sought through internal grievance procedures. When none of these provides any satisfaction – the most common experience – then it's time to approach outside bodies such as government audit departments, regulatory agencies, ombudsmen, anti-corruption bodies, courts and the like. The experience of whistleblowers – as shown in research by William De Maria – reveals these arenas are very unlikely to provide any relief. So eventually, often years down the track, the whistleblower decides to go public: despair over the failure of official channels drives the whistleblower to seek media attention (De Maria, 1999).

The confidential, internal route makes sense if expressing dissent privately turns out to be actually effective. Suppose the boss said, 'You're right, these tax write-offs I've been asking for are inappropriate. I'll immediately rectify the accounts and set up a procedure to make sure nobody – including me – is in any doubt about what's right and proper'. Mission accomplished: the accountant might leave feeling things have been fixed and not even imagine dissent was involved. How often does this happen? No one really knows, because we seldom hear about these cases where private communication promptly leads to a resolution of concerns.

It is safe to say such an ideal outcome is unlikely when something long-standing and deep is involved. If the boss has been fudging the books for years, the accountant is likely to become an immediate target for reprisals, while the boss hides or destroys the evidence. If the accountant pursues internal and external appeal processes, they are unlikely to provide any relief. In such situations, it is more effective to go public as soon as possible, or at least as soon as unimpeachable evidence is available. Going public sometimes can be safer too, because reprisals then become more obvious. The accountant is likely to lose her job whatever she does, but by going public there's a better chance a corrupt boss will be shamed and forced to resign, with vindication for the accountant.

In choosing an arena to express dissent, it's vital to think both of likely opponents and likely supporters. A private meeting sounds good in principle, but will fail if the boss responds by resisting or mounting an attack. What's missing in the private meeting is any way to increase support. Public forms of dissent can serve to mobilize greater support by making both the dissent and any reprisals known to potential allies.

Rationales for Dissenting – Choosing the Music

Another person's dissent can be annoying, distracting, time consuming and wasteful. So why put up with it? Isn't it better to get on with the job? If a group, before taking action, waited until everyone agreed, then it might never get anything done. At some point, disagreement must be set aside or overridden, or the group disbanded. That much is obvious. The key questions are about the appropriate point at which resolution occurs and what should be done about challenges to the establishment in the meantime.

In armies, dissent can be treated as insubordination and severely punished. On the front lines, refusal to fight is considered treason and sometimes penalized by execution. At stake is military success or even survival. Yet even in this life-and-death situation, there is potential value in dissent. Soldiers' rebellions may signal that a war is unwinnable or immoral.

Dissenters can be likened to a body's warning systems. Pain is not pleasant but it is valuable if it prevents a damaging action or draws attention to a serious problem. If pain persists, it may indicate disease. The body is designed so action can be taken despite pain, but it is usually unwise to ignore pain altogether. Any person whose pain receptors are deadened is at grave risk because injury can occur and be aggravated without awareness. Except in rare circumstances, it is unwise to cut off your hand if it is causing severe pain.

Dissenters at times do seem to be a pain in the body politic. A more positive analogy is to say they are like the body's sense of equilibrium, without which a person might fall over. The basic idea here is that dissent can be a valuable form of feedback to a group. It alerts the group to potential downsides of actions, highlights unexplored options and discourages short-sighted decision making. According to this line of thinking, dissenters should be encouraged, not castigated, and certainly not cut off entirely like the painful hand. What's the problem?

What dissenters are up against is a strong social pressure for conformity, which also can have survival value. If a tribe needs all its members to work together to find food, then often it is safer to cast out anyone who threatens the group's unity – or even to cast someone out in a scapegoating ritual in order to create unity. Remaining unified can be more important than getting decisions exactly right.

Whatever conclusions are reached about the dynamics of early human societies, it is certainly true that pressures for conformity continue to exist. The key issue today concerns the level of group cohesion that is necessary or desirable. The dangers of corruption and oppression are well known. The scale of contemporary societies is far greater than anything experienced in human prehistory and likewise the scale of potential and actual corruption and dysfunction is extraordinary. Consequently, it can be argued the need for dissent is greater than ever.

It might seem dissent is safe enough when free speech is protected as a legal right, but this is to confuse law and practical reality. 'Free speech' is the rhetoric but in reality it is hemmed in by all sorts of restrictions. In particular, free speech protections do not apply in workplaces. Deena Weinstein argues that bureaucracies – including corporations – are analogous to authoritarian states, with no rights to form opposition movements or to elect leaders (Weinstein, 1979).

The value of dissent to society is recognized through the respect paid to the principles of free speech, free assembly and the like. These principles can be seen as ways societies have set up early warning systems, to better prepare themselves for changing circumstances. Suppressing dissent can be efficient when the task is simple, unambiguous, and unchanging, and all hands are needed to tackle it. But when tasks are complex and changing, it is more efficient to harness a variety of points of view. Dissent helps make society flexible.

It is often noted that society is becoming more complex and rapidly changing, through processes that include globalization, mass education, technological innovation, diversified communication systems and the quest for personal self-development. In such a turbulent social and technological environment, suppression of dissent becomes ever more dysfunctional. Organizations and entire societies that are able to harness the insights and energy from dissent can better adapt to unpredictable, ongoing changes. Indeed, there is a case for maximizing flexibility by encouraging or even manufacturing dissent. At the small group level this is the familiar role of the devil's advocate; at the organization level it is the role of 'Team B', set up to challenge the dominant perspective represented as 'Team A'. However, there is a long way to go before corporate or government leaders decide to promote greater external scrutiny by funding grassroots opposition groups.

CONCLUSION

The concept of dissent covers a wide range of phenomena, from the intimate to the global and from the subtle to the bombastic. It is possible to restrict the domain of dissent somewhat by distinguishing it from disagreement, rebellion and heresy, but even so its domain is enormous. Dissent can occur in the form of thought alone or appear as the arching of an eyebrow, or it can be manifest in major protest actions. It can challenge the views or edicts of parents, teachers, peers, experts, bosses, national leaders, church leaders or scientific elites. It usually involves a challenge to a dominant view by the less powerful, but occasionally a leader is a dissenter against a pervasive way of doing things. Dissenters can be motivated by altruism, rationality, self-interest or a host of other possibilities.

Dissent is often risky. Some types of dissenters, such as whistleblowers, regularly suffer reprisals. Some dissent passes unnoticed. A few dissenters receive plaudits immediately; others are only recognized years, decades or centuries later. Yet others, probably the majority, are never vindicated and are judged as misguided by both peers and historians.

Is dissent worth having? A society in which all dissent was ruthlessly eliminated would survive only with an omniscient leader. Some level of dissent is necessary to keep an individual, organization or entire society flexible and responsive to change. But how much dissent is needed? And what is the best way to separate useful from damaging dissent? No one has come up with a conclusive answer to these questions. The most common strategy is to try to pick winners, namely to decide which dissent is worthwhile and which is foolish. The trouble with this approach is no one knows for sure which crazy alternative today will be widely accepted as a sensible course later. Attempting to pick winning dissenters is usually a prescription for a low tolerance for dissent.

Yet a balance is needed: too little dissent risks tyranny and stasis; too much risks chaos. What is the optimum level of dissent? My own view is that in many circumstances – such as authoritarian governments, bureaucratic organizations and conformist peer groups – there is a need for more dissent, or rather for more tolerance for dissenters and dissenting ideas. Even dissent that is wrong on the issues can be valuable by triggering an examination that leads to improvement. To ensure there is a reasonable amount of useful dissent, it is more reliable to protect all nonviolent dissent, for example through expansive interpretations and robust defenses of free speech. This means for every vindication of a crazy idea, there are scores of dissenters whose claims are never accepted. That is the cost of being open to challenge.

It is all very well to say more tolerance for dissent is needed. The key question is how to bring this about. Laws protecting free speech or whistleblowers have limited utility because what really counts are attitudes and behaviors. Changing those is more difficult than passing a law. Perhaps more valuable than protecting dissenters through formal processes such as laws is developing better skills in expressing and responding to dissent. Anyone who wants to challenge a dominant viewpoint needs not only powerful evidence and arguments but also skills in expression, negotiation, group dynamics, direct action and self-understanding. In other words, challengers need skills in how to mount an effective challenge. These are not usually taught in families, schools or workplaces!

Just as important are skills for those confronted by dissent. Not everyone is able to separate the message from the messenger, nor to tolerate foolishness while trusting that a few pearls of wisdom will occasionally surface. In all too many cases, managers react to dissent as if it is a personal attack – and sometimes it is, too. The temptation to counterattack can be overwhelming, especially for those with a lot of power. For them changes are needed in attitude, understanding and character, as well as new learning in dialogue skills and in creating a climate where dissent is accepted and harnessed for the greater good.

ACKNOWLEDGMENTS

I thank Steve Banks, Don Eldridge, Sue Curry Jansen and Ken Westhues for valuable comments on earlier drafts of this chapter.

REFERENCES

Deikman, Arthur J. (1990), *The Wrong Way Home: Uncovering the Patterns of Cult Behavior in American Society*, Boston, MA: Beacon Press.
De Maria, William (1999), *Deadly Disclosures: Whistleblowing and the Ethical Meltdown of Australia*, Adelaide, SA: Wakefield Press.
Glazer, Myron Peretz and Penina Migdal Glazer (1989), *The Whistleblowers: Exposing Corruption in Government and Industry*, New York: Basic Books.
Kipnis, David (1981), *The Powerholders*, 2nd edn, Chicago, IL: University of Chicago Press.
Nomad, Max (1932), *Rebels and Renegades*, New York: Macmillan.
Orwell, George (1949), *Nineteen Eighty-four*, London: Martin Secker & Warburg.
Schmid, Alex P. and Janny de Graaf (1982), *Violence as Communication: Insurgent Terrorism and the Western News Media*, London: Sage.
Sharp, Gene (2005), *Waging Nonviolent Struggle*, Boston, MA: Porter Sargent.
Sulloway, Frank J. (1996), *Born to Rebel: Birth Order, Family Dynamics, and Creative Lives*, New York: Pantheon.
Watson, James D. (2001), *The Double Helix: A Personal Account of the Discovery of the Structure of DNA*, Harlow: Penguin Longman.
Weinstein, Deena (1979), *Bureaucratic Opposition: Challenging Abuses at the Workplace*, New York: Pergamon.
Wolpe, Paul Root (1994), 'The dynamics of heresy in a profession', *Social Science and Medicine*, **39**, 1133–48.

3. Dissent in times of crisis

Jean Lipman-Blumen

What I want is men who will support me when I am in the wrong.[1]
(William Lamb Melbourne, British Prime Minister, 1834, 1835–41)

INTRODUCTION

Like Prime Minister Melbourne, few leaders welcome dissent. While stifling dissent is an unabashed hallmark of authoritarian regimes, it occurs in democratic systems as well, despite their avowed openness to debate. When crises occur, dissent is appreciated even less.

Crises shake the ground beneath incumbent leaders. They also give rise to authoritarianism and secrecy. Consequently, crises create hothouse conditions for squelching dissenters and their messages, despite the potential importance of their warnings.

More surprisingly, leaders are not the only ones who cold-shoulder dissenters during crises. In fact, leaders' rejection of dissent frequently infects many of their loyal followers, too. As a result, followers often mimic the hue and cry of their leaders, who routinely subject dissenters and their frustrated brethren, whistleblowers, to professional and personal ostracism or worse (Alford, 2001). They rarely recognize how dissent provides the potential antidote to 'groupthink', that well-documented undertow in which policymakers can be swept away during crises (Janis, 1972).

What leaders, particularly toxic leaders, have to gain by silencing dissenters is quite apparent, even to the casual observer. What followers derive from endorsing the suffocation of dissent, however, is far less obvious and more intriguing. That is particularly the case when the followers' own personal freedoms, even those constitutionally guaranteed, may be in serious jeopardy.

The purpose of this chapter is four-fold: first, to explore several aspects of crisis that set the stage for constituents to accept their leader's quashing of dissent; second, to link the conditions of crisis to ordinary human needs of followers; third, to examine the severe risks to policymaking, including the possibility of groupthink, and the longer-term dangers posed by authoritarian policies embedded in hastily passed legislation; and fourth, to offer several possible strategies for engaging in effective dissent during crises. It should be noted that not all leaders respond to crises by suppressing dissent. Some few, like Mahatma Mohandas Gandhi, rise to the challenge of crisis by seeking out and legitimating dissenting views. Nonetheless, such leaders are noteworthy in part because of their rarity.

SETTING THE STAGE FOR QUASHING DISSENT: NEW LEADERS, AUTHORITARIANISM AND SECRECY

Crises, by their very nature, create several key conditions conducive to crushing dissent. More specifically, crisis is a situation that ruptures the dike of our available responses to run-of-the-mill emergencies (Lipman-Blumen, 1973). In crises, we find ourselves beset by seriously threatening circumstances for which our ordinary resources and coping strategies are patently inadequate. The usual reaction to crisis – doing more of what we normally do or doing it faster and harder – simply won't suffice.

At a minimum, crises promote instability in existing leadership that resorts to its standard emergency repertoire. (Artificial crises provoked by a manipulative leader – like the Spanish-American War allegedly instigated by William Randolph Hearst to boost newspaper circulation – may follow a somewhat different trajectory. A systematic discussion of the additional hazards such crises entail, however, is beyond the scope of this chapter.) Grave threat, sometimes even to our survival, combined with inadequate resources and coping mechanisms, makes participants receptive to leaders and strategies they normally would repudiate. If everything we usually do won't work, then maybe we need to reconsider alternatives we'd typically shun. If the current leader can't supply them, then perhaps a different one can.

Crisis and Leadership

In the initial stages of a crisis, followers typically rally around the leader, propelling the leader's approval ratings into the stratosphere. If the incumbent leader fails to resolve the crisis expeditiously, however, he or she may be toppled or, in democratic systems, voted out of office. Former US President Jimmy Carter learned that lesson the hard way. At the outset of the 1979–81 Iran Hostage Crisis, Carter's decision to oversee the situation from his White House command post (the so-called 'Rose Garden strategy') was met with widespread popular approval. Carter won those plaudits for acting 'presidential' by choosing to remain in the White House above the political fray generated by the upcoming presidential election. That support enabled the president, embattled within his own party, to brush aside Senator Ted Kennedy's election-year challenge to a pre-primary debate in the mid-West. In so doing, Carter completely derailed his Democratic challenger's presidential bid.

Yet, as unrelenting nightly TV coverage counted the days of the 52 hostages' captivity, public support gradually dwindled into impatience and disillusionment. Months passed without any sign of the hostages' release. When Carter's efforts eventually culminated in a disastrous rescue attempt several months shy of the presidential election, the conditions were ripe for the emergence of a new, very different and charismatic leader, Ronald Reagan. As journalist Elizabeth Drew suggested, 'Fairly or not, [the hostage crisis] came to symbolize the question of whether Carter was a leader, whether he was competent, whether he was strong' (Public Broadcast System, 1980).

A more recent crisis, the 9/11 terrorist attack on the World Trade Center, catapulted a faltering Bush presidency into the high approval zone. In the immediate aftermath of the stunning catastrophe, President George W. Bush's approval ratings soared to 90 percent, the highest ever recorded for any American president (Lipman-Blumen, 2005). That strong public confidence enabled Bush to convince a dubious Congress to support the war in Iraq, despite shaky evidence regarding an alleged Iraqi program for weapons of mass destruction.

Over the next four years, as the Iraq war spun out of control, Bush's numbers tumbled dramatically. At the time of writing, Bush's approval rating had plummeted to 27 percent, with members of his own party distancing themselves from the President's policies, both foreign and domestic. Although Bush has 'termed out', most pundits currently believe his inability to resolve the Iraq war or bring Osama bin Laden to justice has spread the public's dissatisfaction with his handling of the crisis to other Republican candidates in the 2008 presidential election. At the end of 2007, many observers from both parties agreed the 2008 election is the Democrats' to lose – a real possibility, considering their frequent demonstrations of this talent.

During crises, new leaders wait impatiently in the wings, practicing their acceptance speech. In fact, charismatic leaders, those charming and seductive characters with radically different solutions, are 'born of distress,' as Max Weber described (Weber, 1946). Because the solutions they offer commonly diverge 180 degrees from the current leader's strategies, disenchanted followers perceive new hope.

Crisis and the Creation of God[2]

Oftentimes, the leader, new or old, insists upon tight, authoritarian changes, purportedly designed to protect the followers in such dangerous times. Because crisis provokes followers to turn to God or human leaders willing to play God, the door to authoritarianism swings open. The followers' ordinary human fears and needs, as I shall discuss below, prompt them to obey the leader's dictatorial commands. The relationship between fear and the creation of gods is hardly new. The Latin poet Publius Papinius Statius (*ca.* AD 45–96) noted it centuries ago when he wrote, 'It was fear that first made gods in the world' [*Primus in orbe deos fecit timor*]; (Latin Library, 2007).

Followers, shaken to their foundations by a crisis for which they have no ready answers, seek protection from an all-knowing, strong leader. They seek gods, both divine and human. They invest fallible human leaders with divine infallibility and omnipotence. They also make a familiar bargain, one learned in childhood with authoritarian parents: safety in exchange for obedience.

So, it is not surprising to see restrictions and conservation of resources during crises. Curfews, food and fuel rationing, travel constraints, salary freezes and other repressive means are introduced – and readily accepted by the majority of followers – when crises occur. Nor is this to say that strong measures are never appropriate in crisis. Nonetheless, most followers' knee-jerk acceptance of unnecessary restrictions lies at the heart of our concern.

Some followers may harbor doubts about the wisdom of obeying the leader's authoritarian commands. Yet, they may find themselves intimidated into remaining silent and following the leader's dictates anyway. Nor is it only the weak and powerless who tap their toes to the rhythms of authoritarianism waltzing with crisis. Even those with considerable political power can be cowed into agreement lest they be labeled traitors, cowards, or worse.

A case in point: in the aftermath of 9/11, many members of the US House of Representatives and the Senate found themselves in the untenable position of voting to send the country to a war they didn't wholeheartedly endorse, lest they be perceived as unpatriotic. In fact, the vote to support the President's plan to invade Iraq was nearly unanimous. This example demonstrates how potential dissenters can be intimidated into censoring themselves.

Followers frequently accept restrictions on so-called 'enemies' that violate some of their own most treasured values. For example, under SEC. 802 (e), (f)[3] of the USA PATRIOT Act also known as The Patriot Act

(HR 3162), passed within 45 days of 9/11, suspected terrorists may be tried by military tribunal without any appeal or review process, so fundamental to American criminal law. Despite complaints by some media and human rights groups, the military tribunal section of the Patriot Act remains in force at the time of writing. President Bush rested his claim for legitimacy on the precedent set by wartime President Franklin D. Roosevelt, who condoned the use of a military tribunal to try Nazi saboteurs after their stealth landing in the US during World War II. Ironically, Roosevelt's action is quite uniformly condemned by contemporary political historians.

Authoritarian leaders often corral their followers by demonstrating their prowess against individuals or members of groups whom the followers despise, fear or resent. The followers can take quiet satisfaction from the leaders' punitive action against those they scorn. For example, many French citizens remained silent as the Nazis deported large numbers of French Jews to concentration camps.

Moreover, in times of crisis, authoritarian leaders can inspire their followers to give vent to their own resentments against a despised group. Consequently, some followers take more than quiet satisfaction; they step up to the plate and swing the bat with gusto. That was the case in the Polish town of Jedwabne, in the summer of 1941. On 10 July, half of the townspeople voluntarily acted out eight Gestapo officers' condemnation of Jedwabne's Jewish citizens – the other half of the population. With unspeakable brutality, they butchered and drowned the hapless Jewish townsfolk with whom they previously had gone to school, shopped in their stores, and generally experienced congenial interaction. Then, they herded the remaining Jews into a barn and set fire to it. One Jedwabne farmer had enthusiastically donated that barn for the occasion. Sixteen hundred Jews died that summer day. By evening, only seven Jews had escaped the murderous rampage. They owed their lives to one family who valiantly hid them from harm. After the war, that family was driven from Jedwabne. To compound the evil, for the next 60 years the town deliberately maintained the myth that the Nazis, not they, had perpetrated the massacre (Gross, 2001).

Beyond condoning authoritarian constraints on those they perceive as 'the enemy' or simply 'the other', followers also tolerate incursions against their own traditionally guaranteed rights and freedoms. In the immediate wake of 9/11, ordinary American citizens demonstrated a clear willingness to trade off some of those rights for the promise of greater security from terrorists. As I have reported elsewhere: '[I]n the two days following the 2001 World Trade Center attack, *New York Times* and CBS News polls indicated that 74 percent of those questioned said they "believed that Americans would have to give up some personal freedoms in order to make the country safe from terrorist attacks"' (Lipman-Blumen, 2005, p. 105).

By the following week, 79 percent of those polled agreed that certain individual freedoms should be forgone to assure greater security from such assaults. In the poll taken within 48 hours of the attack, 39 percent of those questioned agreed that 'regular governmental monitoring of ordinary citizens' e-mail and telephone conversations' was acceptable to them. By the next week, their numbers rose to 45 percent. As if that were not enough, 56 percent reported they were in favor of national electronic ID cards (Lipman-Blumen, 2005, p. 105).

The USA PATRIOT Act includes many provisions the Congress had previously rejected as infringements upon Constitutional protections of citizens' rights. For example, although the Bush Administration assured the public that the Patriot Act would not be used against non-terrorists, within two years of its enactment, according to the *International Herald Tribune* and the *New York Times*, the Justice Department acknowledged the act's helpfulness in prosecuting drug dealers, white-collar criminals and child pornographers – mostly US citizens.

The original 2001 Patriot Act required reauthorization in 2005–6, owing to a sunset clause that served as the gangplank for bringing most stragglers aboard the original legislation. When the bill came up for reauthorization in 2005, the *Washington Post* reported,

> Original action on the bill was blocked in the Senate 2005 by four Republicans and a majority of Democrats who demanded that safeguards be put in place to protect against abuses of the law. Those safeguards included ending the use of 'National Security Letters', which did not require a judge's approval to obtain some forms of electronic information. Senators also added a provision that would allow the recipients of a [*sic*] '215 subpoenas', which are issued by the secret Foreign Intelligence Surveillance Act court, to challenge 'gag' orders that prevented them from disclosing the fact that they had received a subpoena. In the end, the Senate and the House voted overwhelmingly to renew nearly all of the original Patriot Act's provisions, and the president signed the reauthorization bill into law on 9 March, 2006. (*Washington Post*, 2006)

The final vote tallied 89 to 10, split along party lines, with one Democrat abstaining. So, despite the *sturm und drang* about the violation of citizens' freedoms leading up to the vote, to paraphrase T. S. Eliot (1936),

> This is the way the vote ends, not with a bang but a whimper.

Crisis and Secrecy

The danger posed by most crises frequently serves as the rationale, if not the pretext, for authoritarian leaders to shroud their repression of dissension in multi-layered secrecy. In some countries, political dissenters may be imprisoned without specific charges, without access to family or legal counsel, and without any time limit. In fact, families frequently have difficulty gaining information concerning the whereabouts of their dissenting relatives. Moreover, imprisonment may not be the worst fate suffered by political dissenters in some regions of the world.

Transparency evaporates as leaders insist they cannot offer more detailed explanations for their authoritarian actions without divulging key, even state, secrets to the 'enemy'. The murder and disappearance of 9000–30 000 dissenters, known as 'the disappeared', who were murdered or vanished in the 'dirty war' during Argentina's military rule from 1976–83, is but one example of the degree to which authoritarian leadership can impose secrecy during crisis (BBC News, 30 April 2007).

Nor is the crisis-imposed secrecy necessarily limited to the active crisis timeframe. On 30 April, 2007, three decades after their children disappeared, the Mothers of Plaza de Mayo, carrying photos of their vanished offspring, staged their annual march in front of the presidential palace, still demanding to know what had happened to their children.

Dissenters often accept authoritarian decisions based on the leaders' insistence that they know best or at least have critical information to which the followers are not privy – familiar strains from the 'God Is Omniscient Symphony'. The leader's access to secret information offers an irrefutable argument designed to extinguish dissent.

For example, during a 24 May, 2007 presidential news conference, a White House correspondent asked President George W. Bush:

> Mr President, after the mistakes that have been made in this war, when you do as you did yesterday, where you raised two-year-old intelligence, talking about the threat posed by al Qaeda, it's met with increasing skepticism. The majority in the public, a growing number of Republicans, appear not to trust you any longer to be able to carry out this policy successfully. Can you explain why you believe you're still a credible messenger on the war? (Whitehouse.gov, 2007)

The president jauntily responded, 'I'm credible because I read the intelligence' (Whitehouse.gov, 2007).

The Media

While the media's primary role, particularly touted in democratic societies, is to inform the public, even the Fourth Estate may be silenced through intimidation, limited access and other forms of manipulation. Journalists who run afoul of an authoritarian regime routinely lose access to important sources or, worse yet, lose their heads.

Reporters who write articles critical of an authoritarian administration may find themselves shut out by their previously accessible key 'sources'.

Sometimes, the consequences are more dire. For example, in 2006, Anna Politkovskaya, a Russian journalist noted for her criticism of the war in Chechnya, was murdered in her apartment. According to her editors, Politkovskaya's explosive article reporting eye-witness accounts of kidnappings and photographs of tortured corpses in Chechnya had been scheduled for publication the following week. An award-winning reporter, Politkovskaya was the 43rd Russian journalist to be killed under mysterious circumstances since 1993.

Authoritarian regimes often 'manage the news' in various ways. Sometimes, they simply time the release of negative information for specific moments in the news cycle to ensure its lack of coverage by mainstream media outlets. At other times, authoritarian leaders limit the amount and type of news to which journalists have access. The familiar strategy noted above, invoking 'state secrecy', muzzles not only the media, but a wide range of other dissenters as well.

In wartime particularly, governments frequently restrict official military and other state information as 'classified'. Here, too, they insist that informing the general public would simultaneously alert the 'enemy'.

Reporters covering World War II faced major hurdles in their attempts to witness first-hand key battlefield events. Consequently, they were obliged to rely on official government communiqués. In a relevant recent twist, during the second Iraq War, journalists eagerly accepted the government's invitation to become embedded with troops in war zones. Only subsequently did many of these ordinarily savvy reporters recognize the subtle effects their intense interaction with their military comrades had on the objectivity of the reports they filed.

When the mainstream media are silenced, the general public has difficulty ferreting out the issues that demand their dissent. Fortunately, current technology, particularly the internet, offers an alternative source of information, as well as an avenue for drawing the attention and support of other potential dissenters.

In brief, crises, marked by inherent dangers and stresses, create ideal conditions for suppressing dissent. First, they can destabilize leaders whose actions don't resolve the crisis quickly and successfully, largely by increasing the followers' yearning for godlike leaders. Second, crises seed authoritarianism, spawning unquestioned acceptance of leaders' demands, even when those demands muzzle legitimate dissent. Moreover, the dangers inherent in crises provide the rationale for secrecy that also serves to mute disagreement. Even mainstream media, whose official responsibilities include informing the public of issues worthy of dissent, may become targets of authoritarian leaders who wish to suppress dissension.

CRISES AND FOLLOWERS' VERY HUMAN NEEDS AND FEARS

Crises provoke followers' awareness of their very human needs and fears. These ordinary needs and anxieties fit hand-in-glove with the characteristics of most crises, making followers particularly susceptible to the leader's demands. Bowing to the limitations of space, I shall narrow my focus to but a few examples from three major sets of human concerns which crises exacerbate: existential, psychological and pragmatic. By manipulating these three sets of followers' longings and anxieties, leaders lay the groundwork for quelling dissent.

Existential Needs

During the stress of crisis, our most primitive needs and profound anxieties bubble up from our unconscious, making us more vulnerable than ever. According to Sigmund Freud and Ernest Becker, our deepest anxieties surround the unknown timing and circumstances of our inevitable death (Freud, 1936; Becker, 1973). Because these anxieties are so unsettling, even immobilizing, we tend to submerge them in the depths of our subconscious, where they nonetheless quietly drive our attitudes and behavior.

Consciously thinking about our own death, as experimental social psychologists have aptly demonstrated, affects our choices and actions (Pyszczynski *et al.*, 2001). Death dealing crises, like 9/11, propel our existential anxiety to the surface of consciousness and force us to confront these discombobulating concerns. For many of us TV viewers, watching bodies hurtling to the ground from the upper floors of the World Trade Center Towers ripped open the carefully sealed compartment of our unconscious. In that instant, the horrific images compelled most of us to think about how we, too, shall someday die. Nor do we need such extreme catastrophes to awaken the earthquake of our existential dread that controls significant aspects of our behavior.

Psychological Needs

The relevant psychological needs we followers have far exceed the limits of this discussion. So let us settle for a few that make our point. First, as Abraham Maslow's well-known 'hierarchy of needs' suggests, our need for safety or security is only second to our most primal physiological needs (Maslow, 1954; 1971). Leaders who assure us that they have the capacity to shield us from harm, particularly from death, appear particularly attractive during crises. So, in fearsome times, we followers can hardly be blamed for seeking the embrace of leaders who make such promises, even if they can't deliver on their pledges.

Leaders who emphasize the dangers inherent in any particular crisis are likely to witness flocks of followers scurrying to join them. Those leaders who insist the crisis is endless and possibly worldwide can assure themselves of a solid core of fearful followers. Under the circumstances, ransoming their safety, maybe their very lives, with personal freedoms appears to be a minor sacrifice, a reasonable tradeoff, to the threatened. The 'War on Terror', pronounced in the wake of 9/11, is only the most recent example of this strategy. Playing the 'terror card' whenever dissent appears imminent continues to produce a remarkable muffling effect in leadership arenas, from political to corporate and academic.

Second, our yearning to replace those parental figures on whom we could count in our childhood comes into play when crisis strikes. In adulthood, many of us continue to experience the vacuum left by our parents as a serious void. When we hear the familiar strains of authoritarian expectations we learned early in life (for example, 'Children should be seen and not heard'), almost instinctively we begin to dance to that familiar tune. We purchase our security with the coinage of infantilization. We transfer the allegiance and faith we had in our parents to these replacements, authoritarian leaders who teach us to hold our tongues even when we are in the right.

Third, in crises, our need to know and understand, particularly our need for certainty, can be readily manipulated by those leaders who would brook no dissent. Earlier I spoke of the secrecy that authoritarian leaders invoke in crisis. That secrecy is frequently linked to the leader's 'special knowledge'. That undisclosable knowledge, we are told, guarantees the correctness of the leader's strategy. While we, the followers, must be kept in the dark, the leader has information and certainty on his or her side. So we needn't worry.

Other psychological needs – such as our need for community, our fear of ostracism and 'social death', our anxiety about standing alone, our sense of personal impotence in the face of authority, and our need to feel we are among God's or society's 'chosen' – are legion (Lipman-Blumen, 2005). The few we discussed – our need for safety, the hunger to replace parental figures, and our longing for certainty – are merely placeholders for the many psychological needs to which we humans are heir.

Pragmatic Needs

Pragmatic needs have their own hold on us: our jobs, our homes, our children's braces and soccer uniforms. Quotidian concerns about receiving our paycheck, keeping a roof over our heads, and putting groceries on the family table, to name a few, can stifle us, even when we know we have truth, justice and ethics on our side.

Research on whistleblowers suggests that they tend to cast aside such pragmatic concerns, much to the consternation of their families (Alford, 2001). In fact, the breakup of whistleblowers' marriages is one notable side effect of their apparent willingness to ignore pragmatic concerns for the greater good of 'speaking truth to power'.

Pragmatic needs, like their psychological cousins, can bind us like Gulliver in the hands of the Lilliputians. To objective observers, these needs may seem relatively small. In the eyes of the would-be dissenter, however, pragmatic concerns may loom large enough to be incapacitating. When crisis strikes, as noted above, ordinary but critical resources – jobs, food, shelter and other necessities – become scarce. Endangering one's access to these resources by antagonizing the leader through dissent may be more than potential dissenters feel they can afford. Besides, leaders, particularly those who would institute authoritarian restrictions, are wont to hold this threat over potential dissenters' heads in the maelstrom of crisis.

In sum, followers' ever-present human needs escalate in crises. Both real and imagined dangers shimmer in the darkness of hazardous times. Other crisis characteristics – the purported need for secrecy, the potential rise of authoritarianism, and possible restrictions on essential resources – increase leaders' leverage over their shaken followers. By manipulating their followers' existential, psychological and pragmatic needs and fears, leaders can handily throttle dissent.

THE RISKS TO POLICYMAKING

Muffling dissent poses serious risks to policymaking. Here let us treat some representative dangers to policymaking that commonly occur during crises: the likelihood of groupthink (a rush to consensus); the failure to consider secondary, tertiary and other long-term consequences; and the difficulty of reversing hastily enacted policies, particularly those embedded in legislation.

Groupthink

By now, leaders and other policymakers are quite familiar with the concept of 'groupthink', introduced by Irving L. Janis in 1972. Nonetheless, that rush to consensus still recurs in various arenas. The pattern is recognizable: A group of policymakers, acting under an 'illusion of unity', approves the leader's announced preference without considering potential drawbacks and alternative strategies. 'Mindguarding', a key aspect of groupthink, involves one or more members acting as guardians of a limited discussion process to keep would-be dissenters from expressing their concerns. Sometimes, direct pressure is applied to potential dissenters; at other times, the mindguarding process is internalized, and group participants police themselves.

Historians routinely cite the Bay of Pigs crisis, which exploded early in President John F. Kennedy's first term of office, as the paradigmatic case of groupthink. In that April 1961 'fiasco', as it is frequently called, it was Attorney General Robert F. Kennedy who most notably took aside the Administration's sole historian, Arthur M. Schlesinger, Jr., to caution him against expressing his reservations to the president. The attorney general's reasoning: the president had virtually made up his mind, and any dissent would simply derail the process, particularly when 'time was of the essence'. Schlesinger reconsidered and remained mute, much to his subsequent regret (Schlesinger, 1965).

Other subtler aspects of groupthink also play their part in choking off dissent. For example, new or lower status members of the policy group may be reluctant to express their concerns for fear of negative responses from other more established or highly-regarded group members. In retrospect, for example, Schlesinger attributed his failure to confront the president to three major sources: his own sense of newness to the policy group Kennedy had assembled to address the Bay of Pigs crisis; his inexperience with policymaking; and his sensitivity about the unique and ambiguous status he held as an academic historian *vis-à-vis* experienced policymakers.

President Kennedy's anguish about his leadership failure during the Bay of Pigs led him to take deliberate steps to encourage the same set of advisors to air all dissenting views during the Cuban Missile Crisis some 18 months later (Janis, 1972; Kennedy, 1969). Although the historical lens allows us to assess the Cuban Missile Crisis more complexly today than previously, groupthink was deliberately and notably absent from the deliberations of the Executive Committee of the National Security Council.

Failure to Consider Secondary, Tertiary or Longer-term Effects

Even without the full-blown dynamic of groupthink, the real and imagined pressures of time that accompany crises often lead policymakers to ignore the secondary, tertiary or longer-term effects of their decisions. Perhaps the fear, as well as the illusion, that crisis foreshortens the time allowable for decision-making leads policymakers to make short shrift of these less obvious, but potentially grave, sometimes irreversible consequences.

Because the case for secondary, tertiary and longer-term effects of policymaking is often difficult to substantiate, those individuals who raise them may be seen as indecisive Prince Hamlets or, worse, Cassandran prophets of doom. The history of the global warming debate, with early warners pointing to possible long-term and widespread consequences, offers a compelling example of the difficulties inherent in bringing an alternative view to the policy table.

Difficulties of Reversing Crisis-induced Policies

The urgency that marks crisis often prompts policymakers to take action that later becomes exceedingly difficult to reverse. For example, after 9/11, the Bush Administration insisted that eavesdropping was a temporary necessity to keep the US safe from terrorist plots. Many legislators presumably agreed to the initial legislation, calmed by the assurance they could revisit and, if need be, reverse it in 2007. When that opportunity arose, actually just as this chapter was being written, the US House of Representatives voted 227 to 183 to keep the Foreign Intelligence Surveillance Act on the books (*New York Times*, 2007: 1, 14).

Some might argue that the decision was taken because the terrorist threat continues apace. Nonetheless, numerous laws passed decades ago, though seldom used, remain in effect because the political will to remove them is difficult to muster after the crisis dissipates. The political capital necessary to reverse policy decisions concretized in crisis-induced legislation usually is deemed too valuable to squander over long past crisis actions. Still, the danger of such creeping infringements on personal rights and freedoms remains undiminished.

STRATEGIES FOR EFFECTIVE DISSENT DURING CRISES

It would be unduly optimistic to suggest there are many reliable strategies for enacting dissent, even in crisis times. Actually, few robust strategies exist for promoting effective dissent during crises, but let us consider some possibilities.

1. *Create a broad-based coalition.* Being a lone dissenter in times of crisis is rarely successful. In fact, it can be downright hazardous to your health. So, creating a broad-based coalition is probably a wise strategy, if nonetheless difficult to implement. The trade union movement was based on this idea, and, despite the hard times upon which unions more

recently have fallen for a host of reasons, the underlying rationale is still tenable.

2. *Spread the word on the Internet.* Getting the word out to thousands of like-minded individuals and groups has never been easier. The Internet is fast and far-reaching, allowing dissenters – at least in the West – to bypass the mainstream media watchdogs with a click of the mouse. The technology isn't foolproof or completely immune to authoritarian control. Consider the limitations on web access placed on users in The People's Republic of China. Nonetheless, the Internet offers immense advantages. Developing financial and other resources can be accomplished in a surprisingly short time, and polling, coordinating and enlisting supporters can be done globally. Still, it takes considerable Internet savvy to use this powerful communication network effectively. Of course, if dissenters have access to mainstream media who would present their case in a positive light, that too is a powerful route.

3. *Enlist the backing of high-visibility, credible supporters.* Seeking the support of highly respected individuals and groups can lend credibility to the dissenter's position. For example, gathering a group of Nobel Prize Laureates to endorse the dissenter's position can gain considerable visibility with genuinely persuasive clout for the dissenter's cause.

4. *Realize there is more time than you think.* Do not be rushed into ill-considered strategies and pronouncements because of the crisis mindset that insists time is running out. Although time may be short, most crises actually have more decision-making time than either dissenters, followers or leaders usually perceive. Time spent carefully examining all the possibilities is time well spent.

5. *Focus on the constructive, collaborative tone of your message, as well as on a shared goal.* When dissenters frame their disagreement in constructive, reasonable ways, their message is more likely to be heard by policymakers. Framing your dissent as a means of collaborating on a shared goal enhances the possibilities of gaining a serious hearing from decision-makers. Paradoxically, the popular media, preferring a diet of conflict and sensationalism, are less likely to publicize your dissent to the mass of needed supporters.

6. *Because crisis is a time when new solutions are sought, stick to your guns.* Just as charismatic leaders with new solutions are frequently welcomed in times of crisis, so are agendas that may have been rejected in more ordinary times. When stability reigns, leaders and other policymakers may be reluctant to change course, even if the current direction is not leading to great results. That new agenda (regarded as 'dissent' in the stable pre-crisis period) may be welcomed as the perfect solution by harried leaders, desperate for new approaches.

In this chapter, we have necessarily limited our focus to normal crises – situations that arise from human error, poor policy, natural catastrophes and technological mishaps, as well as political and sociological events. Other artificial or manufactured crises, particularly those created or encouraged by toxic leaders, may require additional awareness and strategies. Such induced, facilitated or amplified crises only heighten reliance on fear, secrecy and god-like command. They also exacerbate the existential, psychological and practical needs of followers discussed above. Under such conditions, dissent, if it is to occur at all, becomes even more multi-layered and problematical.

The concerns about quashing dissent in moments of crisis considered here may be read as a cautionary tale about leaders' behaviors and motives, particularly when leadership is most needed. Certainly whenever crises occur, these issues merit serious consideration by followers and other stakeholders. The words of Martin Luther King, Jr. offer a fitting capstone to this analysis: 'Our lives begin to end the day we become silent about things that matter' (QuoteDB 2007).

NOTES

1. The Prime Minister was responding to a politician's pronouncement that 'I will support you as long as you are in the right'.
2. This section is elaborated in Lipman-Blumen (2005).
3. Sections (e) and (f) read: (e) To protect the United States and its citizens, and for the effective conduct of military operations and prevention of terrorist attacks, it is necessary for individuals subject to this order pursuant to section 2 hereof to be detained, and, when tried, to be tried for violations of the laws of war and other applicable laws by military tribunals. (f) Given the danger to the safety of the United States and the nature of international terrorism, and to the extent provided by and under this order, I find consistent with section 836 of title 10, United States Code, that it is not practicable to apply in military commissions under this order the principles of law and the rules of evidence generally recognized in the trial of criminal cases in the United States district courts.

REFERENCES

Alford, C. Fred (2001), *Whistleblowers: Broken Lives and Organizational Power*, Ithaca, NY: Cornell University Press.

BBC (2007), 'Argentine mothers mark 30 years', 30 April, accessed 5 September, 2007 at http://news.bbc.co.uk/1/hi/world/americas/6608871.stm.

Becker, Ernest (1973), *The Denial of Death*, New York: Basic Books.

CBS (2006), 'Russian journalist murdered', accessed 8 September, 2007 at www.cbsnews.com/stories/2006/10/09/world/main2073139.shtml.

Eliot, Thomas S. (1936), 'The Hollow Men', in *Collected Poems (1909–1925)*, New York: Harcourt Brace Jovanovich.

Freud, Sigmund (1936), *The Problem of Anxiety*, translated by Henry Alden Bunker, New York: The Psychoanalytic Quarterly Press and W.W. Norton.

Gross, Jan T. (2001), *Neighbors: The Destruction of the Jewish Community in Jedwabne, Poland*, Princeton, NJ: Princeton University Press.

Janis, Irving L. (1972), *Victims of Groupthink: A Psychological Study of Foreign-Policy Decisions and Fiascoes*, Boston, MA: Houghton Mifflin.

Kennedy, Robert F. (1969), *Thirteen Days: A Memoir of the Cuban Missile Crisis*, New York: W.W. Norton.

Latin Library (2007), 'FRAGMENTA PETRONII QVAE QVIBUS IN LOCIS REPONENDA SINT, INCERTVM EST', fragmenta XXII, accessed 6 August, 2007 at http://thelatinlibrary.com/petroniusfrag.html.

Lipman-Blumen, Jean (1973), 'Role de-differentiation as a system response to crisis', *Sociological Inquiry*, **42** (2), 105–29.

Lipman-Blumen, Jean (2005), *The Allure of Toxic Leaders*, New York: Oxford University Press.

Maslow, Abraham (1954), *Motivation and Personality*, New York: Harper and Brothers.

Maslow, Abraham (1971), *The Farther Reaches of Human Nature*, New York: Viking Press.

New York Times (2007), 'House approves changes in eavesdropping program', 5 August, A1, p. 14.

Public Broadcast System (PBS) (1980), 'People & events: the election of 1980', accessed 6 September, 2007 at www.pbs.org/wgbh/amex/carter/peopleevents/e_1980.html.

Pyszczynski, Tom, Sheldon Solomon and Jeff Greenberg (2001), *In the Wake of 9/11: The Psychology of Terror*, Washington, DC: American Psychological Association.

QuoteDB (2007), 'King, Martin Luther, Jr.', accessed 13 September, 2007 at www.quotedb.com/quotes/3081.

Schlesinger, Arthur M., Jr. (1965), *A Thousand Days*, Boston, MA: Houghton Mifflin.

Washington Post (2006), 'The US Congress votes database', accessed 8 August, 2007 at http://projects.washingtonpost.com/congress/109/senate/2/votes/29/.

Weber, M. (1946), 'The sociology of charismatic authority', in H. H. Gerth and C. Wright Mills (eds), *From Max Weber: Essays in Sociology*, New York: Oxford University Press, pp. 245–52.

Whitehouse.gov (2007), 'Press conference by the president', 24 May, accessed 2 August, 2007 at www.whitehouse.gov/news/releases/2007/05/20070524.html.

4. Dissent and the generational divide

Stephanie Hamel and Ruth Guzley

> Your generations' collective mind-set cannot help but influence you – whether you agree with it or spend a lifetime battling against it.
>
> (Strauss and Howe, 1991: 9)

INTRODUCTION

Leading and dissenting differ across generations. As Greenberg-Walt and Robertson (2001) quip, 'Younger generations always strive to develop their own identities and to make their mark' (p. 148). We know this intuitively and anecdotally, but we need to understand generational differences in a deeper and more disciplined way if we are to promote effectiveness and minimize failures among future leaders. We wonder what today's youth will be able to accomplish on a global scale, given the monumental challenges they face, for both themselves and the generations that will follow.

Pragmatists among us seek to understand those of the newest generation who one day will emerge as leaders. We want to know, can they lead through these challenges? Can they advocate effectively on our behalf and their own? Will they be willing to speak out against injustices? Will they embrace the central tenets of democracy and engage differences through deliberation and dissent? Or will they pave a new way we cannot yet comprehend? We devote this chapter to exploring a fundamental ingredient of democracy – dissent – and learning whether the new generation will seek to embrace, suppress or redefine dissent as they become leaders in our communities, workplaces and global scene.

As professors we interact daily with the newest generation – known variously as 'Generation Y', 'GenNext', 'Echo Boomers' and 'DotNets' but which we will call, adopting Howe and Strauss's nomenclature, 'Millennials'. Just as negative stereotypes abound about this new generation, much has been written about the positive qualities they bring to society (see, for example, Howe and Strauss, 2000). Nevertheless, we have become particularly concerned with an observed trend among our Millennial students toward indifference to (and sometimes repudiation of) the effort required for critical thought and evaluation of ideas and actions necessary for informed debate and deliberation. If generalizable, this trend may indicate a further decline of public interest in debating important issues and expressing well-grounded dissenting views. A 2002 *New York Times* article reflects this concern:

> What are the consequences of students' growing reluctance to debate? Though it represents a welcome departure from the polarized mudslinging of the 90s culture wars, it also represents a failure to fully engage with the world, a failure to test one's convictions against the logic and passions of others. It suggests a closing off of the possibilities of growth and transformation and repudiation of the process of consensus building. (Kakutani, 2002)

We begin this chapter with an examination of the qualities and characteristics that identify the Millennial generation in the United States. We pay special attention to parental, educational and technological influences, particularly as they shape the generation's leaders and their attitudes toward dissent. Next we discuss the manifestations of these influences on Millennials and dissent as they have been reported in three leadership contexts – the community, the workplace and national politics. A clearer understanding of the personal and public influences on Millennials' attitudes toward dissent and citizenship, we argue, is the first step in promoting successful intergenerational communication. We draw conclusions at the end of the chapter about the consequences of Millennials' socialization to dissent and identify further directions for research in this area. It is our hope that readers will find this chapter useful in understanding generational divides in contexts of leadership.

MILLENNIALS: CHARACTERISTICS AND INFLUENCES

Generation researchers Neil Howe and William Strauss argue that Millennials, persons born after 1981, are more numerous (already outnumbering 'Boomers'), more affluent and more racially and ethnically diverse than any other generation. One in five has at least one immigrant parent, and one in ten has at least one noncitizen parent. 'Potentially the largest second-generation immigrant group in US history, . . . they are also becoming the world's first generation to grow up thinking of itself as global' (Howe and Strauss, 2000: 16). The portrait drawn in a recent study by the Pew Research Center (2007) is of a generation whose coming of age has been shaped by unprecedented revolutions in technology (cell phones, iPods, instant messaging and social networking sites like MySpace and

Facebook, for example) and dramatic events both in the US and abroad. The report indicates that although Millennials came of age in the shadow of September 11, they share some characteristics of other generations of young adults in that they generally are happy with their lives and very optimistic about their futures and their ability to shape them.

Omissions and Contradictions

Despite the fact that Millennials appear to be the most studied generation of our time, research contradictions and omissions are common. A striking omission is the tendency in most research on Millennials to focus exclusively on middle to upper-middle class Caucasians, even though this generation is more multiracial than any preceding it (Howe and Strauss, 2000). It is almost as if non-whites and the working class and underclass failed to reproduce in this generation. Shunning overwhelmingly negative stereotypes created (and inflated) by the mainstream media, Millennials are on the one hand a throwback to the 'Great Generation', embracing the positive family and civic values of their grandparents. On the other hand, they are individualistic in the extreme in their excessive material consumption and embrace of potentially socially isolating technologies. These paradoxes have left demographers, sociologists and journalists scrambling to get a handle on the newest generation and their role in American society.

Some research indicates the newest generation is prepared to make significant contributions. For example, Howe and Strauss (2000; also see Beale and Abdalla, 2003; Zemke *et al.*, 2000) see a positive consequence of the Millennials' commitment to community. They predict the nonprofit sector will be a beneficiary of the Milliennials' attention as this generation takes the lead in shaping communities with a for-profit model of efficiency and productivity. Significantly, Howe and Strauss (2000) note that this positive quality of the newest generation can be attributed mainly to non-white Millennials, who, they also argue, are the most important contributors to reversing an array of negative stereotypes about youth, from high crime to profane language to irresponsible sex to low test scores, that have prevailed in America for nearly half a century. They further cite the trend among non-white Millennials of embracing a renewed emphasis on the 'family values' of their respective cultures and neighborhoods, establishing a Millennial tone that is 'assertive, positive, team-playing and friendly' (p. 16). The *Millennial Manifesto*, by Millennials Scott Beale and Abeer Abdalla (2003), concurs and documents the political priorities of Millennials through profiling young leaders, many of whom are non-whites.

Other research evidence, however, indicates the potential contributions of this generation are hard to predict because of conflicting views about

Millennial characteristics and values. For example, studies indicate this generation wants to be civically engaged in projects that matter to them but shuns political activity (Sitaraman and Warren, 2003). Millennials are characterized as uninformed (Mindich, 2005), perhaps more so than any recent generation, but also are more technologically savvy than previous generations (Zemke *et al.*, 2000). They are capable of accessing a wide variety of information electronically, but it is questionable whether they are capable of judging the credibility of information or analyzing it to make sound decisions (Falk and Falk, 2005; Mindich, 2005). Social skills, on the other hand, are seen consistently as a strength of Millennials. Most researchers contend Millennials value consensus building and collaboration but they are also conflict avoidant (Howe and Strauss, 2000; Zemke *et al.*, 2000).

Tending Toward Conformity

A troubling emphasis on consensus building at all costs and a high level of conformity among Millennials militates against the expression of dissent. Most Millennials say they identify with their parents' values, accept authority willingly and are most comfortable following the rules (Howe and Strauss, 2000; Zemke *et al.*, 2000). On the face of it this preference for conformity appears to run counter to Millennials' embrace of pluralism and acceptance of ethnic differences. But the generation's diversity and their acceptance of differences should not be taken as a readiness to challenge the given or normative. The tension between pluralism and conformity is expressed in the now familiar blasé refrain, 'whatever'. The point that is lost for Millennials is, who actually benefits from deliberative dissent and who benefits from conformity, the dissenter or the group? As legal scholar Cass Sunstein puts it:

> Conformists are often thought to be protective of social interests, keeping quiet for the sake of the group. By contrast, dissenters tend to be seen as selfish individualists, embarking on a project of their own. But in an important sense, the opposite is closer to the truth. Much of the time, dissenters benefit others, while conformists benefit themselves. If people threaten to blow the whistle on wrongdoing or to disclose the facts that contradict an emerging group consensus, they might well be punished. Perhaps they will lose their jobs, face ostracism, or at least have some difficult months. (2003: 6)

It is the dissenter who has the most to lose, usually for the good of the group. By all accounts Millennials embrace communal interests and are willing to take risky leadership roles to benefit others, but the desire to avoid conflict wherever it arises is often too strong. Millennials are critical of 'Gen X' and Boomers, whom they describe as all talk and no action. When

Millennials feel strongly enough about an issue, they have the optimism to move beyond criticism to take action, usually in their local communities. Often, however, these are quick fixes by which they can enjoy immediate gratification as having 'acted' instead of addressing the complexities of larger problems. The pressing question about tomorrow's leaders is not whether they will lead and follow – they do lead and they act collectively. Rather it is, will they engage in leadership efforts that optimize dissent and sustain those efforts long enough to produce systemic and lasting change, when as a group they are the most compliant, unquestioning, authority deferring generation to date?

MILLENNIAL SOCIALIZATION

The above characterizations raise a number of concerns about the Millennials' capacity for meeting the challenges that await them (many of which have been left to them by the Baby Boomers), and of advocating for necessary community, workplace and societal changes. We explore these characterizations further by examining three socializing influences on Millennials: their parents, education and digital technology. While the space allowed here prohibits a complete picture of the social, cultural and other influences on Millennials, we have highlighted recent findings from a variety of disciplines that underscore the need for a more thorough review of this generation's willingness and ability to express dissenting views across leadership contexts.

Parental Influences

There is no shortage of child development literature that indicates the role parents play in instilling values in their children. Parents also contribute to their children's behavioral and attitudinal development, contributions that may last a lifetime. We are making an assumption that concerned parents influence their children in ways they hope will benefit them in their private and professional lives and their roles as public citizens. Such is not always the case, however, as David Mindich found in research on declining interest in news. Increasingly families are not watching the news, despite the fact that, '[c]ivic knowledge is one of the best predictors of being a good local citizen' (Mindich, 2005: 86). The children and young adults Mindich interviewed who had little interest in the news were often following in the footsteps of parents who also had a pattern of disinterest. In general these youth paid little attention even to local news. Other studies report a declining interest among Millennials in gathering information about local and nationwide problems. Yet the lack of being informed does not appear to have affected the amount of time Millennials devote to civic engagement, as we will discuss later. It appears that not being fully informed about problems does not deter Millennials from trying to resolve them.

Recent research by the Pew Research Center (2007) indicates that roughly a third of the Millennials surveyed follow civic affairs regularly. The decline in civic engagement throughout the US population began decades ago (Putnam, 2000), but the evidence of that decline now surfacing in Millennials is reason for alarm (Mindich, 2005). Millennials are far less likely than the Baby Boomers to accept such obligations of citizenship as becoming informed and voting (Zukin *et al.*, 2006). Moreover, the differences are less related to age and maturity than to socialization. In other words, this condition is not likely to change as Millennials age.

While Millennials may be unlikely to gain an appreciation for news from their parents, they are likely to know their parents' political views and are to some degree influenced by them. Falk and Falk (2005) report that political issues tend to be more important to older people than to younger ones; nonetheless, political discussions in the home have a significant impact on youth. Zukin and colleagues found that:

> [A]mong young people who are eligible to vote, 38 percent of those from homes with frequent political discussions say they always vote, compared to 20 percent of those without such dialogue. By talking about politics, families teach their children that it is important to pay attention to the world around them – and to take the next step of doing something. (2006, p. 141)

These authors also report that when parents are involved in volunteer organizations, their children are more likely to be highly involved as well, not only in volunteerism but also in organizations and acts of advocacy.

A variety of sources report that Millennials maintain closer ties with their parents and family (Falk and Falk, 2005; Pew, 2007) and spend more time together than in past generations (Howe and Strauss, 2000). Not surprisingly, then, parents of Millennials have shown a strong tendency to be immersed in their children's education in ways not witnessed in previous generations. According to a *Washington Post* article, 'Teachers and principals in the early grades began noticing changes in parents in the 1990s. Parents began spending more time in classrooms. Then they began calling teachers frequently. Then came e-mails, text messages – sometimes both at once' (Strauss, 2006: A8). In years past, when youth went off to college they left their parents behind. College marked the transition into young adulthood when youth matured and learned life skills as well as subject matter away from home and family. They graduated ready to make their own way in the world (at least theoretically).

The Millennial generation, however, is experiencing higher education with significantly more parental involvement than youth of the past. Some of their baby boomer parents are known to college administrators as 'helicopter parents' because of their constant hovering in their children's college lives. The more intrusive parents are known as 'blackhawks'. While it is tempting to believe helicoptering is the exception rather than the rule, current research suggests somewhere between 60 and 70 percent of students' parents exhibit at least some form of helicoptering behavior, and they are not all from middle and upper classes (Jayson, 2007). In these conditions it is difficult for Millennials to develop self-reliance, confidence and skills to make their own decisions and to solve problems, and gain the ability to manage conflict effectively – all of which are necessary to engage in responsible dissent.

This interference with life-skill development follows Millennials into the workplace. *Fast Company* magazine provides an account of a 22-year-old pharmaceutical employee (and Harvard graduate) who was denied a promotion. 'His mother called the human-resources department the next day. Seventeen times' apparently in an attempt to fix the problem (Sacks, 2006: 72). Potential employers of Millennial graduates have perhaps delayed their development as adults further by including parents of interns in office tours and providing parents with information packets about their companies, encouraging parents to be involved in their child's future employment decisions. An editorial in the *Christian Science Monitor* sums up the situation: 'That parents care deeply about their adult children, and that many of these young people consider their parents friends, is good news. But if employers involve parents with hiring, when do young people learn from mistakes and act for themselves?' (*Christian Science Monitor*, 2007: 8).

Some noteworthy counter-examples exist, however, where Millennials exhibit a different kind of inspiration derived from their parents. For example, Mari Oye and Leah Anthony Libresco are two of 141 Presidential Scholars who, in 2007, were honored in a ceremony at the White House. Mari Oye handed President Bush a letter and spoke on behalf of approximately one-third of the scholars in telling President Bush during the ceremony that they were opposed the torture of detainees. Libresco coauthored the letter and later recounted, 'if I'm going to be in the room with the president, I've got to say something, because silence betokens consent, and there's a lot going on I don't want to consent to' (as cited in Goodman, 2007, paragraph 13).

Educational Influences

One of the primary goals of higher education, though not always overtly expressed or realized, is the development of responsible citizens. It is in classrooms where students are often inspired to care about the news (Mindich, 2005), examine the advantages and drawbacks of conformity, and explore – even express – dissent. Steven Shiffrin, one of the country's leading FirstAmendment theorists, advances a dissent-based theory of free speech and discusses the importance of promoting dissent in the classroom:

> Any society committed to encouraging dissent must begin its encouragement in its system of education. . . . If our citizens are not educated with a sense of justice, they are less likely to acquire it. Indeed, a sense of justice and of injustice is typically a prerequisite for progressive dissent. In addition, our educational system must educate not only autonomous thinkers prepared to reject the habits, customs, and traditions of the larger society but also citizens who generally regard dissent against injustice as virtuous behavior. (Shiffrin, 1999: 113)

But how well does our educational system currently prepare Millennials to dissent productively? According to Shiffrin (1999) it falls seriously short. Rather, an overwhelming push toward conformity, peaceful collaboration, conflict moderation and consensus building may communicate to our students that there is no appropriate space for dissent at all and no need for skills in argument and deliberation. It is not that these qualities are unimportant to effective citizenship; if left unbalanced by critical thinking and willingness to question the status quo, however, they may erode into group think or mindless obedience (Sunstein, 2003).

A variety of scholars have questioned whether educational institutions may have abdicated responsibility for citizenship development and critical thinking as they have become more immersed in the world of corporations. Stanley Deetz, for example, argues that textbook companies require authors to simplify formatting by using boldface, summary boxes and other devices to the point where students are required to think very little, if at all, about the material they read. Students are literally told by the formatting what to think about the material, leaving little opportunity to question an author's point of view or reach different conclusions than those provided by the author's summary (Deetz, 1992). Jeffrey Schmidt argues that graduate programs are rife with requirements of obedience and subordination, hoops to jump through, which prepare students for professional lives of conformity in organizations. He concludes that students can resist such academic indoctrination by knowing how the indoctrination works and maintaining and exercising voice in opposition when necessary. Such resistance is not easy, however, particularly given that professional training 'is set up to turn students into good self-adjusters or else get rid of them' (Schmidt, 2000: 213). In addition, awareness requires critical thinking, for which Millennials may be receiving less than adequate preparation, by both the education system and their parents.

When we stand these shortcomings in academic life derived from research next to recent empirical observations about characteristics of Millennials that are likely to affect their learning, a disturbing image emerges. Even in America's celebrated hotbeds of intellectualism – Ivy League schools – critical thinking and dissent may be on the way to becoming passé. Joseph W. Gordon, Dean of Undergraduate Education at Yale, observed: 'My sense from talking to students and other faculty is that out of class, students are interested in hearing another person's point of view, but not interested in engaging it, in challenging it or being challenged' (Kakutani, 2002). Jeff Nunokawa, a Professor of English at Princeton University, states, 'Debate has gotten a very bad name in our culture. It's become synonymous with some of the most nonintellectual forms of bullying, rather than as an opportunity for deliberative democracy' (Kakutani, 2002).

About 70 percent of high school students regularly receive civic instruction, but some 40 percent of those students indicate the courses are having no impact on them (Zukin *et al.*, 2006). The numbers change, however, when lively discussion and debate of issues are encouraged in classes by instructors. Under these circumstances, students are more likely to become civically involved (that is, to join organizations outside of school and follow political news). Far fewer college students reported taking civics courses (40 percent), and approximately half of those students indicated the courses increased their interest in civic involvement. While the majority of college students indicate they are encouraged by instructors to reach their own conclusions on issues, less than half report that instructors encourage open discussion.

In tandem with the view of Millennials as conformists who shun debate and dissent, John Flower argues that in recent years student incivility has masqueraded as debate and represents a 'lack of respect for the structures of society' (Flower, 2003: 85). While it is unclear how widespread the incivility may be, Flower relates its emergence to the increasing degree to which students view education from a consumerist perspective and their right to demand 'service' as they want it. It also may be related to a retreat from social engagement. '[T]he diminished debate syndrome mirrors the irony-suffused sensibility of many millennial-era students. Irony, after all, represents a form of detachment; like the knee-jerk acceptance of the positions of others, it's a defense mode that enables one to avoid commitment and stand above the fray' (Kakutani, 2002).

According to Amanda Anderson, an English Professor at Johns Hopkins University and author of the book, *The Way We Argue Now*, there is more going on than taking an ironic stance: 'It's as though there's no distinction between the person and the argument, as though to criticize an argument would be injurious to the person' (quoted in Kakutani, 2002). Overcoming young people's reluctance to engage in productive debate is critical to sustaining healthy democratic practice, and the educational system plays a crucial role in that process. While there is evidence that parents of Millennials are socializing them to be less than adequately prepared for advocacy and dissent, the system of higher education undoubtedly also has participated in this lack of preparation. Conditioning both these influences is the unprecedented intrusion of digital technologies into the coming of age experience.

Technological Influences

Falk and Falk (2005) describe the Millennials as the cyberspace generation. They have grown up using computers, the Internet and cell phones and are more likely to turn to YouTube than the television for entertainment (*Guardian Unlimited*, 2007). The Pew Research Center has found that 86 percent of Millennials use the Internet at least occasionally and that college graduates in this generation are somewhat more likely to use the Internet than those who have not attended college. While Millennials' Internet use may not be as high as some would expect, they more than exceed expectations for cell phone use. The Millennials surveyed were nearly twice as likely to have sent or received a text message on a cell phone in the past 24 hours (51 percent) as their Gen X counterparts (26 percent). Of the Millennials who had previously used a social networking website, 82 percent reported having created a personal profile; however, only 38 percent said they used the social networking website as often as once a day or weekly. There were some intriguing contradictions in Millennial respondents' answers as well. While 67 percent indicated these technologies increase isolation, 64 percent indicated they improved the closeness with old friends and family, and 69 percent responded that making new friends was easier with technology. It might be that critical reflection has not been applied to their own use of technologies.

More surprising, it is the function of the technology, rather than the display of its use, that matters most to Millennials. Epstein (1998) notes 'they care about what technology can do for them. Unlike Boomers [*sic*], N-Geners [Millennials] view glitz and high-tech buzzwords as less important than benefits' (p. 14). If they are the first in line to purchase the newest version of the iPod or iPhone or the newest video game, it is because they expect change that can benefit them. As Epstein observes, they have been influenced by 'years of TV channel surfing as well as Internet surfing, [and so] they have come to expect a world of almost limitless choices' (p. 14). They also have come to expect immediate payoffs (Falk and Falk, 2005).

The outcome of this technological savvy is debatable, drawing both praise and ridicule. For example, while Katz and Rice (2002) argue that the birthright of growing up with the Internet may well be a higher level of literacy, creativity and social skills, Falk and Falk lament that 'more illiterate than previous generations, the "millennials" know only what they see on a screen. They have rarely held a book in hand' (Falk and Falk, 2005: 63). What is not debatable is the attraction of technology remains strong, particularly with regard to social networking websites. Patrick White reported earlier this year that 'Over the past eight months, Facebook has transformed from an online *Animal House*, exclusive to a few million high-school and college kids, to the world's seventh-most popular website – a 30-million strong social networking portal open to all ages and branches of the family tree' (White, 2007, p. L1).

Of particular interest to our topic is the manner in which Millennials use computer-mediated communication. For example, the Internet is reported to increase the ease of students communicating with instructors as well as with other students and to facilitate discussion of sensitive issues in particular (Katz and Rice, 2002). The potential for anonymity may provide motivation for online openness while at the same time shielding the message sender from judgments that would be apparent in face-to-face conversations (Katz and Rice, 2002). On a more sinister level, it may also contribute to cyberbullying, which has become a significant problem on social network web sites such as MySpace and Facebook (Lelchuk, 2007).

In a recent study centered on college students' use of impression management in chat rooms, Jennifer Becker and Glen Stamp found three motivating factors for this behavior: 'desire [for] social acceptance, relationship development and maintenance, and desire for identity experimentation' (Becker and Stamp, 2005: 246). The desire to conform to the norms of one's social group is clearly high for Millennials, as is typically the case for youth. This doesn't bode well for the encouragement of dissent unless one's social group is already drawn to such behavior. Mindich (2005) points out it is unwise to compare virtual communities with real ones, given the degree of anonymity virtual communication affords versus face-to-face interactions, where one is directly accountable for one's actions and ideas. 'Real communities require a level of work, sacrifice, and accommodation that virtual ones do not always share. This is quite simply because in the real world you often encounter a lot more opposition than you do in the virtual' (p. 90). It follows then that engaging in real communities, rather than virtual ones, provides better training in effective, productive dissent. 'In the real world we struggle against or compromise with neighbors because they will be our neighbors tomorrow, too. On the Internet, we are more likely to drop our virtual neighbors completely to get someone else who will agree with us' (Mindich, 2005: 91).

One aspect of the Internet that is increasingly, though still minimally, being used by Millennials to express dissenting views is blogs. Whereas previous generations may have engaged in civic organizations with people who held geographic ties, Millennials engage with virtual and face-to-face community members who hold ideological and cultural ties. As Keren (2006) describes the aggregation of millions of online diaries, blogs (short for web logs) are an outgrowth of the desire of ordinary people wanting to speak out after September 11. For many, blogs appear to satisfy a need to express dissenting views and do so in an expedient, convenient and anonymous fashion. Blog researchers note this form of dissent usually does not have direct political impact, but on several occasions they have and 'bloggers' continue to search for creative means to employ the medium in instrumental ways (Keren, 2006). For example, blogs can keep alive negative news stories about politicians that were mostly ignored by the mainstream media until the person in question is forced to resign or voted out of office. However creative, the scope of the majority of political blogging is still local and anecdotal. They seek quick, local expression and easy solutions to what are complex problems rather than institutional change (Keren, 2006).

It may be tempting to assume Millennials use the Internet to read the news, but this is not the case. Mindich's work reveals a disturbing trend in American's knowledge of news events relating to local, national or world affairs.

> Across the news industry, executives fret over the future of news and its declining audience. But the United States is facing a crisis that extends far beyond the news industry. While math and reading skills of young Americans remain relatively stable, their average political awareness has become remarkably shallow. While the Internet has allowed many to develop expertise in their own narrow interests, fewer are willing or able to develop a generalist's gaze. Knowledge of sports and celebrities continues to rise, but local and national political literacy has plummeted. (2005: 4)

Despite this dim view of diminishing knowledge of public issues and problems, Millennials' early mastery of new technologies and their creative applications of such technology still have the potential to transform democracy as we know it. Forums for dissent abound, yet informed dissent remains fleeting and inconsistent.

MILLENNIALS IN THE COMMUNITY, AT WORK AND IN POLITICS

The Civic Life of Millennials

A fundamental difference between Boomers, who also grew up in an era of rising affluence, and Millennials is their view of public institutions and their role in public life. Boomers widely regarded their economically prosperous upbringing as institutionally planned and a result of growing income equality. They witnessed a growth and prospering of the middle class and were concerned with trends toward conformity. In contrast, Millennials have been raised to believe it is their job to fix civic institutions that are in danger of collapse and global problems that require all the creativity and innovation they can muster (Howe and Strauss, 2000; Zemke *et al.*, 2000). Millennials have turned pundits on their heads and demonstrated a 'can do' attitude, responding with loyalty to government and civic organizations in disarray. This response most resembles their grandparents' pragmatism and work ethic, attracting the label 'The Next Great Generation'. Another important contrast exists between the mindsets of Millennials and 'Generation Xers', those who are most likely to be working closely together in public and private organizations. Millennials are unlike their older Gen X siblings (or for some, Gen X parents) who were discontented with the establishment or disillusioned by civic life, and who turned their attentions to the marketplace to focus on their immediate family and social needs. Those born in the 1980s and after are consistently outward-looking.

Not all research paints a picture of this generation as inherently committed to public life, however. For example, Sitaraman and Warren argue that this generation was once characterized as apathetic but has been catapulted by recent events into an interest in public involvement. The interest, however, may be fleeting.

> A once-insular, once-apathetic generation has been forever transformed by catastrophe. America's young have been awakened from the consumerist slumber of the 1990s to face a redefined world. Overnight we have been reshaped into 'Generation 9/11', ready to take up the mantle of leadership and face our nation's destiny. It's a familiar tale . . . but this tale is as manipulative as it is inviting. It avails itself of our country's need for patriotic optimism in a time of trouble rather than confronting the less comfortable reality: 9/11 is not a defining moment for this generation of young people. (Sitaraman and Warren, 2003, p. 14)

Sitaraman and Warren (2003) further argue that young people's disinterest in political participation has to do, in large part, with the increasing gap between citizens and the politicians who purportedly make decisions on their behalf and impoverished system-wide information being delivered via increasingly sensationalized news programming. We do not disagree with the authors' conclusions, but we would add that their parents and technology have also been significant influences.

While Millennials may not be stampeding for leadership positions in high level public life, there is some evidence that community is the new polity for Millennials. A survey conducted by Harvard University's Institute of Politics in 2000 found that 85 percent of young people feel that community volunteerism is better than political engagement for addressing issues facing them. Studies reporting unusually high levels of volunteerism among Millennials abound, which might be seen as evidence of the generation's idealism and commitment.

The attraction of community activism among Millennials seems easy to understand when one recognizes how accessible and personal this platform is for acting on political views. Edward Chambers describes civil society as 'the place where people come together voluntarily to act in and around shared interests. . . . Civil society is . . . where values and traditions are instilled and fostered. The state and the market came later and exist to support it' (Chambers, 2003: 61). The organizations that make up civil society include families, congregations, schools, social clubs, citizen organizations, athletic groups, parent-teacher associations, block clubs, unions, and fraternal, social and other local organizations. These institutions are often described as the glue that holds society together, but that alone doesn't illuminate their attraction for Millennials. Chambers (2003) contends they respond to a much deeper and more intimate need for connection with others at a local level, and that need is heightened when citizens are depersonalized as consumers and government becomes remote. 'When the state doesn't keep the market in its place, but instead gets bought by it, as we see all around us in the era of Enron, Tyco, and WorldCom, civil society is all that's left to initiate change' (p. 63).

A sense of justice and commitment to the practice of democracy may very well be what motivates baby boomers and Generation X to engage in their communities, as is consistent with their views of institutions and personal obligations. But what about Millennials? High school and college civic outreach requirements are motivating an entire generation of young people to engage in their communities in the name of advancing their educational and professional goals. Others look to the Internet first to engage with their local communities virtually. As Katz and Rice (2002) note, individually focused motives draw individuals to experience community engagement as an online activity. Communities can still benefit from this involvement, but at what cost to democracy and the practice of dissent?

> [T]he Internet draws people who are interested in advancing their personal interests and not necessarily in promoting community per se. This does not mean that community benefits will not be forthcoming, only that motives are individually centered. Thus the pursuit of individual interests leads to new and unexpected forms of social interaction and group activity. (Katz and Rice, 2002: 353)

Is it no wonder then, that Millennials are most likely to engage national politics and the marketplace on a community-sized scale they can relate to and trust – whether virtual or not? These Millennial trends augur well for mitigating civic leadership failures at the local level of communities. They suggest the opposite for larger scale issues and global leadership failures.

Millennials at Work

Speaking out against the status quo or voicing a dissenting view in the workplace has always involved risks, along with potential benefits. Despite the risks, almost all of the rights that workers enjoy today are consequences of hard won battles that began with simple acts of worker dissent alone or in union with others. As technological advances and cultural changes influence the requirements of work and surveillance techniques, new protections for workers' rights will need to be established. Are Millennials up to the challenge? How will they respond to initiating change and working with older generations in the workplace?

In *Generations at Work*, Ron Zemke *et al.* (2000) argue the Millennials will most resemble the 'Veterans', those born between 1922 and 1943, in the workplace. Similar to their seniors, they have a 'belief in collective action, optimism about the future, trust in centralized authority, a will to get things done, and a heroic spirit in the face of overwhelming odds' (p. 144). Economists are predicting a dramatic increase in productivity with this generation and they appear more than willing to sacrifice their own personal pleasure for the common good of the group. Their capacity for and skill at working in teams is unprecedented, as are their multitasking capabilities and technological savvy. However, they bring some limitations to the workplace that will likely be exacerbated in intergenerational interactions and affect their transition into leadership roles.

The first liability for Millennial workers is their need for supervision and structure. Given the highly scheduled and closely supervised childhood of this generation, their desire for structure and direction is pervasive and not surprising. The implications for dissent among Millennials in the workplace, given their willingness to acquiesce to authority figures, is less than encouraging. Intergenerational collaborations at work, however, can transform this liability into an asset. In a *Wall Street Journal* article on getting the generations to close the culture gap at work, one IBM manager cites the benefits of mixing perspectives and drawing on the strengths of each generation. Pairing a 20-something employee hired from a start-up with a Baby Boomer for work on a new product turned out to be a match made in heaven, after both came to appreciate each other's strengths:

> The young employee 'has dozens of out-of-the-box ideas and a great sense of, "Let's change the world right now"', Mr Brown says. By contrast, the Baby

Boomer is more steadfast 'but knows our company's processes and our sales force,' he adds. Encouraged by Mr Brown to pool their strengths rather than to get into a tug of war about whose talents were more vital, the two employees got the product launched in a record three months. Mr Brown thinks his own close relationships with several older IBM executives have helped him manage across generations. 'Listening and communicating is key to this', he adds. (Hymowitz, 2007: 10–11)

A second liability is the Millennials' avoidance of interpersonal conflict, such as often happens with difficult people at work. In contrast, Baby Boomers place a high value on relationship building and maintenance and social networks they rely on for guidance and ideas. Generally though, these relationships are formed with other Baby Boomer peers who hold the same values of hard work and trust. Attempts to pair Baby Boomers with younger generations in mentoring programs do not always fare well, as a mutual disinterest in the other's life experiences prohibits Boomers and Millennials from developing strong relationships (Greenberg-Walt and Robertson, 2001).

Millennial Politics: The Climate Activists

Much has been written about the declining voter turnout among America's youth. The most recent data report a slight rise in participation but nowhere near the potential impact this group could have if they decided to act en masse. However, the story of Millennials' political involvement does not end with voting booth tallies; rather, it continues with the growth of a particular social movement. Youthful idealism is alive and well, and apparently it's green. Each generation has rallied passionately, and sometimes successfully, behind political and humanitarian causes, and the leaders in these movements have often moved into key organizational positions that shape American life. For many though, their commitment to issues begins to wane with the onset of mid-life financial pressures and family obligations. Whether Millennial leaders will turn their passion for the environment into a sustained and successsful political movement is yet to be seen. So far, the predictions look good.

Social scientists, politicians and business leaders say student-led climate activism could be the third youth movement to alter the course of national history, following the civil rights movement and anti-war demonstrations of the 1960s. 'Unlike the Earth Day kids of the 1970s, climate activists who belong to the 80 million-strong demographic bulge known as the Millennials aren't hard left or anti-business' (Green, 2007: 62). The tools and skill sets they bring to the table are far more sophisticated than earlier generations and their strongest asset may be their willingness to work within the system to affect change. Their commitment to collaboration and focus on accumulating 'small wins' to achieve larger goals gets them a seat at the bargaining table that other youth movements were less likely to get, pursue or desire. The tools they bring to the climate change movement include Excel spreadsheets, administrators' numbers on cell-phone speed dials and blogs. Their ranks are diverse and fast-growing, including such groups as Engineers for a Sustainable World, the Evangelical Youth Climate Initiative and Net Impact, a network of environment-focused business school with 130 chapters. 'Student groups at 570 schools signed up to take part this year [2007] in the Campus Climate Challenge, a campaign sponsored by 30 environmental groups' (Green, 2007: 62). A common refrain from organizers of the climate movement is, 'Be cynical, or be effective', which provokes otherwise nonpolitical youth to get involved. Yet whether Millennials can sustain their enthusiasm for any one issue is still questioned by today's analysts and leaders. In their defense, Bill McKibben of Step It Up, a nationwide campaign rallying students behind a single environmental banner, argues Millennials represent a broader societal shift and will bear the brunt of any climate catastrophe: 'There are a lot of people who are educated about global warming and want to figure out what to do' (quoted in Green, 2007: 62).

Anya Kamenetz argues that Millennials are working toward small and achievable goals, rather than pursuing radical, systemic change. She describes the efforts of Billy Parish, the 23-year-old leader of Energy Action, who cofounded the nation's largest youth environmental coalition as a Yale junior in 2003. Energy Action conducts national campaigns on clean energy and global warming and claims an email list of 30 000 and member organizations on 1500 campuses. ' " The next generation of advocates are solution-oriented," says Parish. "They're interested in things like biodiesel, etc." – instead of the radical ecology of the '70s. This pragmatism may seem alien to those who equate youth with uncompromising zeal' (Kamenetz, 2005: B3).

The Millennials' entry into the political arena through the issue of climate change has not been lost on the organizations who hope to hire the best and brightest of this generation. According to US Labor Department data, by 2012 there will be just one person entering the workforce for every four who leave, because of the exodus of Baby Boomers by retirement. It is no surprise that companies anticipating the shift to a Millennial workforce are keen to understand what motivates climate activists (Green, 2007). Businesses that want to attract the most qualified Millennials are aware their newest employees view the environment as twice as important as the economy and seek to compliment their business acumen with a green sensibility.

DISSENT AND MILLENNIALS: READY OR NOT . . .

The purpose of this chapter has been first and foremost to provide insights about Millennials and their socialization, particularly with regard to how that socialization has influenced their attitudes about and aptitude for dissent. We have taken Millennials as representative of oncoming generations. These insights are important for a variety of reasons. First, the Baby Boomer generation is fast approaching retirement age. As a generation they are living longer than their ancestors and intend to work longer, to be more active and involved in their communities, and to engage in life-long learning (Castro, 2007). These predictions indicate there will be a significant amount of interaction between Baby Boomers and Millennials across a number of contexts, and the potential for conflict exists because of generational differences.

A second, and related, reason the insights presented in this chapter are important is that they direct researchers to a broader examination of not only the strengths and weaknesses of the Millennial generation but also to how their weaknesses may be exploited by power holders at local and national levels. While it is valuable for Millennials to understand previous generations' similarities and differences to their own generation, it is also important they understand fully the implications and consequences of their own socialization, particularly as it relates to exercising voice in communities, the workplace and national issues.

Finally, the characterization we found of Millennials in reviewing the literature presented here tends to be homogeneous. Just because Millennials have been described as a generation that values diversity in ethnicity and in viewpoint does not mean that dissenting voices in this generation are or will be equal across class and ethnicity. To ignore this point in future research will not serve us well in what we need to know about this generation.

In sum, three outcomes of Millennials' socialization come to the fore: a tendency toward conformity, avoidance of conflict and lack of complexity in problem solving. These characteristics of Millennials are likely to be the cause of much conflict in collaborating with other generations and in restricting the likelihood of productive dissent. We offer a brief description of each outcome here.

Tending Toward Conformity: Being Accepted is Better than Being Just

Throughout this chapter evidence abounds that Millennials are drawn to conformity. Certainly, generations of the past have exhibited their fair share of conformity; however, the characteristic of Millennials we have described as conformity proneness puts them at particular risk of poor decision making. Sunstein (2003) warns of the injustices that occur as a result of seemingly benign conformity:

> The problem with conformity is that it deprives society of information that it needs. I have emphasized the same problem with social cascades, in which people follow others and fail to disclose what they actually know. As a result of cascades, both individuals and groups can blunder badly. When grave injustice exists, it often persists only because most people have a false impression of what other people think. They silence themselves, thinking that others must be right or simply wanting to avoid social disapproval. The tragedy is that blunders and injustice could be avoided if only people would speak out. (Sunstein, 2003: 210)

Avoiding Conflict

An aversion to conflict and lack of dispute management training give dissent a bad name. The inherent conflicts that exist in a democracy and are present in our work, civic and political lives require dialogue that negotiates differences and keeps democracy alive (Carter, 1998). A long line of research on decision-making tells us that the presence of disagreement and a multiplicity of viewpoints enhances the quality of decisions such that performance is improved – but more importantly, the democratic process is upheld. Counter to what many Millennials may expect, dissent is not the antithesis of harmony. 'Differing values and experiences can often lead to conflict, of course, but the "constructive abrasion" of the diverse styles also is likely to lead to new forms of value creation' (Greenberg-Walt and Robertson, 2001: 152).

If we want to maintain a democratic society we will need to persuasively demonstrate to Millennials the importance of dissent and model effective forms of dissent in our communities and workplaces. While we may be tempted to conclude that since Millennials are averse to conflict, so too will they be averse to dissent, we needn't see that as a necessary conclusion. Deliberative, collegial dissent and debate is a cornerstone of change efforts and effectively persuading others to one's own differing point of view. The collective orientation of Millennials and the apparent drive to work on behalf of the common good may persuade them to adopt more assertive forms of communication than those to which they have been socialized.

Lack of Complexity

A 'quick fix' will not solve all problems. It appears Millennials neither embrace nor suppress dissent in the way previous generations understand and engage in it. Instead they appear to have redefined dissent for their generation. One way Millennials express their disagreement with the status quo is in forming ad hoc but technologically sophisticated social networking groups acting in concert with civic organizations to address problems through local action (Beale and Abdalla, 2003). Older generations' criticism of this approach is that Millennials' actions confront symptoms of larger problems but not the problems themselves. In the workplace this symptoms oriented approach reveals itself in Millennials' tendency to jump head-first into tasks without asking for clarification and assistance or carefully researching problems to understand their complexity and how to appropriately address it (Zemke *et al.*, 2000). Millennials argue that at least they are 'acting', whereas older generations appear to be failing at finding solutions to problems (Beale and Abdalla, 2003).

Yet rushing to apply remedies to symptoms while ignoring underlying causes has been the hallmark of contemporary leadership and its 'wars' on such ills of humanity as drugs, poverty and terrorism. And failing to understand the complexity of issues often is one of the critical preconditions of failed leadership. In this sense Millennials are not so different from the generations who will bequeath leadership positions and responsibilities to them. If we wish today's student generation to improve over the record of failed leadership and to vigorously exercise productive dissent, what can we teach them and what can we learn from them? Put differently, what lessons for advancing dissent-sensitive leadership can be derived from this examination of Millennials?

An essential list in response to that question must include the advocacy of parenting that fosters self-reliance and rewards critical reflection in coming generations. Educators, including especially those in higher education, need to actively dissent from administrative models and delivery modalities that preclude advocacy, debate and dissent. Teachers need to model responsible dissent, civil resistance and deliberative decision-making in their own lives. Unfortunately, a revolution is needed in the administrative structure, culture and production of mainstream news organizations. It is possible that with diligence, the Internet will remain open and become more powerful as an alternative source of information about current affairs and social alternatives. Millennials and later generations are likely to take some advantage of such a source.

As Millennials strive to make their mark in this world they may yet become 'The Next Great Generation'. Becoming a 'great' generation, however, comes with costs. Hard-won battles of informed dissent and investing in the success of future generations, while perhaps not realizing the benefits of those decisions in one's own lifetime, is the stuff of great legacies. As we argued throughout this chapter, effective intergenerational communication can help balance the newest generation's shortcomings with their strengths and help not only assure their success as leaders in civic and work contexts but also increase their capacity to give voice to dissenting views and undertake leadership that invites dissenters into problem solving, deciding and action. It is certain that without a robust culture of dissent in the coming generation, a culture of leadership failure will persist.

REFERENCES

Anderson, A. (2006), *The Way We Argue Now: A Study in the Cultures of Theory*, Princeton, NJ: Princeton University Press.

Beale, Scott and Abeer Abdalla (2003), *Millennial Manifesto: An Activist Handbook By, For, and About the Millennial Generation*, Collierville, TN: Millennial Politics.

Becker, J. A. H. and G. H. Stamp (2005), 'Impression management in chat rooms: a grounded theory model', *Communication Studies*, **56** (3), 243–60.

Carter, Stephen L. (1998), *The Dissent of the Governed: A Meditation on Law, Religion and Loyalty*, Cambridge, MA: Harvard University Press.

Castro, Tony (2007), 'Are we ready for the golden age of boomers?', *The Daily News of Los Angeles*, 19 May, N1.

Chambers, Edward T. (2003), *Roots for Radicals: Organizing for Power, Action, and Justice*, New York: The Continuum International Publishing Group.

Christian Science Monitor (2007), 'Liftoff for "helicopter" parents', 3 May, 8.

Deetz, Stanley A. (1992), *Democracy in an Age of Corporate Colonization: Developments in Communication and the Politics of Everyday Life*, Albany, NY: State University of New York Press.

Epstein, Jeffrey H. (1998), 'The net generation is changing the marketplace', *The Futurist*, **32** (3), 14.

Falk, Gerhard and Ursula A. Falk (2005), *Youth Culture and the Generation Gap*, New York: Algora.

Flower, John A. (2003), *Downstairs, Upstairs: The Changed Spirit and Face of College Life in America*, Akron, OH: University of Akron Press.

Goodman, Amy (2007), ' "We do not want America to represent torture": high school presidential scholars deliver Bush a message on human rights', accessed 3 July, 2007 at www.democracynow.org.

Green, Heather (2007), 'The greening of America's campuses', *Business Week*, 9 April, 62.

Greenberg-Walt, Cathy, L. and Alastair G. Robertson (2001), 'The evolving role of executive leadership', in Warren G. Bennis, Gretchen M. Spreitzer and Thomas G. Cummings (eds), *The Future of Leadership: Today's Top Leadership Thinkers Speak to Tomorrow's Leaders*, San Francisco, CA: Jossey-Bass, pp. 139–57.

Guardian Unlimited (2007), 'Learning to love the bloggers', 3 April, 2.

Howe, Neil and William Strauss (2000), *Millennials Rising: The Next Great Generation*, New York: Vintage Books.

Hymowitz, Carol (2007), 'Managers find ways to get generations to close culture gaps', *The Wall Street Journal*, 9 July, B1.

Jayson, Sharon (2007), 'Helicopter parents appear to defy socioeconomic pegging; study: mothers of sons do most of the hovering', *USA Today*, 4 April, 5D.

Kakutani, Michiko (2002), 'Debate? Dissent? Discussion? Oh, don't go there!' *The New York Times*, 23 March, B7.

Kamenetz, Anya (2005), 'Call this passive?; We're young and we do it our way', *The Washington Post*, 28 August, B3.

Katz, James E. and Ronald E. Rice (2002), *Social Consequences of Internet Use: Access, Involvement, and Interaction*, Cambridge, MA: The MIT Press.

Keren, Michael (2006), *Blogosphere: The New Political Arena*, Lanham, MD: Lexington Books.

Lelchuk, Ilene (2007), 'School bullies' new turf: Internet', *San Francisco Chronicle*, 17 March, A1.

Mindich, David T. Z. (2005), *Tuned Out: Why Americans Under 40 Don't Follow the News*, New York: Oxford University Press.

Pew Research Center (2007), *How Young People View Their Lives, Futures and Politics: A Portrait of 'Generation Next'*, 9 January, Washington, DC: Andrew Kohut.

Putnam, Robert D. (2000), *Bowling Alone: The Collapse and Revival of American Community*, New York: Simon and Schuster.

Sacks, Danielle (2006), 'Scenes from the culture clash', *FastCompany*, January, 72.

Schmidt, Jeff (2000), *Disciplined Minds: A Critical Look at Salaried Professionals and the Soul-battering System that Shapes Their Lives*, Lanham, MD: Rowman & Littlefield.

Shiffrin, Steven H. (1999), *Dissent, Injustice, and the Meanings of America*, Princeton, NJ: Princeton University Press.

Sitaraman, Ganesh and Previn Warren (eds) (2003), *Invisible Citizens: Youth Politics After September 11*, New York: iUniverse.

Strauss, Valerie (2006), 'Putting parents in their place: outside class', *Washington Post*, 21 March, A8.

Strauss, William and Neil Howe (1991), *Generations: The History of America's Future, 1584 to 2069*, New York: William Morrow & Co.

Sunstein, Cass R. (2003), *Why Societies Need Dissent*, Cambridge, MA: Harvard University Press.

White, Patrick (2007), 'About face; parents who go online to snoop on their kids are having the tables turned on them', *The Globe and Mail*, 12 June, L1.

Zemke, Ron, Claire Raines and Bob Filipczak (2000), *Generations at Work: Managing the Class of Veterans, Boomers, Xers, and Nexters in Your Workplace*, New York: AMACOM.

Zukin, Cliff, Scott Keeter, Molly Andolina, Krista Jenkins and Michael X. Delli Carpini (2006), *A New Engagement? Political Participation, Civic Life, and the Changing American Citizen*, New York: Oxford University Press.

5. Organizational totalitarianism and the voices of dissent

Howard F. Stein

INTRODUCTION

Corporate executives – no less than national leaders – use language in an effort to manage (which most commonly means to control) dissent. Their tactics include denying, constraining, subverting, transforming, quashing and discrediting challenges that oppose orthodox ideologies and policies. Dissent management by leaders is a central activity in creating and maintaining totalitarian workplace management styles. I shall argue that language does not independently stamp out dissent. Rather it is the instrument and medium of the heavy boot that tramples thinking itself.

The viewpoint I bring to my analysis of totalitarian discourses in organizations is that of a psychoanalytically oriented anthropologist who gains insights into workplace dynamics through day-to-day work as an ethnographer in medical and other settings, and as someone engaged in action research. In this chapter I first discuss how totalitarianism finds expression in American culture. I then identify core psychological features of totalitarianism, and I conclude by offering three vignettes to illustrate these processes.

TOTALITARIANISM AMERICAN-STYLE

Fascism traditionally has been viewed as a nationalist ideology. For instance, Richard Falk defines historical fascism as 'the convergence of military and economic power of an ultranationalist ideology that views its enemies – internally and externally – as evil and subject to extermination or extreme punishment' (quoted in MacKinnon, 2003). Not all totalitarian forms, however, look alike ideologically, although ultimately they act alike. Just as during the Cold War communist and socialist ideology was largely tailored by the nation in which it was adopted, the same is true of fascism. Falk articulates what I have long felt about an emerging American national style and language of totalitarianism: One must examine both the cultural *act* and the cultural *disguise*.

> In many ways, the language is very careful. No one today has the bluntness of a Hitler or a Mussolini. . . . [I]t is important to acknowledge that if this fascist threat exists, it exists in a distinctive form both in the United States and in the world, and that it is conditioned by the American political culture – which is resistant to the language of fascism. Certainly the people who are the architects of these policies would reject my analysis, and probably sincerely so. They think they're doing something else; it will all be done in the name of democratization. It's a very deceptive and confusing style of political domination, because it pretends to be the opposite of what it is. There is an ambiguity, because this is a concealed fascism that is occurring within the framework of a constitutional democracy. (MacKinnon, 2003)

I shall argue that a cultural ethos pervades many kinds of social institutions within that culture, with the result that workplace organizations are as likely to be regulated by fascist attitudes and relationships as are nations. Shortly after the September 11, 2001, terrorist attacks, United States President George W. Bush declared that 'Either you are with us, or you are with the terrorists' (Bush, 2001). Rationalized by relentless economic competition and globalization, countless business, corporate and industrial leaders have uttered the same sentiment, although in reference to different enemies.

Albert Dunlap, former CEO of Scott Paper and then Sunbeam, is a case example. He called himself 'Rambo in Pinstripes' (see Sunbeam and 'Chainsaw Al', 2005). His tactics included loud confrontation, public humiliation and put-downs. He earned the epithets 'Chainsaw Al' and 'The Shredder' by turning around troubled companies through relentless employee firings and numerous plant closings. As these names imply, he treated people as if they were inanimate things. The only thing he cared about was increasing – in fact temporarily inflating – shareholder value and pleasing stockholders. In 1996 he published a book titled *Mean Business: How I Save Bad Companies and Make Good Companies Great*. Indeed, he polarized the world into shareholders (the 'good' people, who were to be placated) and workers (the 'bad' people, who were disposable).

During Dunlap's reigns from the 1970s through the 1990s, he enjoyed being cruel to those who stood in the way of his ambitions. Shareholders were his 'allies', and employees were his 'enemies'. His compatriot P. Newton White characterized Dunlap's approach to managing subordinates: 'Piss all over them and then build them up' (Byrne, 2003, p. 3). The more people he fired, the higher climbed the stock prices. The more he rid the company of 'them', the more he pleased 'us'.

So relentless is the search for 'enemies', that as a national culture the US has made many of 'us' (employees, workers) into enemies as well as the officially designated 'them' in the 'war on terror' (Lotto, 1998; Stein, 2005). The once-ubiquitous psychological contract between employer and employee has been summarily cancelled since the mid-1980s, and workers have been virtually abandoned to fend for themselves. Wave upon wave of downsizing, reductions in force (RIFing), restructuring, reengineering, outsourcing and deskilling are heir to this cultural war against and sacrifice of those deemed to be threats to the reified nation or organization. Monikers are quite revealing: 'Neutron' Jack Welch of General Electric, who reputedly got rid of people like a neutron bomb; and 'Chainsaw' Al Dunlap of Scott Paper, who 'cut' people out of organizations like a chain-saw. Seth Allcorn has also observed that the dynamics and language of totalitarianism are hardly limited to the nation's political apparatus: 'Those who study organizations are also no longer surprised to find suppressed, dominated and controlled, and alienated employees. More recently (1990s through 2005) downsizing, rightsizing, reengineering, globalization and corporate scandals have diminished the ideal of freedom, dignity and democracy in the workplace' (Allcorn, 2007: 40).

In American literature, Captain Ahab of the ship *Pequod* in Herman Melville's novel *Moby Dick* is perhaps the quintessential bully-leader – and American hero. Ahab is the single-minded narcissistic CEO of his enter-prise seeking revenge on the great white whale Moby Dick for amputating his foot on an earlier voyage. He intimidates his crew into wildly endorsing and fulfilling his ultimately suicidal mission and diverting themselves from their work-task of hunting whales for whale oil. Had Ahab been a corpor-ate executive of the late twentieth century, he no doubt would have exhorted his whalers to be uncritical 'team players', not only to obey his command, but to make his obsession their own.

No amount of guile, cajoling, or public humiliation was beyond Ahab. Late in the novel, the casks of oil sprung leaks in the hold. First Mate Starbuck urged Captain Ahab to change course and have the leaks repaired. This is not the first time that Starbuck's is the voice of reason, reality, dissent and protest, while Ahab's is the voice of obsessive pursuit of Moby Dick. 'Thou art always prating to me, Starbuck, about those miserly owners, as if the owners were my conscience. But look ye, the only real owner of anything is its commander; and hark ye, my conscience is in this ship's keel. – On deck!' Ahab orders (Melville, 1961: 449).

Emboldened, Starbuck comes closer in Ahab's cabin and presses his case. Ahab grabs a loaded musket and points it towards Starbuck, exclaiming, 'There is one God that is Lord over the earth, and one Captain that is lord over the Pequod. – On deck!' (p. 449). As he leaves the cabin, Starbuck respectfully warns Ahab of his greatest foe, himself: 'I ask thee not to beware of Starbuck; thou wouldst but laugh; but let Ahab beware of Ahab; beware of thyself, old man' (p. 449). Ahab briefly reconsiders Starbuck's caution, then upon reaching the deck, raises his voice to the crew, ordering them to do what Starbuck had advised him – but as if it were his own idea. In the American corporate world, it is not unusual for executives to co-opt the original ideas of their subordinates, and then to demand adulation for their brilliance.

Much earlier on the voyage, with the entire crew assembled on deck, Ahab rages toward his men with the true purpose of the voyage, to pursue Moby Dick to his death and avenge Ahab's lost leg. 'I'll chase him round Good Hope, and round the Horn, and round the Norway Maelstrom, and round perdition's flames before I give him up. And this is what ye have shipped for, men! To chase that white whale on both sides of land, and over all sides of earth, till he spouts black blood and rolls fin out. What say ye, men, will ye splice hands on it, now! I think ye do look brave' (p. 166). Ahab is trying to shame them into colluding with him. Starbuck, again, the voice of reason and realism, counters, 'I came here to hunt whale, not my commander's vengeance. How many barrels will thy vengeance yield thee even if thou gettest it, Captain Ahab? It will not fetch thee much in our Nantucket market'. Ahab is aroused: '. . . my vengeance will fetch me a great premium *here*! . . . Talk not to me of blasphemy, man; I'd strike the sun if it insulted me' (p. 166).

Ahab sets out to isolate and humiliate Starbuck and rally the crew to his single-minded mission: 'Are they [the crew] not one and all with Ahab, in this matter of the whale?' Ahab rubs it in: 'Stand up amid the general hurricane, thy one tost sapling cannot, Starbuck!' (p. 167). Ahab then devises a ritual to seal his victory, the crew's acquiescence. He orders the pewter, filled with alcohol, passed so that the entire crew will drink a draught of this communion.

To seal the vow, he further orders the mates to flank him in a circle with their lances, and cross lances in front of him. Ahab is now the undisputed center of the circle of fealty. He thunders triumphantly, 'Oh, my sweet cardinals! Your own condescension, that shall bend ye to it. I do not order it; ye will it' (p. 169). In a frenzy, Ahab binds them to an oath: 'Drink, ye harpooners! Drink and swear, ye men that man the deathful whaleboat's bow – Death to Moby Dick! God hunt us all, if we do not hunt Moby Dick to his death!' (p. 170).

A more fitting example of what Heinz Kohut called 'chronic narcissistic rage' (1972) could not be found. Forged on the anvil of intimidation, Ahab's crew are no longer individual, thinking beings. Now identified with Ahab and each other, they are a single – unthinking – will. For all the world,

Ahab's voice could have been that of Jack Welch (GE), Al Dunlap (Sunbeam), Joe Nacchio (Qwest), Dennis Kozlowski (Tyco), Harold Geneen (ITT) or Donald Trump (dealmaker and demanding boss of the popular reality television show, 'The Apprentice'). If Ahab is a classical figure, he is also uncannily modern.

Slightly over a century and a half later, American cartoonist Scott Adams depicts and evokes the intimidating corporate atmosphere of America in his long-lived newspaper series 'Dilbert'. Since 1989, Adams's newspaper comic strip and his 1996 book, *The Dilbert Principle* and its successors have portrayed, mocked and caricatured the dominant management and organizational change styles in vogue. 'Dilbert' as an art form is culturally symptomatic of the way of life it evokes and rebukes. Its wide appeal, measurable by newspaper syndication and book sales (not to mention its presence in photocopy form as social commentary on break-room bulletin boards and refrigerator doors), cross-cuts a wide array of organizational types, aggressively capitalist and nurturantly service-oriented alike. Adams's genius in his characters' words, gestures and facial expression is to reveal the viciousness and brutality behind supposedly inexorably good business sense. His ever-present image of the workplace 'cubicle' depicts the austere, lifeless, deadening mental geography of confinement and constriction. In this world, work is prison with pay. 'Dilbert' at once parades our business euphemisms before us and exposes them. The cartoonist is in fact a moralist. 'Dilbert portrays corporate culture as a Kafkaesque world of bureaucracy for its own sake and office politics that stand in the way of productivity, where employees' skills and efforts are not rewarded, and busy work praised. Much of the humor emerges as we see the characters making obviously ridiculous decisions that are natural reactions to mismanagement' (Wikipedia, 2005).

A few examples (without full benefit of cartoon) must suffice. In a 1995 'Dilbert' cartoon, Dogbert, Dilbert's pet, acting as a downsizing consultant, demonstrates how to notify employees that their jobs will be outsourced by having his consulting partner, Ratbert, bend over. At the edge of a desktop, Dogbert kicks Ratbert in the buttocks into the trash can. In the final scene, the 'Pointy-Haired Boss' asks Dogbert, 'How do I get them all stooped over?' Dogbert recommends 'a program of very bad ergonomics' (Adams, 1996).

In a 1996 cartoon, Catbert, the evil human relations director, advises Wally, a stressed-out worker, to start smoking cigarettes, since in that way he would 'have frequent company-sanctioned breaks throughout the day'. Wally asks: 'This is your strategy for downsizing, isn't it?' In another 1996 'Dilbert' cartoon, Catbert's tail is twitching, which is his sign that it is time to write more evil company policies. This time the directive is: 'Employees must wear shoes that are one size smaller than their feet'. Later he says: 'This is my favorite part: "We must do this to be competitive" '. Finally, to the inquiry as to whether anyone has complained about the 'footsizing' program, Catbert replies: 'I haven't listened to a single complaint'. The bullying and sadism are obvious as (counterproductive) 'motivating' methods for achieving greater productivity and profitability (Adams, 1996).

More recently, in the 'Dilbert' cartoon of 17 October, 2005, the scene is a staff meeting around a table. A man says, 'Our shareholders are suing us for misleading them about our financial problems'. The Pointy-Haired Boss replies, 'Since when is it illegal to shaft innocent people for personal gain?' Turning to Wally, the man replies, 'Don't put that in the minutes' (Adams, 2005a). The egregious misleading of shareholders and employees at Enron, WorldCom, Global Crossing, Tyco and other large companies finds its way to cynical caricature in this cartoon.

In another cartoon, Catbert, the evil director of HR, informs staff of new guidelines of who are permitted to fly on the same plane. 'We can't risk losing too many key employees'. First, 'The CEO and the president are not allowed to be on the same flight'. Second, 'No more than three vice presidents may be on the same flight'. Asok, an intern in Dilbert's company, asks, 'What are the guidelines for interns?' Catbert replies, 'Infinite interns are allowed on the same flight. You are also allowed to run with scissors and put plastic bags over your heads' (Adams, 2005b). Not only are employees of lower status expendable, but the sadistic HR director encourages them to harm, if not kill, themselves.

In a similar vein, a different 'Dilbert' cartoon depicts yet another meeting, this time presided over by the Pointy-Haired Boss. He reads, 'Management is pleased to announce that it has a plan to make your pension fund solvent'. In the next cartoon cell, the corporate building is shown, accompanied by the words, 'In unrelated news, the guidelines for workplace safety have been relaxed'. In the final cell, back at the meeting table, the Pointy-Haired Boss says, 'Our CEO reminds you that smoking is cool' (Adams, 2005c). Here the corporate brutality is transparent and undisguised. The faltering corporate pension fund will be made solvent through the accelerated deaths of workers. It should be clear that business is about far more than rational economic decisions based on self-interest. 'Dilbert,' like Captain Ahab, is uncannily current.

The success of 'Dilbert', then, is a reliable social barometer of mass discontent with organizational totalitarianism. It resonates with the cynicism, the mistrust, the dread in many American workplaces. Adams's comic strip is popular humor's closest approximation to dissent and social protest. It is the closest our grim age comes to satire. Because it resonates so truly and pervasively, 'Dilbert' tells us as well as, if not better than, any scholarly essayist of our time that people are nonpersons, only 'workers' and 'producers'. They are only as good as they are useful, so long as one can exact work from them – then toss them aside as disposable, expellable waste. If the reader objects that I make too much of a mere comic strip and its creator, I can only reply that the meanings I infer are those that mass culture has created. The data are already there; I am only pointing them out. In a sense, American culture has created Scott Adams and the 'Dilbert' characters and scenarios in which we recognize ourselves – and pay to recognize this portrait of ourselves.

'Dilbert' speaks to and gives form to a whole way of life that has come to be regarded as rational business-as-usual. 'Dilbert' unmasks our self-deceptions and smoke screens. Adams refuses to go along with the crowd, with the officially imposed corporate worldview. He tells us what we know but are afraid to admit directly: things are as bad as, if not worse than, they seem; cruelty more than rationality rules many American workplaces.

UNIVERSAL AND ORGANIZATIONAL PSYCHODYNAMICS OF TOTALITARIANISM

Ideological systems such as 'managed social change' and its related nomenclature do not stand or act on their own. Likewise popular cultural forms such as Scott Adams's 'Dilbert' cartoons continue to occupy newspaper and bookstore space because they appeal to the fantasies and fears of those who read and purchase them. They perform psychological functions vital to keep anxiety at bay and to fulfill unconscious desires. They are part of 'organizations in the mind' as well as external structure. That is, 'organizations and [other] groups exist . . . predominantly, *but not solely*, as an outcome of dynamic and changing individual and collective projections rooted in unconscious fantasies and emotions' (Diamond *et al.*, 2004: 32, emphasis in original). In a 2003 essay on 'fascism resurgent' in the United States, psychoanalyst and psychohistorian David Lotto explores deep beneath the political, cultural and ideological veneer of fascism and identifies certain universal psychodynamic features. He writes:

> I suggest that fascism involves an exaggerated tendency toward the use of primitive splitting mechanisms, dividing the world into good and evil, and externalizing the evil by projecting it onto the alien enemy other while claiming exclusive possession of the good for oneself and one's cohort. This way of looking at fascist impulses and actions allows us to see the commonality among a number of apparently disparate types of political activities. (Lotto, 2003: 297)

Lotto situates the ideological spread of American fascist ideology in relation to the psychological as well as physical and political injury of the attacks on the United States on September 11, 2001. 'In times such as these, when we have been attacked and feel threatened and passions run high, there is a strong pull to respond to our narcissistic injury with narcissistic rage – to lash out against those we see as responsible for our pain' (2003: 305).

One could expand this argument in space and time to include the responses of many businesses, corporations, industries and other organizations to the now-chronic external climate of ruthless competition and the threat to organizational survival, rampant since the 1980s. Under such circumstances of psychological siege and attack, narcissistic leaders appeal to an us/them polarization, demand unquestioning loyalty, and quash all internal dissent. With their frequent threats of danger to the organization, they help induce regression and dependency upon their beneficent protection, which amounts to increased vulnerability in the guise of safety.

A similar process occurred in the American federal government's immediate response to the devastating hurricanes Katrina and Rita in the late summer of 2005, and to the enormous flooding following the breaches in the levees protecting New Orleans. In an ABC 'Good Morning America' interview on 1 September, 2005, President George W. Bush declared 'I don't think anyone anticipated the breach of the levees'. Two days later, Homeland Security Secretary Michael Chertoff argued: 'That "perfect storm" of a combination of catastrophes exceeded the foresight of the planners, and maybe anybody's foresight'. He described the disaster as 'breathtaking in its surprise' (Chertoff, 2005).

Despite the fact that the federal government had been abundantly warned about the precarious condition of the levees, federal officials insisted on their innocence, ignorance, and goodness, while vilifying local New Orleans and Louisiana governments for making a delayed and incompetent response to the disaster. 'Mother Nature', too, became labeled as the unpredictable enemy. In this national scenario, as in organizational life, leaders often resort to psychological splitting between us/them and good/bad, and count on frightened loyalty in return from followers.

Allcorn writes of the critical role of corporate ideology in establishing this either/or process: 'Those who study organizations are also no longer surprised to find suppressed, dominated and controlled, and alienated employees (Stein 2003). More recently (1990s through 2005) downsizing, rightsizing, re-engineering, globalization and corporate scandals have diminished the ideal of freedom and dignity in the workplace (Allcorn et al., 1996)' (Allcorn, 2007: 40). Through ideology, leaders psychologically 'bind' workers to the organization, whereby all opposing views are rejected and doubt is eliminated. For psychoanalyst Christopher Bollas, in the fascist state of mind, '[t]he mind ceases to be complex, achieving a simplicity held together initially by bindings around the signs of ideology' (Bollas,

1992: 201). Followers are recruited and subsequently 'bound' to the ideology by the promise of alleviating intense anxiety and radically splitting the perceptual world into 'good' people (us, insiders) and 'bad' people (them, others).

Organizational leaders' appeal to grave danger and offer of a magical solution is illustrated by the following story from Seth Allcorn:

> I recall hearing of a meeting in a large teaching hospital that was called to formally announce that downsizing was about to ensue with the help of a notorious downsizing consulting group. The hospital CEO was speaking to all of upper and middle management, approximately 150 people. He explained the downsizing process this way. 'You are standing on a train station platform. You have three choices. You can get on the train that is going where I want to go. You can wait just a little bit before deciding what you want to do. Or, you can get on the second train that is leaving the hospital'. Since I studied downsizing in depth as a researcher . . . I can bear witness to the fact that the metaphorical trains both lead to a man-made hell on earth. (Allcorn, 1998: xii)

As I have described elsewhere (Stein 1998, 2001), Nazi Holocaust-era trains are a widespread metaphor used by leaders, victims, and survivors to describe the harrowing experience of downsizing, reductions in force, rightsizing, and other forms of 'managed social change'. The CEO offers Captain Ahab's choice: follow me, and you live; don't follow me, and you're dead. The irony, of course, is that to follow Ahab is to doom oneself to death. Firm belief in the totalitarian ideology and the cause that it champions becomes more vital than life itself.

A few words about the psychodynamics of what is 'total' in the ideology and practice of totalitarianism are in order. The work of a number of psychoanalytic writers converges to help us to understand the psychodynamics of organizational and political totalitarianism and, hence, the appeal of its ideology and its ability to mobilize people in its service. In his pioneering work on the adolescent quality of either/or, inside/outside, thinking that characterizes totalitarian ideologies, Erik Erikson distinguished between exclusivistic 'totalistic' thinking from inclusivistic 'wholism' in identity formation (Erikson, 1968: 74–90). In totalistic thinking an ideology is created and embraced that radically simplifies the world, repudiates if not destroys all opposing views, and is intolerant of all doubt.

Erikson described the universal process of dividing the world into what he called 'pseudospecies' (1968: 41–2), by which all peoples to some degree describe themselves as *the* human beings, and others as lesser and lower life forms. That is, there is a split in affect such that affiliative 'good' feelings are associated with one's own group, and disaffiliative 'bad' feelings are associated with others. 'Inside' is idealized and 'outside' is demonized. The others 'were at least useful as a screen of projection for the negative identities which were the necessary, if most uncomfortable, counterpart of the positive ones' (p. 41). Erikson continues: 'The pseudospecies . . . is one of the more sinister aspects of all group identity' (p. 42).

This process becomes exaggerated and ossified in times of crisis, anxiety and massive large group regression, as Vamik Volkan (1997, 2002) and I (Stein, 2004) have described. Under such circumstances, people come to rely on emergency psychological measures to protect themselves. What George Devereux (1955) called 'catastrophic' thinking tends to seize the group, and the reduction of (psychotic) anxiety becomes the central obsession of the group and its leaders. Great effort is mobilized to revitalize the loss- and death-obsessed group (see La Barre, 1972). Under these simultaneously inner and outer circumstances, people come to re-experience annihilation anxiety, against which they defend by the use of some of the developmentally earliest defense mechanisms such as splitting, massive projective identification and externalization. Identity rigidity replaces continuous identity development. 'Total immersion in a synthetic identity' goes hand in glove with 'a totally stereotyped enemy of the new identity' (Erikson, 1968: 89). Erikson continues: 'The fear of loss of identity which fosters such indoctrination contributes significantly to that mixture of righteousness and criminality which, under totalitarian conditions, becomes available for organized terror and for the establishment of major industries of extermination' (p. 89).

What W. R. Bion called unconscious 'basic assumption'-type thinking, especially 'fight-flight' vigilance and readiness to attack, tends to prevail. Likewise, Pierre Turquet's (1974) fourth basic assumption of group 'oneness', and what Michael Diamond and Seth Allcorn (1987) call 'group homogenization' overtake the functioning of the group. That is, one willingly relinquishes critical faculties and self-differentiation and integration in the quest for absolute safety and certainty – a safety as much from one's unconscious as from the reality one unconsciously provokes into attacking. For example, under the spell of 'oneness', group members 'seek to join in a powerful union with an omnipotent force, unobtainably high, to surrender self for passive participation, and thereby feel existence, well-being, and wholeness [cohesion]' (Turquet, 1974: 357). A transferential contract is struck between charismatic, shaman-like leader and group: the narcissistic leader promises to elevate the status of the emotionally deflated group, while the group promises to mirror and confirm the leader's needy greatness (La Barre, 1972; Pauchant, 1991).

The totalitarian group is paralyzed with an inability to 'learn from experience' (Bion, 1962), and its reality testing capacity is impaired, since the external world is now mostly defined and inhabited by the evacuated contents of the unconscious, which is to say, the rejected parts of the self.

At the individual level, the ego, impaired in its integrative function, constricts into an endless vigil of boundary maintenance to protect it from the enemies it finds everywhere. Corporate leaders like Albert Dunlap, Jack Welch, Joseph Nacchio and Dennis Kozlowski arrive uncannily on the cultural and corporate scene to rescue and revitalize the organization – only to debase it. The protection they offer is in fact a protection racket.

I turn now from a discussion of theoretical issues to a consideration of three vignettes taken from the real corporate world. The vignettes will put flesh on the more literary and abstract discussion of organizational totalitarianism thus far.[1]

THREE ILLUSTRATIONS OF TOTALITARIAN DISCOURSE

Vignette 1: The Jew in their Midst

The following vignette illustrates the operation of patently nationalistic and totalitarian thinking in ordinary workplace institutions such as businesses, corporations and universities. It shows how mundane organizational fascism can be. The vignette entails a conflict between a unit director and a social scientist working in his unit in a large research and development institute. The social scientist employee, Dr Frankel, is widely known to 'have a mind of his own' and to often express a dissenting view in workplace meetings. The unit director likes to have tight control of his projects and workers, and regards Frankel as a 'loose cannon' in his institute.

The supervisor is a brilliant, ambitious academic medical researcher who is building his own institute and a wide regional network. The language of their conflict points to the presence of unconscious as well as political issues fueling the strife. In the employee's narrative, the supervisor constantly degrades his worker, often humiliating him in private. Although Frankel's ostensible job description was to serve as an applied sociologist on R&D projects, the supervisor forbade him even to use the concepts of 'culture' or 'society' in his work because 'Nobody will understand you'. He dictated the language of discourse the social scientist was permitted to use. Frankel was widely published in the supervisor's field, but the supervisor often said to him:

> You've published a lot, but very few people in the field can understand what you're saying. . . . You keep asking for respect, but you don't deserve any. . . . You've received numerous national awards for your work, but they are given by the wrong organizations. Don't you understand that they don't count around here?

Oddly, many of the ideas Frankel proposed and championed, and which the supervisor publicly ridiculed or harshly condemned, the supervisor later adopted as his own in projects, grant applications and publications. When Frankel would try to inquire about this mysterious appearance, the supervisor would insist that the ideas were his own or had come from an entirely different source. He separated, dissociating himself from his employee's influence. On one occasion the supervisor temporarily softened and confided in the employee:

> Maybe I envy you a little. I've always wanted to be a field and stream biologist, not a hard driving researcher and administrator responsible for the production of a large group of people. I look at you and I see what I'd like to be: here's a guy who does what he likes and doesn't listen to anyone. I sure would like to have the job description where I could devote 50 percent of my time to writing and publishing.

For a moment, the supervisor had allowed himself to identify consciously with his worker. Quickly, admiration returned to envy. What he could not have or be in himself, he had to destroy in his employee. The colleague came again to embody what Erik Erikson spoke of as the 'negative identity', that is, the condensed image of all one rejects about oneself and one's internal representations. On a later occasion, while Frankel was driving the supervisor to an affiliate R&D site, the supervisor engaged in lecturing him as to the nature of his problem. He was diagnosing Frankel's problem, and then offering him help:

> What is it with you Jews? You act just like the other Jews I've known. I've never been able to understand why you act as if you're so special. Look at the history of the Weimar Republic before Hitler came into power. Jews were overrepresented in government, in the arts, in science, in medicine, in the media, in everything. They were in control of the whole country. Can't you understand why Germans wanted to get rid of them, to get their own country back? It seems to me like the Jews bring persecutions upon themselves. I know it's terrible to say – and I'll deny that this conversation ever took place if you say anything about it – but the Jews push their way into everything. What happened to them was horrible, but much of it owes to their own doing. It's the same here in America. Jews have infiltrated the government, the news media, the arts, science. They want to control everything. And you're just like them. You act as if everyone is against you, and it is not true. You get surprised when we push back. I don't know how to get you to realize that I'm on your side. You just need to downplay your writing projects in the home office. You've got to realize that few R&D specialists anywhere can read and understand your papers. Your future here in the corporation depends on your ability to be less rigid and to trust me.

In this corporate diatribe, the protection the supervisor proffered was a protection racket. The fee exacted from the employee was his own independent thought and judgment. The supervisor had also touched something raw in himself. Dr Frankel had come to represent something sinister to him – that part of his own self that he had rejected in favor of the pursuit of success in the corporate world. Hypernationalist (Nazi) stereotypes and xenophobia played a central role in the supervisor's perception and experience of the workplace conflict. The supervisor's conflict with Frankel was heavily colored by his own inner conflict. Organizational fascism took on an ordinary face even as it used the language of the Holocaust. The employee represented the voice of dissent which the supervisor had to co-opt or silence.

Vignette 2: Dissent and Eradication

For my second vignette, I want to focus on a single text, one that although not statistically representative is nonetheless thematically representative of the numerous workplace biographies I have heard and witnessed since the mid-1980s. A man I will call Dr Paul Opal had long been an accomplished academic physician in an urban medical center. He was consistently an outspoken critic of accepting without reflection or comment statements from the chairman, dean and provost. His was a voice of dissent in a place that increasingly demanded lockstep thinking. In 1999 he was without warning summarily fired. In early October 2003, Dr Opal wrote a poignant, articulate letter to me. From an instrumental, that is, practical, point of view, the writer of the letter had found a new job after his firing – arguably a better one than he had before. From an expressive, that is, symbolic, viewpoint, however, he languished in a grief no one wanted to hear or acknowledge, what Kenneth Doka (2002) calls 'disenfranchised grief', losses that culturally do not merit acknowledgment and mourning, and are hence unsupported socially.

> It is now more than four years since I last spoke with you. It was in late January of 1999 that I told you of my being *exiled* from my company. After telling you some of my story, you suggested that I should write about my experience. This is the first piece of writing I have done in four years.
>
> My exile was executed in a chillingly, callous manner. The official explanation to me was that I was not a 'team player'. I was told to leave the building immediately, lest the police be called. I was not allowed to gather my personal belongings, including my books, papers and photos of my family and friends. I was told my belongings would be catalogued and returned to me.
>
> Others were told that they were forbidden to talk about me. To inquiries about me, the official response was, 'Dr Opal no longer works here'. There would be no discussion of the circumstances of my exile. My name was not to be uttered, nor my accomplishments and contributions ever acknowledged, or even mentioned. In effect, I was 'painted out' of the organization's history. Stalin, who

airbrushed Trotsky's picture out of any official representation of the Russian Revolution, perfected this technique. As an organizational sacrifice, I was not killed. I was terminated. I had simply become a non-entity. I had metamorphosed into a 'bug' [allusion to Franz Kafka's story, 'The Metamorphosis'].

Friends told me that after I left, it was as if I never existed in the land of the corporation. The person who replaced me, after asking, 'What happened to Dr Opal?' was told, 'Don't ask'. My name was never spoken, and one person said, it was as if one day the sea parted, I fell in, and I was never to be heard from again.

I lost more than a job. My world stopped making sense. I was forever asking myself, and others, 'How did this happen?'; 'Why did this happen?'; 'What did I do?' I simply could not explain what happened to me. My sense of unreality was fed by the silence of many around me. I was expected to 'get over it', to 'deal with it', to 'get on with my life'. But if I was to 'move on', I needed to talk about what happened. Lacking an audience to hear my story, I was deprived of what Rafael Moses calls the *balm* of narcissistic injuries -- acknowledgment.

My dreams mirrored my reality. Repeatedly I dreamt of being with former colleagues, people I thought of as friends, who 'turned away from me' whenever I asked them what had happened to me. I found some solace when I read Primo Levi who wrote in *Survival in Auschwitz* of his own reoccurring dream, where he is telling others of his camp experience, and they are completely indifferent, as if not there. Levi asks: 'Why is the pain of the everyday translated so constantly into our dreams, in the ever-repeated scene of the *unlistened*-to-story?'

I can attest to the assertion made by a variety of authors that being treated with *indifference* is the cruelest form of punishment. Indeed for me, there has been no greater pain than being ignored, rejected, unwanted, deemed insignificant and the like.

Although I did receive some support from a few people . . ., I often ask myself if the people who I thought were my friends ever wondered how I was, if I was surviving, if I was employed again, or even if I had committed suicide. I wonder what sort of euphemisms, rationalizations, justifications, or excuses they might make for not dropping a note or making a phone call to inquire about me and wish me well. (16 October 2003, all emphases in original.)

Dr Opal's story can be read and heard as both singularly unique and as an exemplar of narratives voiced by many victims and survivors of corporate totalitarianism's violence. Here I will discuss several themes common to both. To begin with, there is a loss of a 'world' (identity, sense of place) not merely a 'job'. Moreover – and common to RIFs and related disruptions – one is literally severed from the job and workplace. One is virtually thrown out ('exiled') and abandoned with little or no warning or preparation. A third theme is the terrifying feeling of being transformed from a living human subject into a dead object, from a person to a non-person, a thing, a bug. Coupled with this is the withdrawal by others, a condemnation to the void of silence. No one is willing to listen to, to validate and give witness to one's story. It is as if it never happened. One's very existence is obliterated. Another theme is the evocation of Holocaust imagery and narrative as a trope with which to represent and comprehend one's own experience. There are as well other emotionally raw images and metaphors of violent attack upon oneself (for example, Stalin's eradication of Trotsky from official Russian Revolutionary history).

Yet another theme is the coercion one has and feels from others – superiors, colleagues, friends – to let go of the past and move on without first the necessary affirmation of having been listened to. There is no bridge, only rupture. Memory itself is discounted. The story is too disturbing to be heard. Further, the story touches anyone who was in contact with the writer, a 'touch' which they anxiously try to rid themselves, lest they be 'contaminated' with the same fate. They are admonished not to speak further of him, to kill him in their memories. Partly from fear of sharing his fate and from feelings of guilt and shame, they withdraw from him and from any memory of him. Personally and organizationally, he is obliterated. It no longer matters to them whether he is dead or alive.

Such is the power of projective identification and its counterpart in the victim or survivor, introjective identification. Riddance and haunting presences are the twin facets of this organizational scapegoating and sacrifice. As if this all is not enough, personal factors in one's developmental, family, and ethnic history are reawakened and played out on the stage of current workplace atrocity (see Terry, 1984). Still, despite the wide diversity of individual biographical experience, the narratives are strikingly similar. Further, this vignette distills the experience of American corporate *desaparacidos* (originally, Argentinians who were brutally 'disappeared' during the 'dirty wars' of the 1980s) in the late twentieth and early twenty-first centuries (see Suarez-Orozco, 1990).

Vignette 3: I *am* the Corporation

For my final vignette, I turn from local, individual, even private corporate experiences to a public, national and international example of corporate totalitarianism and the suppression of dissent, the era of Leo Dennis Kozlowski of Tyco International, from 1976 to 2002. This vignette shows how the Kozlowski era at Tyco typifies and personifies corporate greed and corruption, and how corporate totalitarianism was an instrument of achieving them. For Kozlowski, people were exclusively a means to achieving personal aggrandizement. His corporate acquisitions numbered some 200 per year. Under Kozlowski, Tyco came to include health care products, security systems, electronics, disposable diapers, and fiber-optic cables. In 2001, he fired 11 500 people and cut annual costs by $350 million. Kozlowski was on the cover of *Business Week* in 2001, under the headline 'The Most Aggressive CEO' (BusinessWeek Online, 2001).

As leader of Tyco, with the help of CFO Mark Swartz, he obliterated the boundary between personal and corporate interest, manipulating Tyco's books to steal hundreds of millions of dollars, using stock options and outright grants, hiding unauthorized bonuses, and forgiving loans to himself. Reason and dissent were forbidden; only an idolatry of the leader was permitted. On the surface, Kozlowski ran a 'successful lean conglomerate' (Maremont and Cohen, 2003). Behind the scenes, he 'transferred massive sums of wealth to himself at the expense of shareholders'. He sought managers who were 'smart, poor, and [who] want[ed] to be rich'. He made frequent reference to his working-class roots in Newark, NJ, and his work ethic, as though these thereby justified his excesses.

Kozlowski practiced humiliation in the service of profit. As president of Tyco's largest division, Grinnell Fire Protections Systems Company, he 'cut overhead to the bone', set salaries low and offered a bonus tied to profit – but with a twist. 'Kozlowski held a banquet at which he presented awards not only to the best warehouse manager but also to the worst one. "It was kind of embarrassing watching a guy to go up," says R. Jerry Conklin, a former Grinnell executive. "It was like his death sentence" ' (BusinessWeek Online, 2002).

Kozlowski claimed to be aligning the interests of management with those of the shareholders, whom he robbed. In deed if not in word, the few in management were the 'us' to be looked out for, and investors, workers and retirees were the 'them' who were readily disposable. He invoked the American work ethic while secretly undermining and mocking it. His grandiosity was bounded only by his ambition. Repeatedly he 'proclaimed his desire to be remembered as the world's greatest business executive, as a "combination of what Jack Welch put together at GE and Warren Buffett's very practical ideas on how you go about creating return for shareholders" ' (BusinessWeek Online, 2002).

Seventeen days before he was indicted for tax evasion, he said in a commencement speech at Saint Anselm College in New Hampshire, 'You will be confronted with questions every day that test your morals. . . . Think carefully and, for your sake, do the right thing, not the easy thing' (Kozlowski, 2002). He accepted huge pay raises while 'pronounc[ing] his distaste for runaway executive pay' (Maremont and Cohen, 2003). Declaring in 1997, '[Stock] options are a free ride' in his advocacy of a pay-for-performance program at Tyco, Kozlowski shortly thereafter received 3.3 million options. He extolled the virtues of austere workplaces while building for himself palatial offices at Boca Raton, FL. He told one visitor to Tyco's official and simple two-story headquarters in Exeter, NH, 'We don't believe in perks, not even executive parking spots' (BusinessWeek Online, 2002). The split between public pronouncement and private behavior could not be more obvious.

The $6000 shower curtain for his extravagantly furnished Manhattan apartment fits well with his pattern of conspicuous consumption that included a $15 000 umbrella stand. He held a million-dollar birthday party on Sardinia for his wife, a part of which featured a life-sized ice sculpture of Michelangelo's 'David' urinating Stolichnaya vodka into cups. In interviews, he disavowed his own excesses, denying, for instance, that he knew anything about the shower curtain. 'People think that I'm a greedy guy; that I was overcompensated. . . . Greed, I think, is the key word. But while I did earn enormous sums of money, which for a poor kid from Newark was spectacular, I worked my butt off and it was all based on my performance in Tyco's long established pay-per-performance culture. . . . I firmly believe that I never did or intended to do anything wrong. . . . I never thought in my wildest imagination I or any of us did anything wrong my entire time there. I still cannot believe that they say words like larceny (Sorkin, 2005).

Since Kozlowski had fused personal interest with what he saw as corporate interest, he was certain he did no wrong. 'They' – no doubt a dissociated guilty part of himself – are the ones who use words like 'larceny'. What is more, Kozlowski could not have done his brazen deeds without collusion with lawyers, accountants, other executives and the board of directors. Kozlowski and his inner circle engaged in their secretly-run corporate totalitarianism, while believing that it was good for the company. Kozlowski publicly espoused corporate meritocracy and moderation, while secretly practicing organizational tyranny and excess.

A recent paper, 'The Corrupt Organization,' by David P. Levine (2005), sheds considerable light on the widespread practices of which Kozlowski was a cultural exemplar during the heady 1980s through the early 2000s. Levine begins by saying that

> our motivation is to assure that we are good, which is to say worthy of love, rather than bad, which is to say unworthy of love. Psychically, those apparently varied things to which our greed attaches itself 'all ultimately signify one thing. They stand as proofs to us if we get them, that we are ourselves good, and so are worthy of love, or respect and honor, in return' (Riviere, 1964: 27). The language of corruption, by pointing us toward greed also points us toward moral thinking. But, it does so without acknowledging that greed can be defined within rather than in opposition to a moral world. (Levine, 2005: 736)

He continues by observing that the paradox between a CEO pillaging his company and professing small-town values

> disappears when we bear in mind that the CEO did not conceive the company as something separate from his self, which is to say, he could not conceive a reality independent of his subjective experience and hope-invested fantasies.

Since these hope-invested fantasies were fantasies about being identified with the good, they operated in a moral universe. The fantasized identification of the self with the good, or the fantasized realization of hope, meant that the personal good was the good, and what appeared from outside as self-aggrandizement was not more than the reward for being good. (2005: 737)

Thus, in engaging in the practice of organizational totalitarianism, Kozlowski, like many of his contemporaries, could be terrorizing and ruining the lives of millions while being convinced that he was serving the highest good. At the cultural level, he could engage in totalitarian discourse and practice, while believing that he was living out the all-American work ethic of 'pay-per-performance'. Dissent was prohibited; the only voice allowed was his and echoes of his. For all the world, Kozlowski could have been Captain Ahab on the *Pequod*.

Certainly one cannot generalize in a quantitative sense from these three vignettes. Nevertheless, they are culturally exemplary for our times. They illustrate psychological terror in the American workplace from the perspectives of both the victims and perpetrators. Not unlike Starbuck on the *Pequod*, the researcher Frankel in the first vignette and Dr Opal in the second vignette are minimized, discounted, and either symbolically eliminated or threatened with elimination. And not unlike the driven Captain Ahab, Tyco's Dennis Kozlowski relentlessly chased his symbolic whale of shareholder value, fame and fortune – only to be brought down by the object of his obsession.

Lest we forget, even though American-style organizational totalitarianism has primarily symbolic casualties, they are casualties of terror nonetheless. One should never say that these are 'only' the victims of psychological oppression. And even though most of those who have been disposed of are resilient and find other jobs (often of lesser pay, benefits and status), they carry the emotional scars of betrayal and of having been treated as inanimate 'dead wood' or as 'fat' to be trimmed. Once we recognize the official language of economics to be the smokescreen that it is, we have no trouble in discerning the brutality – even sadism – that it has obscured.

In the broader view, the short-term economic surge of stock value has become our central cultural defense against death-anxiety (Becker, 1973), just as the corporation for many has become our predominant immortality-symbol. Organizational totalitarianism has been the key instrument to make all the 'sacrifices' necessary to keep the corporation 'alive'. In this atmosphere of dire emergency, no voices of dissent are permitted.

Finally, we would do well to inquire into who, precisely, are the victims of organizational totalitarianism. The most obvious answer is that they are those who are terminated (by whatever corporate euphemism), and their families. Upon further reflection, we must add those who remain left ('alive') on the job, from line-workers to managers, who also are victims of often brutal oppression. They are pressured to incorporate in their jobs the work that remains from those who were fired or restructured, to perform it more efficiently, and therefore to be more productive. All the while, they labor under the constant threat, and accompanying anxiety, of being made redundant and disposable. Ultimately, in fact, no one is safe, from the worker on the factory floor to the CEO in the corporate penthouse, because anyone can be fired at any time – a breeding ground for abandonment and annihilation anxiety.

It is necessary also to ask what happens internally, interpersonally, as a work group and as an organization, to those who have been through often multiple firings and who are 'waiting for the second shoe to fall'? What do the 'survivors' (as they often call themselves) give up of themselves – of personal integrity, values, ethics – in order to survive? What do they become, to themselves, and to others? My sense is that many turn into virtually symbolic *Muselmann* characters, emotionally devastated if not destroyed, continuing in a kind of living death. The term *Muselmann* was originally used to describe men and women inmates in the Nazi death camps 'who had been broken psychically and physically by life in the camp' ('Muselmann', 2006). There is the quality of brokenness amid the manic pace of contemporary organizational life.

Although there is no literal blood to be found, everyone knows nonetheless that there is blood on the walls and floors (Allcorn *et al.*, 1996). Common expressions such as 'organizational Siberia', 'career-limiting decision' and 'the walking wounded' all speak to a common emotional if not visceral experience under the domination of organizational totalitarianism. Under such menacing circumstances, the official and legal protection offered to whistleblowers offers little comfort to those who now silence themselves.

CONCLUSION

In sum, this chapter has offered a psychodynamically grounded ethnographic approach to understanding and explaining totalitarian discourses in American workplaces that have emerged since the 1980s. I have focused on the language, argumentation and metaphors of dissent management, and have offered three vignettes that illustrate the brutality of this process. It is my hope that I have not only helped to portray and account for organizational totalitarianism, but to also validate the experience of readers who have been reluctant to assign so ideologically foreign a label to something now pervasive in American work life.

NOTE

1. These vignettes are drawn from publicly available documents or are described here with permission granted by the subjects. Names of private persons have been changed to protect confidentiality. The R&D supervisor talk derives from organizational observation and action research, and is part of a database I use for organizational discourse analysis.

ACKNOWLEDGMENTS

I would like to express my gratitude to Drs Stephen Banks, Seth Allcorn and Michael Diamond for their reading of this chapter and their valuable suggestions. An earlier version of this chapter was presented at the 2006 Annual Colloquium, Center for the Study of Organizational Change, University of Missouri-Columbia, 6–7 October, 2006 and published in *The Journal of Organizational Psychodynamics*.

REFERENCES

Adams, Scott (1996), *The Dilbert Principle: A Cubicle's-eye View of Bosses, Meetings, Management Fads and Other Workplace Afflictions*, New York: HarperBusiness /HarperCollins.

Adams, Scott, (2005a), Dilbert cartoon, accessed 12 November, 2005 at http://unitedmedia.com/comics/dilbert/archive/dilbert20051017.html.

Adams, Scott (2005b), Dilbert cartoon, accessed 12 November, 2005 at www.unitedmedia.com/comics/dilbert/archive/images/dilbert2005102104653.jpg.

Adams, Scott (2005c), Dilbert cartoon, accessed 12 November, 2005 at www.unitedmedia.com/comics/dilbert/archive/images/dilbert2005183151027.gif.

Allcorn, Seth (1998), 'Foreword', in Howard F. Stein, *Euphemism, Spin, and the Crisis in Organizational Life*, Westport, CT: Quorum Books, pp. ix–xiv.

Allcorn, Seth (2007), 'The psychological nature of oppression in an American workplace', *Organisational and Social Dynamics*, 7 (1), 39–60.

Allcorn, Seth, Howell S. Baum, Michael A. Diamond and Howard F. Stein (1996), *The Human Costs of a Management Failure: Organizational Downsizing at General Hospital*, Westport, CT: Quorum Books.

Argyris, Chris (1960), *Understanding Organizational Behavior*, Homewood, IL: Dorsey Press.

Armstrong, David (2005), *Organization in the Mind*, Robert French (ed.), London: Karnac.

Becker, Ernest, (1973), *The Denial of Death*, New York: Free Press.

Benedict, Ruth F. (1934), *Patterns of Culture*, Boston, MA: Houghton Mifflin.

Bion, Wilfred R. (1959), *Experiences in Groups*, New York: Basic Books.

Bion, Wilfred R. (1962), *Learning from Experience*, London: Karnac.

Bollas, Christopher (1992), *Being a Character: Psychoanalysis and Self Experience*, New York: Brunner-Routledge.

Bush, George, W. (2001), 'Address to a joint session of Congress and the American People' United States Capitol, Washington DC, accessed 29 October, 2007 at www.whitehouse.gov/news/releases/2001/09/20010920-8.html.

BusinessWeek Online (2001), 'Dennis Kozlowski, Tyco International', 8 January, accessed 20 November, 2005 at www.businessweek.com:/2001/01_02/b3714009. htm?scriptFramed.

BusinessWeek Online (2002), 'The rise and fall of Dennis Kozlowski', 23 December, accessed 11 November, 2005 at www.businessweek.com/magazine/content/02_51/b3813001.htm.

Byrne, John A. (2003), *Chainsaw: The Notorious Career of Al Dunlap in the Era of Profit-At-Any Price*, New York: Collins.

Chertoff, Michael (2005), 'Chertoff: Katrina scenario did not exist', accessed 11 November, 2005 at www.cnn.com/2005/US/09/03/katrina.chertoff/.

Devereux, George (1955), 'Charismatic leadership and crisis', *Psychoanalysis and the Social Sciences*, **4**, 145–57.

Diamond, Michael A. and Seth Allcorn (1987), 'The psychodynamics of regression in work groups', *Human Relations*, **40** (8), 525–43.

Diamond, Michael A., Seth Allcorn and Howard F. Stein (2004), 'The surface of organizational boundaries: a view from psychoanalytic object relations theory', *Human Relations*, **57** (1), 31–53.

Doka, Kenneth (2002), *Disenfranchised Grief: New Directions, Challenges and Practices*, Champaign, IL: Research Press.

Dunlap, Albert J. (1996), *Mean Business: How I Save Bad Companies and Make Good Companies Great*, New York: Times Books, US.

Erikson, Erik H. (1968), *Identity: Youth and Crisis*, New York: Norton.

Kohut, Heinz (1972), 'Thoughts on narcissism and narcissistic rage', *The Psychoanalytic Study of the Child*, **27**, 36–400.

Kozlowski, Dennis (2002), commencement speech at Saint Anselm College, New Hampshire, accessed 21 November, 2005 at www.fastcompany.com/online/62/speedometer.html.

La Barre, Weston (1972), *The Ghost Dance: The Origins of Religion*, New York: Dell.

Levi, Primo (2000), *Survival in Auchwitz*, New York: Collier Books.

Levine, David P. (2005), 'The corrupt organization', *Human Relations*, **58** (6), 723–40.

Levinson, H., C. R. Price, K. J. Munden and C. M. Solley (1962), *Men, Management and Mental Health*, Cambridge, MA: Harvard University Press.

Lotto, David (1998), 'The corporate takeover of the soul: the current state of the American health care system', *The Journal of Psychohistory*, **26** (2), 603–9.

Lotto, David (2003), 'Fascism Resurgent', *The Journal of Psychohistory*, **30** (3), 296–305.

MacKinnon, James (2003), 'Interview with Richard Falk: early signs of fascism', accessed 10 May, 2005 at http://adbusters.org/magazine/48/articles/early_signs_of_fascism.html.

Maremont, Mark and Laurie P. Cohen (2003), 'Executive privilege: how Tyco's CEO enriched himself . . .: The Pulitzer Prize winners 2003', *The Wall Street Journal*, 7 August, accessed 20 November, 2005, at www.pulitzer.org/year/2003/explanatory-reporting/works/wsj6.html.

Melville, Herman (1961), *Moby Dick, or The Whale*, originally published 1851, New York: Bantam.

'Muselmann' (2006), accessed 7 February, 2006 at www.wsg-hist.uni-linz.ac.at/Auschwitz/HTML/Muselmann.html.

Pauchant, Thierry C. (1991), 'Transferential leadership: towards a more complex understanding of charisma in organizations', *Organization Studies*, **12** (4), 507–27.

Riviere, J. (1964), 'Hate, greed and aggression', in M. Klein and J. Riviere (eds), *Love, Hate and Reparation*, New York: W. W. Norton & Co., pp. 3–53.

Sorkin, Andrew Ross (2005), 'Tyco ex-chief is humbled, but unbowed', *The New York Times*, 16 January, accessed 21 November, 2005 at www.nytimes.com/2005/01/16/business/16koz.html?ex=1263531600&en=751b234295ea335b&ei=.

Stein, Howard F. (1998), *Euphemism, Spin, and the Crisis in Organizational Life*, Westport, CT: Quorum Books.

Stein, Howard F. (2001), *Nothing Personal, Just Business: A Guided Journey into Organizational Darkness*, Westport, CT: Quorum Books.

Stein, Howard F. (2003), *Beneath the Crust of Culture: Psychoanalytic Anthropology and the Cultural Unconscious in American Life*, New York: Rodopi.

Stein, Howard F. (2004), *Beneath the Crust of Culture*, Amsterdam and New York: Rodopi.

Stein, Howard F. (2005), 'Corporate violence', in Conerly Casey and Robert Edgerton (eds), *A Companion to Psychological Anthropology: Modernity and Psychocultural Change*, Malden, MA: Blackwell, pp. 436–52.

Suarez-Orozco, M. M. (1990), 'Speaking of the unspeakable: toward a psychosocial understanding of responses to terror', *ETHOS*, **18** (3), 353–83.

Sunbeam and 'Chainsaw Al' (2005), accessed 27 November, 2005 at www.e-businessethics.com/sunbeam2.htm.

Terry, Jack (1984), 'The damaging effects of the "survivor syndrome"', in S. A. Luel and P. Marcus (eds) *Psychoanalytic Reflections on the Holocaust: Selected Essays*, New York: Holocaust Awareness Institute, Center for Judaic Studies, University of Denver, and KTAV Publishing House, pp. 135–48.

Turquet, Pierre M. (1974), 'Leadership: the individual and the group', in G. S. Gibbard, J. J. Hartman and R. D. Mann (eds), *The Large Group: Therapy and Dynamics*, San Francisco, CA and London: Jossey-Bass, pp. 349–71.

Volkan, Vamik (1997), *Blood Lines: From Ethnic Pride to Ethnic Terror*, Boulder, CO: Westview Press.

Volkan, Vamik (2002), *Blind Trust: Large Groups and Their Leaders in Times of Crisis and Terror*, Charlottesville, VA: Pitchstone Publishing.

Wikipedia (2005), 'Dilbert' entry, accessed 12 November, 2005 at http://en.wikipedia.org/wiki/Dilbert.

6. Leading, dissenting and public relations

Stephen P. Banks

INTRODUCTION

It might seem odd to find a chapter on public relations in a book about dissent and leadership. Why public relations? And what is its relevance to failed leadership and dissent? The answer to the first question is that public relations often acts as the voice and conscience of leaders. In its 'official statement on public relations' the Public Relations Society of America asserts that the 'public relations practitioner acts as a counselor to management . . . with regard to policy decisions, courses of action, and communication, taking into account their public ramifications and the organization's social or citizenship responsibilities' (http://www.prsa.org/aboutUs/officialStatement.html). To the extent that managements lead institutions, public relations (hereafter PR) is a key communicative go-between for leaders and relevant others. The answer to the second question is more complicated and is what most of the rest of this chapter will address.

As to the voice of leadership, in mass-mediated societies PR is a necessary, if not always appreciated, tool of civic discourse. As Amy Goodman assesses those who use the mass media for communicating, 'in a society where freedom of the press is enshrined in the Constitution, our media largely acts as a megaphone for those in power' (Goodman, 2004: 7). Nonetheless, institutional communication in every sector – commercial and industrial, religious and educational, governmental and military, for-profit and voluntary – and from all positions of advocacy use public relations. To illustrate this point, consider that both Wal-Mart and its critics use PR. For decades Wal-Mart's PR unit was all but invisible. But in early spring 2006 the company began recruitment to fill two new PR executive positions. The senior director of campaign management is responsible for overseeing campaigns and 'opposition research' from the corporate 'war room' to counter growing criticism potentially damaging to Wal-Mart's reputation. The other executive position, director of media relations, is responsible to 'oversee crisis communications' and manage press relations 'in rapid response mode'; the executive also must be able to 'mobilize resources' in a 'crisis situation' (Barbaro, 2006b).

Clearly, Wal-Mart leaders see critics as enemies that warrant an aggressively militaristic response from the corporation, and boosting their PR capability is seen as key in that response. In addition to building its own in-house PR force to mount the counter-offensive, Wal-Mart also retains PR consulting giant Edelman Public Relations, at $9 million a year. Edelman operatives provide numerous services for their fees, including expertise for communicating in the blogosphere. When bloggers write pieces favorable to Wal-Mart they might subsequently receive an email from Marshall Manson, congratulating them on their perspicacity and offering Wal-Mart insider stories and breaking news, and possibly a visit to the corporate headquarters in Bentonville, AR. Manson is a senior account supervisor at Edelman, and he monitors and provides material for blogs related to Wal-Mart (see Barbaro, 2006a). Edelman also is responsible for 'Working Families for Wal-Mart', an advocacy organization that has the appearance of coming from grassroots consumers but actually is created by the PR firm. Such strategic communication groups are called 'front organizations', or 'false-front organizations', and their use goes back to the nineteenth-century origins of modern PR.

Wal-Mart's increased PR firepower is prompted by PR successes achieved by their recent adversaries – grocery store unions and consumer advocate organizations, like Wal-Mart Watch and Wake Up Wal-Mart, who have been making headway with PR campaigns to change Wal-Mart's policies on employee compensation, health benefits and community relations, among other issues. Wake Up Wal-Mart, for example, is a coalition of consumers, former Wal-Mart employees and other activists who use the techniques of PR to advance their agenda to change Wal-Mart – press releases, video news clips, television advertising, blogs and speakers. Wake Up Wal-Mart leaders also organize letter-writing campaigns, supply their version of facts and guide the formation of community activist groups to take on Wal-Mart's expansion. WakeUpWalMart.com is not the creation of a PR firm but is an authentic grassroots organization.

More about front organizations and activists comes later, but first I wish to flesh out the definitions and typical practices of PR, so that the relationship between position-leaders and PR can be further explored. I then will analyze leadership, PR and dissent as a circuit of positions and actions animated by the creation and deployment of power, both personal and institutional. Along the way, I will identify five key tensions and controversies within the education, research and practices of PR, all of which influence the effectiveness or ineffectiveness of leaders. This chapter concludes by evaluating claims that PR practitioners can be effective dissenters and dissent facilitators, and that they can be mobilized to counter the prevailing antagonisms toward dissent and dissenters among position-leaders and old-guard PR people.

PR FUNCTIONS, DEFINITIONS AND HISTORIES

Monitoring blogs, supplying text for like-minded citizens to use in their letters to the editor, and setting up advocacy organizations are only a few of the myriad techniques a typical PR agency or corporate shop uses. Nearly all do publicity – creating and disseminating positive news about the client organization or individual, typically by creating press releases to run as print news, electronic news releases, blogs and other media. An online tour of the website of any major PR firm, however, will give a more complete view of what the (self-attributed) profession identifies as services properly within its scope. A good example (because it has a strong reputation for innovation and creativity and is one of the first to offer 'thought-leadership' services) is Ruder Finn Public Relations, a privately owned, medium-sized agency of about 600 employees worldwide. Listed on the Ruder Finn website are the following functional areas: corporate reputation, social responsibility, public affairs, financial [communication], arts and culture, global issues, crisis and issues management, ethics, employee relations, branding and executive thought-leadership. These categories are broad and encoded in jargon, almost to the point of being incomprehensible even when the firm's own descriptions are added. Consider 'executive thought-leadership', for example:

> The more the world changes, the more important it is that CEOs articulate their visions. Ruder Finn's corporate trust advisors work with today's top CEOs to develop their Executive Thought-Leadership positioning to build trust and credibility with their most important stakeholders. Executive Thought-Leadership is a critical reputation-management tool that creates unique leadership platforms for members of the executive teams to shape their image relating to the key issues of impacting their business strategies in an era of increasing scrutiny. Our work has included: [bulleted] Branded Leadership platforms; Speaker Platforms and Networking Programs; Board Memberships; Media Outreach Programs; Leadership and Management Book Deals; CEO Transitions: Retirements, Resignations, Departures and New Arrivals; Corporate Communications Training. (Ruder Finn, 2007)

One way of restating this is: Ruder Finn helps executives communicate so they will be perceived as more trustworthy, which will improve their image and reputation, with the expectation that improved image and reputation will enhance their effectiveness as executives; Ruder Finn also provides career guidance for executives. But inscribed within the agency's language are clues about the posture taken by PR toward the occupation's work and clients. It isn't just enhancing leaders' image or reputation; it is 'shaping their image relating to key issues impacting their business strategies in an era of increasing scrutiny'. Here, the image work is instrumental for responding to scrutiny that, arguably, can adversely affect the business or the way of doing business. One deflects scrutiny by polishing up one's reputation. Thought-leadership is not mainly for inspiring others, improving processes and products or solving problems; it is for strengthening impression management to inspire potential critics so that criticism will be minimized. Thus one central function of PR is creating identities through communicative activity, and the identities created are strategically instrumental in the achievement of the client's goals. Note that PR serves institutions, like corporations and churches and governments, as well as individual leaders, like CEOs.

Creating identities to achieve the client's goals, however, is only one aspect of PR's more fundamental purpose, which is to persuade 'targeted' publics to assent. Wilcox *et al.*'s popular textbook was most plainspoken on this fundamental role: 'The dominant view of public relations, in fact, is one of persuasive communication actions performed on behalf of clients' (1995: 264). The 'father' of public relations, Edward Bernays, called public relations 'the engineering of consent' (Bernays, 1955), which says that deliberation with dissenters is the antithesis of PR's objective. PR has been defined most conventionally as 'the management of communication between an organization and its publics' (Cutlip *et al.*, 2006; see also Lattimore *et al.*, 2004; Seitel, 2006). The key term, 'management', is prominently featured in the Public Relations Society of America's (PRSA) expansive description of the profession, indicating that such persuasive communication is both intentional and strategic – it is planned communication executed in the interests of the client institution or individual (see www.prsa.org/aboutus/). In the United Kingdom, the Chartered Institute of Public Relations (CIPR) offers a two-part definition for PR that merits quoting:

> Public relations is about reputation – the result of what you do, what you say and what others say about you. Public relations is the discipline which looks after reputation, with the aim of earning understanding and support and influencing opinion and behaviour. It is the planned and sustained effort to establish and maintain goodwill and mutual understanding between an organisation and its publics. (CIPR, 2007).

Evincing the 'asymmetrical model' of PR communication (discussed further below) the CIPR definition of the field holds that the purpose of

PR is to establish harmonious relations with 'publics' by influencing them through the management of reputation. It should be apparent that diverse views exist of what PR is, how it is done and why it is undertaken. What is common to both national professional associations, however, is the sense that it is persuasive communicating in service to an institutional client to enhance the client's strategic position (see Pfau and Wan, 2006). This view of the dominant PR role is confirmed in research on definitions of public relations, which concludes that 'it is generally accepted that public relations is strategic communication between an organization and its publics' (Vasquez and Taylor, 2000: 324). Kevin Molony argues that all PR practice in all sectors consists of campaigns of 'weak propaganda' (Molony, 2006).

This sort of strategic persuasive communicating has been practiced since earliest humans first tried to shape public opinion (Byerly, 1993). Indeed most histories of PR envision an orderly development of the practices of weak propaganda into the contemporary occupation described by PRSA and CIPR. Historians of PR and most PR textbooks combine a significant events approach and an eras or periods approach to argue for a progressive narrative from primitive governmental and ecclesiastical campaigns through reputation management for medieval lords and kings through the press agentry and deception of the nineteenth century and into the emergence of social science and mass media of the twentieth (see Cutlip, 1994; Vasquez and Taylor, 2001).

The historiography of PR, however, is not a mature or unitary field. A recent study of major PR textbooks finds that the idea of the progressive development scheme of PR's history is widely believed and taught as fact, but there is little historical or theoretical foundation to substantiate that progressivist view. Instead, the dominant basis for perpetuating that idea appears to be occupational storytelling (Hoy *et al.*, 2007), whose authority has been long forgotten. Critics of the progressive narrative of PR's history see contemporary PR as using new technologies and sophisticated rationalizations to conduct a practice that holds the same goals and strategies as have always been its hallmarks – propaganda, strong or weak, and winning public opinion for the advancement of self-interests (see Olasky, 1987); or as an instrument of legitimation in ever more complex and changing social milieux (Holmström, 2005; L'Etang, 2006).

Circuits of Leadership, Dissent and PR

Legitimation, from the PR perspective, is accomplished through managing the reputations and identities of what Ruder Finn calls the 'members of the executive teams' and thereby legitimating their actions. These members, in most organizations, are the positional power-holders, or what are packaged routinely in PR theorizing as the 'dominant coalition' (Daugherty, 2001). Bruce Berger observes that 'the dominant coalition is a pivotal concept in mainstream public relations theory' (Berger, 2005: 5). However, he and others challenge that concept: contrary to the widely held assumption that the dominant coalition is a single group of an organization's position-leaders, Berger's research demonstrates that there are multiple, interrelated and intersecting dominant coalitions. All, however, are perceived by organizational members and PR practitioners as leaders because they control vital operations and rules of the organization.

Grounded in this sense of control, power reveals the identification of leaders for PR workers, and to the extent that task-, policy-, and position-leaders engage in communicating with groups, PR is activated as leaders' agent of communication. Reciprocally, Curtin and Gaither (2005) argue, identity work always implicates power relations and disciplines of control. Power as control over others – the most commonplace, zero-sum, power-over view of power – uses PR to maintain or increase leaders' control; consequently, PR's weak propaganda function treats dissent as a threat to the client power-holder. In PR-speak, dissenters outside the client organization are termed 'activists' and are 'targeted' for message reception as enemies. In a circular definitional logic, some PR analysts have likened activists to 'adversaries' (Grunig and Hunt, 1984: 309), 'anarchies [conducting] insurgence against leadership' (Lesly, 1992: 327), and 'dissidents' (Brody, 1991: 188).

While the conventional view of activists is as a threat to power-holders, some PR scholars conceive activists as organized groups who work to influence others 'through action that may include education, compromise, persuasion, pressure tactics, or force' (Grunig *et al.*, 2002: 446, quoted in McCown, 2007: 52). In other words, activists can be any group who wish to influence others by using these techniques: not a very useful distinction. In practice, and implicitly in research reports, activists are individuals and groups who want some sort of change from an organization's assumed leadership. They are a 'public' of PR because PR practitioners identify them as meriting communication or strategic silence. In the prescribed PR communication process, one critically important step is 'segmenting publics', which means identifying the cluster of individuals or groups of individuals who will receive a particular 'message' or be exempted from communication (see any current PR textbook for details). The 'public' of public relations is not the public of 'public sphere', which is the communicative space that's open to anybody in a democracy to participate (Ihlen and van Ruler, 2007). Ironically, in the application of the PR process it often is the case that activists are created by the very people who believe they are under threat, sometimes erroneously aggregating groups of people whose only trait held in common is the desire for some change from leadership.

From a 'standard' power-over view, then, one circuit linking leaders, PR and dissenters is a set of links that direct flows of control toward dissenters (and other, more benign publics) from position-leaders through the communicative intermediation of PR specialists. While less frequently recognized as such, a reverse flow can occur in the same circuit, as dissent pushes back against authority or power-holders. Here, circuits are conceptual models that are a close metaphor based on power circuits in electricity. In using the circuits metaphor I am adapting a simplified version of Stewart Clegg's (1989) extensive analysis of power. This standard view conceives established authority, position, direct force, rules, and so on, as the generative source of power. PR conditions power and provides conductance, representing it to targets and connecting them with power sources, with an expectation that outcomes will happen according to the circuit design. Design in this standard view may be likened to a line diagram with directional flows of communication and influence. Dissent is treated as circuit resistance, an impurity and a rival to effective functioning of the system. System is key, because the normative PR paradigm is grounded in social systems theory (Pieczka, 2006).

Clegg is careful to point out, however, that this is only one of a range of possible circuits of power in operation. He argues that authority generates power only if it is empowered by others in the circuit. Reaching back to Macchiavelli, Clegg points out that power always is relational and thus always is generated in the meanings persons hold about actions, intentions and consequences. In this more subtle and potent view of power, the circuit's generative source of power is the interpretations of actions by people in relationships. PR is one node in this much more multidirectional and complex circuit – complex because PR cannot be conceived as a unitary practice or interest (as discussed in the following section). In this circuit, PR is always also a potential source of power, depending on its validation by others, the same way validation empowers position-leaders. It can also be an annoyance, a translator, a facilitator or, arguably, a dissenter. Leaders also cannot be conceived as unitary occupiers of positions; empirical studies, including those cited by Clegg, argue that leaders might be emergent, task-specialized, coalition-based, consensual, or identified as something else. Design in this view can be thought of as the circuit's disciplines, disciplines both in the sense of Foucault's and Weber's notions that regulated and rationalized practices may be internalized as the way a responsible person does things; and in the sense of the regulation of contextual factors, such as occupational routines and the constraints of architecture and traditions, customs and cultural assumptions. On this point, Curtin and Gaither (2005) have proposed a closely related model based on the circuit of culture. While it is not inconsistent with the circuits of power approach, the culture circuit model focuses more on relational and discursive factors than on power as the central concern for the analysis of dissent.

Finally, Clegg's formal model links up three modalities or 'levels' of power as a system of flexible, distinctive but interrelated circuits. One level focuses on episodic power relations activated in the here-and-now. In this modality, outcomes of communication are influenced by and reciprocally influence social relationships. Outcomes also are conditioned by people's beliefs about direct control over resources and other situational factors that reflect authority. Clegg says that power at this first level 'is the most apparent, evident and economical circuit of power. It is "power over"' (1989: 215). At the same time, a second modality of power fixes meanings for interpretations and rules for action. This 'dispositional' power provides for social integration through struggles over interpretations of meanings and 'membership categories' (or identities). The third modality of 'facilitative' power fixes relations of domination by the establishment of discipline. Discipline is more than just normalized routines and accepted positionalities; it also includes 'rationalized obedience', or people's acceptance and internalizing of the logic of action and meanings. Facilitative power provides for system integration through struggles over 'the source of resources of power' (p. 239) and acceptance or rejection of innovations. Each modality exerts pressure on the others for both stability and change; Clegg warns that power circuits are dynamic, inconsistently activated and only partially predictable.

In this model, greatly simplified from Clegg's elaboration, dissent can occur as resistance in any modality and often across all three concurrently. An activist group who challenge a retailer's practice, for example of hiring only part-time workers to avoid paying health benefits, resists episodic power at the store's front door or in the op-ed page of the local newspaper. It also, implicitly or explicitly, challenges the assumed meaning of the labor contract and of just compensation; in addition, it might propose a new disciplinary form for community involvement in commercial activity, thus challenging the authority of private enterprise. This multiple level approach to power accounts more effectively for PR's relation to leaders and dissenters, because it includes struggles for control over meanings, identities and disciplinary conditions, and not just objective win/lose struggles over strategic issues. Within each circuit, the persuasive communication function is an instance of PR at work, linking power-holders and dissenters.

CONTROVERSIES AND TENSIONS WITHIN PR

Unfortunately, the prevailing theories of PR and almost all PR 'professional' practice are guided by functionalist views of power, organizations and communication. The normative view of power underpins most of the key controversies or problems in the PR field. In the following section I identify and discuss five PR controversies or problems that can influence the relationship of leaders and dissenters: (a) Weaknesses in prevailing theory; (b) professional status and adversarial practice; (c) communicating dirty tricks; (d) biases toward management and other dominant interests; and (e) PR education.

Some Problems with PR Theories

In recent years several books and special issues of academic journals have revealed dissatisfactions with the dominant line of theory about PR (see, for example, Aldoory, 2005; L'Etang and Pieczka, 2006; Ihlen and van Ruler, 2007; Spicer, 1997). That approach is pervasively functionalist and prescriptive in nature and is most elaborately formulated in the work of James E. Grunig and his colleagues (Grunig, 1992; Grunig and Grunig, 1989; Grunig *et al.*, 2002; Grunig and Hunt, 1984). Despite the emergence of alternative views on theory in PR, an examination of PR research, practice and education amply demonstrates the persistence of the Grunig tradition as the guiding rationale and descriptive and analytic tool (see Botan and Taylor, 2004: 659). I will refer to this tradition as the normative approach, because it conceives the world fundamentally as a set of hierarchical systems of practices and positions.

New alternatives show that the normative approach to PR theory has two major sorts of problems. First is its conception of communication. The model for communication that dominates the field is message-centered and mechanistic, at its most highly developed a primitive version of a cybernetic system. As such, the normative approach to PR conceives communication to be some form of transmitting messages between senders and receivers, allowing for system interference, noise and feedback. Privileging messages, cognitive coorientation and feedback, Grunig has argued for a symmetrical version of this cybernetic scheme as the highest form of communicating, in which senders and receivers enjoy parity in initiating, evaluating and responding to one another by jointly orienting to communication contexts (see Grunig, 2006). Calling it his 'comprehensive general theory of public relations', he recently has expanded the symmetry idea to include 'cultivation' of good relationships: 'I now believe that the concept of relationship cultivation strategies is the heir to the models of public relations and the two-way symmetrical model, in particular. Cultivation strategies identify specific ways in which symmetrical communication can be used to cultivate relationships' (2006: 168). This circular reasoning doesn't free the model from its variable-analytic, cybernetic presuppositions. Moreover, Grunig goes on to assert that two-way symmetrical communication is not good for engaging dissenters: 'In developing the concept of symmetrical communication, I believe it is necessary to acknowledge that publics often are not willing to collaborate with organizations and often behave in ways that are destructive to the relationship and to society in general' (2006: 168). In such cases, coercion can be ethically inserted into symmetrical communication, according to Grunig.

This limited conception of communication as cybernetic theory, while popular in the 1970s and 1980s, has been superseded by much more complex elaborations on self-organizing systems and cellular automata (Contractor and Monge, 2003; Wheatley, 2005). The normative approach to PR, furthermore, neglects or marginalizes subjective meaning, relational processes and political dynamics (Spicer, 1997). Perhaps even more consequential is the defense of the two-way symmetrical model, which perpetuates existing power relations (Roper, 2005), impoverishes the concept of relationships (Jo, 2006) and obviates true dialogue (Durham, 2005; also see Duffy, 2000). Finally, Grunig's functionalist application of systems-theoretic communication invokes a functionalist application of systems-theoretic operations research. Because the method is self-confirming and reinstates its own theory, it hampers possible change of both PR practice and PR theory.

The second main criticism of normative PR theory is about publics and social responsibility. The 'publics' of PR are creations of PR operatives – audiences at whom messages are targeted. While the symmetrical theory claims to aspire to advancing civic discourse and social equitability through ethical communication, the practice focuses on segmenting publics and persuading them to assent to the visions, actions and policies of the client. That segmenting function is, in normative theory, based on PR operatives scanning the environment for relevant stakeholders and identifying those who should be targets of strategic communication plans (including non-interaction). The possible range of publics is dictated by the 'situational theory', which is based on a categorical matrix of types of audiences. As a consequence, 'most public relations theorists are concerned with relationships of an organization with its publics and not much with the problem of how an organization relates itself to the public arena and society at large' (Ilhen and van Ruler, 2007). The lesson for leaders and dissent here should be obvious: the voice and conscience of leadership by design focuses leaders' attention toward persuading targeted stakeholders and away from the larger societal concerns of many dissenters, who might be viewed by PR specialists as non-collaborative or a danger to society.

Two caveats about PR theory are necessary. First, James Grunig should be praised for bringing PR into the arena of legitimate scholarly research and theory. His work is perhaps the most important of the second half of the twentieth century for PR. Second, much of the extant PR theory is *prescriptive* – deriving propositions and corollaries about how PR *should* be practiced and assessed, however weak those prescriptions might be in theory. What is most important to leadership and dissent is *descriptive* theory that accounts for PR as it actually is practiced and rationalized by what those in the occupation refer to as 'professionals'.

PR as a Profession

PR in the United States is a self-styled profession. Practitioners, PRSA and PR educators often say they practice, represent or teach a 'profession'. In the 1980s PRSA established a 'Code of Professional Conduct', which was superseded in 2000 by a 'Member Code of Ethics'. Both documents claim to establish professional standards of ethical practice. What is implied is that only members of PRSA can be deemed professionals and, further, that compliance with the Code actually results in professional behavior. Neither is true. PRSA membership represents only a tiny percentage of PR practitioners in the US. Some critics argue that they aren't professsionals, anyway (Parkinson, 2001). Most professions require examinations, certification and licensure from an agency of government or overseers who are specifically designated to do so. Attorneys, medical professionals and public accountants are examples; it is not legal to practice these professions without first having the requisite qualifications. On the contrary, no particular education, experience, certification or licensure is needed before hanging out the PR counselor shingle.

The PRSA Member Code of Ethics and the earlier Code of Professional Conduct, according to analysis by Michael Parkinson (2001), 'may neither reflect actual public relations practices nor establish standards appropriate for a profession' (p. 27). He argues that a profession must explicitly recognize the ethical obligations the professional is required to meet. He then demonstrates that the codes demand mutually contradictory allegiances of PR practitioners – to serve one's client, which is supportable from a public choice theory point of view, and concurrently to serve the interests of the public (in the sense of the commonweal or of democracy). Advocates, Parkinson says, cannot operate in the public interest: that is a matter for the larger system – the courts of law or the courts of public opinion – to decide following advocacy. More central to the weakness of the codes, there are no penalties or enforcement provisions, other than terminating PRSA membership and certification. For those practitioners who are not PRSA-invested, outside of breaking a law anything goes.

An expert wordmeister who knows the ways of mass media and has no professional constraints on tactics and techniques is just the ally leaders who see their relationships in terms of win/lose outcomes would want. And often what leaders who seek to silence dissenters or co-opt other activists use is PR dirty tricks.

Communicating Dirty Tricks

I have mentioned front organizations and ghost-writing grassroots correspondence. Those are only two of the repertoire of practices that give PR its overwhelmingly negative reputation (Banks, 2000) and give conscientious and good-intentioned PR practitioners nightmares. Among the more prominent PR dirty tricks is intentional lying, more politely called disinformation. The most famous case is Hill & Knowlton (H&K) PR's scheme for 'Nurse Nariyah' to testify before the US Congress's Human Rights Caucus in 1990. She told the legislators that she had witnessed Iraqi soldiers killing hundreds of infants in Kuwait City's al-Addan Hospital. This testimony was part of H&K's effort to sell then-President G. H. W. Bush's Operation Desert Storm to the Congress and American people. Congress came across with funding for the war, and American sentiments were turned against the Iraqis, partly based on Nariyah's dramatic story, shown repeatedly on evening television news. The problem is that the story was created by H&K and Nariyah was actually Nijirah al-Sabah, daughter of the Kuwaiti ambassador to the US. H&K claimed to be working for the Committee for a Free Kuwait, which was a front group they had created to mask their retainer relationship with the Kuwaiti royal family (PR Watch, n.d.).

Other forms of deception include unattributed video news releases (VNRs). While VNRs can be legitimate tools for organizations to tell their stories in television and online formats, it is not unusual for PR workers to produce VNRs with fake newscasters and without identifying the pieces as advocacy for the institution the news is about. This was the case when the nonpartisan Government Accountability Office took the George W. Bush Administration to task for creating 'covert propaganda' in VNRs used to promote the prescription drug amendments to Medicare and changes to national drug policies. In a related policy advocacy deception, the US Department of Education secretly paid political commentator Armstrong Williams $240 000 to promote on-air the Administration's 'No Child Left Behind Act'. These and other scandals of deception are reported regularly in the pages of *PR Watch*, a project of the Center for Media and

Democracy (also a website, www.prwatch.org). *PR Watch* has become an oppositional cottage industry whose growth and influence would not have been possible without the ethical lapses of PR 'professionals'.

Other relevant lapses of PR ethics include 'neutralizing opposition groups', the term used in Shandwick Worldwide's campaign plan to harvest protected trees in New Zealand (Hager and Burton, 1999); selective distortion of client records, as PR workers did in 2005 for the American Chemistry Council by lauding the client's economic contributions while lobbying for the same client to weaken the annual reporting requirement on producers of toxic substances (Farsetta, 2006); and staging media events, which was the backstory of the Jessica Lynch 'rescue' from a hospital in Nassiriya, Iraq (*The Guardian*, 2003). These and other abuses have not only perpetuated PR's reputation for unethical practice, they also have contributed to accusations of systemic biases in the occupation.

PR Biases

PR practices around the globe are dominated by occupational standards and normative academic theories originating in the West. I have highlighted the practitioner associations from the United States and United Kingdom, because that is where PR has been most defended by its own occupational organizations. Nonetheless, scholars, journalists and intellectuals from Europe, Australasia and the Americas have begun to speak back to the established practices and theories of PR. Among the strongest voices of critique are those arguing that PR as an institutional practice is neocolonialist and has a bias toward the advanced Western capitalist societies, to the disadvantage of all developing nations and less technologized societies.

Recently one main aspect of that critique challenges corporate image manipulation, whereby public relations campaigns create reputations for firms as being highly responsive to environmental, ethical and social responsibility issues. Such campaigns, called 'greenwashing', forefront the virtues of organizations' proenvironment and prosocial actions so as to direct attention away from past wrongdoings, subvert scrutiny of present strategies and deflect future criticism (Beder, 2000). Greenwashing is seen as part of a larger global PR practice that favors a dominant organizational core of Western interests against the marginalized interests of poorer, less developed societies:

> Seen through a postcolonial lens, the discourse of sustainable development is promoted by dominant coalitions [of Western institutions]. This discourse draws upon ecological narratives to save the Earth, but in practice retains the divisions between the colonizer and the colonized that effectively endorse the

continued exploitation of the Third World. This lens brings into view how the corporate discourse of sustainable development deliberately suppresses resistance to colonizing pressures. (Munshi and Kurian, 2005: 515)

When leaders in the West resist developing nations' efforts to reject toxic waste transfers; when they promote World Bank projects that are socially and environmentally damaging to Third World countries; when they 'rebrand' themselves as green and socially responsible by targeting only key stakeholders in the buying and selling decisions and not resistant 'publics on the periphery', those leaders are served by mainstream PR (Munshi and Kurian, 2005).

A related bias, also generated by both the practices and theories of PR, is the bias toward the existing power structure of institutions (sometimes called the 'managerial bias'; see Holtzhausen and Voto, 2002). Grunig recently wrote, 'our research showed that involvement in strategic management was the critical characteristic of excellent public relations. We found that public relations must be empowered through representation in the dominant coalition or from having access to these powerful members of the organization' (Grunig, 2006: 160). Even advocates of PR activism recognize the dominance of the modernist vision of PR serving the needs of a soulless, bottom-line driven corporate leadership:

> This [modernist] approach recognizes the importance of public relations as a management function, membership in the dominant coalition, and strategic planning of public relations with measureable outcomes, preferably in economic terms. The modernist, or functionalist . . . approach to organizations remains largely dominant in North America . . . and most likely in most Western countries. (Holtzhausen and Voto, 2002: 59)

The managerial bias is attributable to an occupational culture and practices that favor client defense over impartiality and self-defense for PR over reflexive self-critique. Lastly, the practice, but not necessarily the theories, of PR evinces a bias toward mass audiences, media technologies and conflict, and against small groups, face-to-face interaction and collaboration. For this reason PR is often considered out of place in neighborhood regulation controversies, local development projects and conflicts at the grassroots level, where small groups come together in face-to-face deliberation. As media change, however, this bias appears to be evolving, too: even in my home area of Idaho, where population centers are small towns and villages, the tools of modernist PR are beginning to show in uses of highly targeted websites and blogs, often to form grassroots organizations to influence public policy debates. The colonialist and managerial biases, however, persist through the inertia of modernist practice and, tellingly, in the new educational curricula in PR.

Education for PR

I have long been a critic of PR education in US colleges and universities (see, for example, Banks, 2000). Despite the relative disinterest of the PR industry in job candidates with PR degrees, the politics of disciplines in higher education have spawned a rapidly growing number of degrees, departments and graduate programs in PR education. The problem is that the basic curriculum continues to teach the normative theory and practices of PR and eschews education in the humanities, other social sciences, critical thinking and philosophy beyond basic PR-focused ethics. In a special edition of *Public Relations Review* (Coombs, 2001), the struggles of PR educators to define their territory and design an adequate core curriculum are evident. Alas, the only article in the volume that advocates expanding the scope and theoretical ambition of the PR curriculum is Maureen Taylor's argument for internationalizing the discipline (Taylor, 2001).

An assessment of PR education in the UK has found that much of the curricular emphasis has been on skills development and legitimation of the occupation as a profession (L'Etang and Pieczka, 1996: 10). Indicting the lack of breadth and depth in PR education, L'Etang and Pieczka advocate 'that public relations education should be integrated and interdisciplinary, taught by academics who can move comfortably between the traditional disciplines as they help students learn to see different perspectives and the varied implications of any particular situation' (p. 13).

The implication for leaders and dissenters is this: if a growing number of PR practitioners come from university programs that teach the modernist, normative theories and techniques of the occupation, then the likelihood of leadership failure will be exacerbated by more technically savvy but less worldly communicators. Further, dissenters will be less likely to be seen as legitimate collaborators and more likely to be treated as adversaries and insurgents.

REVITALIZING PR FOR DISSENT AND LEADERSHIP

At the beginning of this chapter I said, paraphrasing PRSA's Official Statement on the occupation, PR is the voice and conscience of leaders. The conscience part, however, is more ambition and fantasy than routine practice. If PR is to truly become the conscience of client organizations and leaders, the occupation needs to redefine itself and its role in executive action by becoming officially instrumental in screening decision criteria, evaluating client ethics and practices, and monitoring relationships and cultural trends. These surveillance and quality control roles usually are handed off to legal staff or are coopted by command level executives, sometimes by establishing ombuds officer positions to neutralize dissenters or by delegating responsibility without commensurate authority.

Some contrary evidence shows that a dissent-friendly transformation of PR's role is at least partially possible: Nance McCown (2007) details a case in higher education where PR facilitated expression of employee dissent and in turn helped produce changes in leadership and relationships. Nonetheless, in that case the PR director was propelled into a 'conscience' role by employee activism, and only when she had the top leader's trust and authority to direct communication activities was she effective in that role: 'Overall, employee activist tactics forced the organization to "listen" to employee concerns and to revamp internal public relations practices to increase opportunities for input, shared decision-making, and trust and relationship building' (McCown, 2007: 63).

It need not take an internal crisis to shift the PR role from servant-megaphone to activist-conscience. A recent study based on surveys of PRSA members and interview data has found that practitioners say they would exercise dissent under certain conditions within their own client organizations (Berger and Reber, 2006). In expressing dissent, PR people say they would be most likely to assertively confront management, when they believe there has been an illegal or unethical action; other dissent expressions include agitating others to take positions against management, using facts selectively and, to a much lesser extent, leaking information and sabotaging implementation of bad decisions (pp. 176–8). Berger and Reber also found that greater age, tenure in the occupation and seniority of position predicted likelihood of practitioners saying they would assertively express dissent. In arguing for increased influence of PR practitioners on executive decisions and actions, however, Berger and Reber observe that

> It's unsettling that the profession still cites *defining itself and its relevancy* as one of its most important issues for the next decade. . . . It's also no small irony that a profession so adept at constructing images for other individuals and organizations has failed to advance its own professional aura. . . . Too many people still equate practitioners with shady publicists and spin masters who can always figure out a way to put a favorable twist on an unfavorable truth, or create a buzz about something inconsequential. . . . In addition, though practitioners are valued symbol producers and tactitians, there is scant empirical evidence to suggest that professionals today exert any more influence on strategic decision making than they ever have, or that they hold more power or are in better positions of power to advise and help organizations do the right things. (p. 219)

If PR continues to have a poor reputation and continues to have low influence on decision making and hold low power positions, how do communication specialists rise to the role of activist-conscience for their clients? The key is found in reforming power relations. Berger and Reber observed that '[m]ost of the professionals we interviewed expressed concerns about power relations and their corresponding deficiencies. They indicated that the presence or absence of power affected the practice of public relations in many ways in their organizations, and accepting and understanding that reality was a necessary first step in becoming more influential' (p. 225). The interviewees' solutions to this problem, however, were passive, nonconfrontational and unpolitical – basically to do a better job of showing executives PR's value and to strengthen their own political skills and will. The authors move far beyond the practitioners by advocating activism and dissent, including unsanctioned influence techniques, such as whistle-blowing (see Ihlen, 2007). For both the respondents and the authors, however, power is conceived as normative, power-over relations at the episodic circuit level.

PR practitioners, however, cannot start with normative power. To attempt reconstitution of power relations initially at the episodic circuit level would be tantamount to insubordination and disloyalty. At the more deeply embedded and constitutive levels of dispositional and facilitative power, however, PR can change power dynamics and create openings for dissent to be heard. This is so because PR people by definition are boundary-spanning environmental scanners; as such they are primary and official interpreters of external factors and internal relationships that can influence leaders' understandings and actions. To function in this way, though, PR people must see their responsibility to their clients differently than most actually operate today, and clients must be willing to adapt to an activist PR role that requires power sharing.

CONCLUSION

In mass mediated societies comprised of complex institutions, PR is an inescapable activity and a crucial node in the circuits linking leadership and dissent. In its present configuration – relying on normative theories about communicating and power, largely technical education and self-defining regulation – PR mainly serves clients to oppose dissenters as targeted activist publics. How can this practice and applied area of theory be transformed so that it mitigates the possibilities of failure and enhances likelihood of leadership success, if that is possible? In this analysis, what can be done to reframe PR in the power circuits involving leadership and dissent?

Considerable encouragement is being produced by theorists who advocate that PR practitioners become activists to transform their occupation and organizational roles (Berger, 2005; Holtzhausen, 2000; Holtzhausen and Voto, 2002). None, however, says what specifically needs to be done to change the power relations in the distributive and facilitative circuit levels. While placing the burden on the moral character, boldness and passion of PR practitioners, none of the advocates for PR activism seems willing to challenge directly the way PR is theorized, taught, regulated and practiced. Only when those significant weaknesses of the occupation are changed is there a possibility for truly changing power relations. Here are four proposals for making PR an effective instrument for recasting dissent as a positive and necessary element in leadership. Only the last requires individuals to take responsibility for change.

First, scholars and practitioners will work together to open up the scope of theorizing – move beyond the normative view of communication and the PR process to position post-structuralist, social constructionist and postmodern ideas at the center of analysis. An incipient move in this direction already is under way; however, such theory and analyses still are self-labeled as coming 'from the margins' (Holtzhausen and Voto, 2002; see also *Journal of Public Relations Research*, 2005, Volume 1).

Second, PR curricula in higher education will move away from the normative, narrow journalism- and PR technician-based education model and toward a broad and inclusive range of coursework in the humanities and social sciences. This refocusing will include courses in history, political science, business, international studies, philosophy and others that emphasize social responsibility and cultural differences in broader contexts than just PR practice.

Third, both PR educators and practitioners will become activists in demanding licensure and certification by a body other than their PR 'professional' association; and without licensure an individual and agency will not be allowed to do business. In the mistaken belief that the official use of drugs is more powerful and consequential for society than the official use of the electronic media, most political entities license nurses but not public relations communicators.

Fourth, practitioners will insist on being leaders – not position-leaders or members of a core dominant coalition, but leaders in creating institutional power for the practice of PR. This means moving beyond the self-identity as technician, technician's boss or expert consultant to one of authentic collaborator and professional. It also means refuting the entrenched occupational identity that holds PR to be the voice of leadership. Or worse, merely marketing through propaganda: Wes Pedersen, a member of PRSA's Hall of Fame, recently wrote that

> PR is really all about selling an idea, a product, a personality, a government policy, a candidate, maybe even a war. PR is always selling. Sometimes these days

we are even selling the idea that our corporate chief is not a crook, or that the church is not really a haven for sinful priests, or our glorious leaders have feet of clay [*sic*], or that our own PR agency is as transparent as Saran wrap and as pure as Ivory Flakes. (Pedersen, 2006: 2)

A more fitting argument for the need to reform PR would be difficult to find.

REFERENCES

Aldoory, Linda (2005), 'Preface: identity, difference and power', *Journal of Public Relations Research*, **17** (2), 89–90.

Banks, Stephen P. (2000), *Multicultural Public Relations: A Social-interpretive Approach*, London and Ames, IA: Blackwell/Iowa State University Press.

Barbaro, Michael (2006a), 'Wal-Mart enlists bloggers in PR campaign', 7 March accessed 16 July, 2007 at www.nytimes.com/2006/03/07/technology/07blog. html?ex+1299387600&en=ae7585374bf280b9&ei=5088.

Barbaro, Michael (2006b), 'Wal-Mart begins quest for generals in PR war', 30 March accessed 16 July, 2007 at www.nytimes.com/2006/03/30/business/media/ 30walmart.html?ex=1301374800&en=31a3f9d8014f8e9a&ei=5088&partner=rs snyt&emc=rss.

Beder, S. (2000), *Global Spin: The Corporate Assault on Environmentalism*, Darlington: Geen Books.

Berger, Bruce K. (2005), 'Power over, power with, and power to relations: critical reflections on public relations, the dominant coalition, and activism', *Journal of Public Relations Research*, **17** (1), 5–38.

Berger, Bruce K. and Bryan H. Reber (2006), *Gaining Influence in Public Relations: The Role of Resistance in Practice*, London and Mahwah, NJ: Lawrence Erlbaum.

Bernays, Edward (1955), *The Engineering of Consent*, Norman, OK: University of Oklahoma Press.

Botan, Carl H. and Vincent Hazelton (eds) (2006), *Public Relations Theory II*, London and Mahway, NJ: Lawrence Erlbaum.

Botan, Carl H. and Maureen Taylor (2004), 'Public relations: state of the field', *Journal of Communication*, **54** (4), 645–61.

Brody, E. W. (1991), *Managing Communication Processes: From Planning to Crisis Response*, New York: Praeger.

Byerly, Carolyn M. (1993), 'Toward a comprehensive history of public relations', paper presented at the annual meeting of the Association for Education in Journalism and Mass Communication, August, Kansas City, MO.

Chartered Institute of Public Relations (CIPR) (2007), 'Careers and education', accessed 18 July, 2007 at www.cipr.co.uk/education/index_home.asp.

Clegg, Stewart R. (1989), *Frameworks of Power*, London and Newbury Park, CA: Sage.

Contractor, Noshir and Peter R. Monge (2003), 'Using multitheoretical multilevel models to study networks', in R. Brelger, K. Carley and P. Pattison (eds), *Dynamic Social Network Modeling and Analysis: Workshop Summary and Papers*, Washington, DC: National Research Council, pp. 324–44.

Coombs, Timothy (2001), 'Resources for public relations teaching: facilitating the growth of public relations education', *Public Relations Review*, **27** (1), 1–2.

Curtin, Patricia A. and T. Kenn Gaither (2005), 'Privileging identity, difference, and power: the circuit of culture as a basis for public relations theory', *Journal of Public Relations Research*, **17** (2), 91–115.

Cutlip, Scott M. (1994), *The Unseen Power: A History of Public Relations*, Hillsdale, NJ: Lawrence Erlbaum.

Cutlip, Scott M., Alan H. Center and G. M. Broom (2006), *Effective Public Relations* (9th ed.), Upper Saddle River, NJ: Prentice Hall.

Daugherty, E. L. (2001), 'Public relations and social responsibility', in Robert Heath (ed.), *Handbook of Public Relations*, Thousand Oaks, CA: Sage, pp. 389–402.

Duffy, M. E. (2000), 'There's no two-way symmetric about it: a postmodern examination of public relations textbooks', *Critical Studies in Media Communication*, **17**, 294–315.

Durham, Frank (2005), 'Public relations as structuration: a prescriptive critique of the StarLink Global food contamination case', *Journal of Public Relations Research*, **17** (1), 29–47.

Farsetta, Diane (2006), 'It was a very false year: the 2005 Falsies Awards', *PR Watch*, **13** (1), 1–15.

Goodman, Amy (2004), *The Exception to the Rulers* (with David Goodman), New York: Hyperion.

Grunig, James E. (2006), 'Furnishing the edifice: ongoing research on public relations as a strategic management function', *Journal of Public Relations Research*, **18** (2), 151–76.

Grunig, James E. (ed.) (1992), *Excellence in Public Relations and Communication Management*, Hillsdale, NJ: Lawrence Erlbaum.

Grunig, James E. and Larissa A. Grunig (eds) (1989), *Public Relations Research Annual, Volume I*, Hillsdale, NJ: Lawrence Erlbaum.

Grunig, James E. and Thomas Hunt (1984), *Managing Public Relations*, New York: Holt, Rinehart & Winston.

Grunig, Larissa A., James E. Grunig and D.M. Dozier (eds) (2002), *Excellent Public Relations and Effective Organizations: A Study of Communication Management in Three Countries*, Mahwah, NJ: Lawrence Erlbaum.

The Guardian (2003), 'The truth about Jessica', 15 May.

Hager, Nicky and Bob Burton (1999), *Secrets and Lies: The Anatomy of an Anti-environmentalist Campaign*, Nelson, NZ: Craig Potton Publishing.

Holmström, Susanne (2005), 'Reframing public relations: the evolution of a reflective paradigm for organizational legitimization', *Public Relations Review*, **31** (4), 497–504.

Holtzhausen, Derina R. (2000), 'Postmodern values in public relations', *Journal of Public Relations Research*, **12** (2), 93–114.

Holtzhausen, Derina R. and Rosina Voto (2002), 'Resistance from the margins: the postmodern public relations practitioner as organizational activist', *Journal of Public Relations Research*, **14** (1), 57–84.

Hoy, Peggy, Oliver Raaz and Stefan Wehmeier (2007), 'From facts to stories or from stories to facts? Analyzing public relations history in public relations textbooks', *Public Relations Review*, **33** (2), 191–200.

Ihlen, Øyvind (2007), 'Book review: gaining influence in public relations: the role of resistance in practice, by Bruce K. Berger and Brian H. Reber', *Journal of Communication Inquiry*, 194–6.

Ihlen, Øyvind and Betteke van Ruler (2007), 'How public relations works: theoretical roots and public relations perspectives', *Public Relations Review* **33** (3) (special issue on social theories and public relations), 243–8.

Jo, Samsup (2006), Measurement of organization-public relationships: validation of measurement using a manufacturer-retailer relationship', *Journal of Public Relations Research*, **18** (3), 225–48.

Lattimore, Dan L., Otis Baskin, Suzette T. Heiman, Elizabeth Toth and James K. Van Leuven (2004), *Public Relations: The Profession and the Practice*, Boston, MA: McGraw Hill.

Lesly, Philip (1992), Coping with opposition groups, *Public Relations Review*, **18** (4), 325–34.

L'Etang, Jacquie (2006), 'Public relations as theatre: key players in the evolution of British public relations', in Jacquie L'Etang and Madga Pieczka (eds), *Public Relations: Critical Debates and Contemporary Problems*, Mahwah, NJ and London: Lawrence Erlbaum, pp. 143–66.

L'Etang, Jacquie and Magda Pieczka (eds) (1996), *Critical Perspectives in Public Relations*, London: International Thompson Business Press.

L'Etang, Jacquie and Magda Pieczka (eds) (2006), *Public Relations: Critical Debates and Contemporary Problems*, Mahwah, NJ and London: Lawrence Erlbaum.

McCown, Nance (2007), 'The role of public relations with internal activists', *Journal of Public Relations Research*, **19** (1), 47–68.

Molony, Kevin (2006), *Rethinking Public Relations: PR Propaganda and Democracy* (2nd edition), London: Routledge.

Munshi, Debashish and Priya Kurian (2005), 'Imperializing spin cycles: a post-colonial look at public relations, greenwashing, and the separation of publics', *Public Relations Review*, **31** (4), 513–20.

Olasky, Marvin N. (1987), *Corporate Public Relations: A New Historical Perspective*, Hillsdale, NJ: Lawrence Erlbaum.

Parkinson, Michael (2001), 'The PRSA Code of Professional Standards and Member Code of Ethics: why they are neither professional nor ethical, *Public Relations Quarterly*, **46** (3), 27–39.

Pedersen, Wes (2006), 'PR's "implausible deniabilities" ', *Public Relations Quarterly*, **51** (2), 3–5.

Pfau, Michael and Hua-Hsin Wan (2006), 'Persuasion: an intrinsic function of public relations', in Carl H. Botan and Vincent Hazelton (eds), *Public Relations Theory II*, Mahwah, NJ: Lawrence Erlbaum, pp. 101–36.

Pieczka, Magda (2006), 'Paradigms, systems theory, and public relations', in Jacquie L'Etang and Magda Pieczka (eds), *Public Relations: Critical Debates and Contemporary Problems*, Mahwah, NJ and London: Lawrence Erlbaum, pp. 333–57.

PR Watch (n.d.) 'How PR sold the war in the Persian Gulf', www.prwatch.org/books/tsigfy10.html.

Roper, Juliet (2005), 'Symmetrical communication: excellent public relations or a strategy for hegemony?', *Journal of Public Relations Research*, **17** (1), 69–86.

Ruder Finn (2007), 'Executive thought-leadership', accessed 20 June, 2007 at www.ruderfinncom/ corporate-public-trust/executive-thought-leadership.html.

Seitel, Fraser (2006), *The Practice of Public Relations*, 10th edn, New York: Prentice Hall Business Publishing.

Spicer, Christopher (1997), *Organizational Public Relations: A Political Perspective*, Mahwah, NJ: Lawrence Erlbaum.

Taylor, Maureen (2001), 'Internationalizing the public relations curriculum', *Public Relations Review*, **27** (1), 73–88.

Vasquez, G. M. and Maureen Taylor (2000), 'Public relations: an emerging social science enters the New Millenium', in William B. Gudykunst (ed.), *Communication Yearbook 24*, Thousand Oaks, CA: Sage, 319–42.

Vasquez, G. M. and Maureen Taylor (2001), 'Research perspectives on "the public"', in Robert L. Heath (ed.), *Handbook of Public Relations*, London: Sage, 139–54.

Wheatley, Margaret (2005), *Finding Our Way: Leadership for an Uncertain Time*, San Francisco, CA: Berrett-Koehler Publishers.

Wilcox, Dennis L., Phillip H. Ault and Warren K. Agee (1995), *Public Relations: Strategies and Tactics*, 4th edn, New York: HarperCollins.

7. Women, leadership and dissent

Patrice M. Buzzanell, Rebecca Meisenbach and Robyn Remke

INTRODUCTION

A small group of faculty members gathered in a conference room to discuss prominent individuals at their universities and lessons the faculty members had learned from being on all-university committees. One professor described her participation on a top officer search committee. After a summary of candidates' official records, 'Sue' said that the discussion among deans and VPs centered on the candidates' leadership styles and administrative successes. All the records displayed outstanding achievements and all the names being ranked for the short list were middle-aged white men – except one. When Sue questioned why the lone woman to have survived previous screenings was not listed in the top three despite her considerable accomplishments, the committee members remarked that she did not seem to have a take-charge attitude and forceful style.

Sue related this story with a smile. In the meeting, Sue acknowledged that the woman had a different style from the other candidates, but she also was able to point out all that this woman had done in a relatively short time, with accolades from those who reported to her. Sue remarked that if she had not been on that committee, the female candidate would never have been offered the top officer position. And that university would have missed a huge opportunity to bring in talent that helped move the university strategic plan in innovative directions and with member commitment in the process.

So what was really going on in Sue's story? Were the male committee members simply trying to hire someone like them? In a sense, yes. We all have a tendency to be attracted to, hire, and develop others who have qualities, values, and appearances similar to our own. In these ways, interviewers and other organizational members reproduce themselves and the organizational status quo (Kanter, 1977). However, much of this process is unconscious.

When called to task about decision criteria, the other committee members could list a number of characteristics that they considered essential for a university leader. This list often includes: assertiveness, even aggressiveness; single-minded devotion to bottom-line and related results; inspiring presence and vision; take-charge attitude; ability to direct and delegate; and a record of individual contributions that instills immediate confidence. The list usually does not focus on qualities that center on nurturing, power-sharing and consultation. For if it did, how could one know whether the person can lead a huge enterprise or significant task force? How could one know if the individual with authority simply had the good sense to surround herself with brilliant direct reports and advisors? Moreover, when push came to shove, how would one know that this individual can muster all the resources and commit the time needed to handle the crisis or deadline if she had children and other family and community responsibilities?

These questions are logical ones to ask. They speak to the enormous time, skill acquisition and networking commitments that leadership in any venue entails. And they also speak to the fears that organizational members have – for the decision to invest in the development and promotion of high-potential individuals is a considerable one. Members want some assurance that their investments and selections will pay off. The hedge against this uncertainty is to rely on tried-and-true characteristics and people. As a result, the vast majority of the top officers in major US corporations and throughout the world are men. The pattern is replicated in every major industry and institution. Whether called the 'glass ceiling', the failure of the 'pipeline' and diversity initiatives or the 'opt-out' revolution, the percentages of women in leadership positions and of women earmarked as having leadership potential falls short of their numerical representation in many advanced educational programs, in entry- and mid-level corporate positions, and population statistics as a whole. The questions are: why, and what can be done?

In this chapter, we analyze these questions about women's leadership by looking first at the ways in which women are marginalized through habitual processes that block assessments of women's abilities through stereotyping, tokenism, structural barriers and exclusionary organizational cultures. We next define and propose dissent as a previously unconsidered way of challenging traditional gendered thinking, behaving and structuring organizational life. We conclude with a comprehensive program whereby corporate leaders can capitalize on the potential of dissent.

POSITIONING WOMEN AT THE MARGINS

Before we share our thoughts on the ways that people – both men and women – position women at the margins of organizational life, we ask each reader to take a sheet of paper and draw a line down the middle. To the left of the line, readers should list the names of people whom they consider to be exemplary leaders, past or present. To the right, they should write down what actions or events they associate with each name. These names should be the ones that come to mind upon first thought and *not* upon reflection. Only when this task is completed do we ask our readers to continue this chapter.

The researchers who originally designed this exercise, Kouzes and Posner (1993), asked their readers to do this in order to demonstrate how people tend to praise leaders for handling a crisis or turning a situation around. We adapted this exercise to display the extent to which women and leadership do not mix. One of the authors of this chapter constructed a list that included Jack Welch, Aaron Fuerstein and Herbert D. Kelleher – CEOs of General Electric, Malden Mills and Southwest Airlines, respectively. The lone woman on her list was Mother Jones. This response is not unusual and in fact is typical.

Life Magazine's (1997) list of 'the 100 people who made the millennium' included only ten women. The Catalyst organization released study findings in October 2005, highlighting the continued existence of gendered stereotypes regarding leaders and leadership. In particular, the study found that both men and women rate men leaders higher than women leaders at upward influence and delegating tasks. These perceptions do not necessarily match the actual leadership behaviors of male and female leaders. What these perceptions might reflect is that the popular media dangerously reinforce already existing stereotypes about women leaders and their abilities, which in turn maintain the gender gap in leadership.

What does this marginalization look like? Robert Hopper (2002) provides countless examples of how everyday interactions and constructions of gender disadvantage women, including instances where females achieve and find their accomplishment attributed to luck or an abnormality. The positioning of her accomplishments (as either luck or as abnormal or unique for women) reinforces the existing stereotypes of women as less capable than men. These stereotypes are further accomplished through interoffice memos and jokes such as 'How can you tell the difference between a businessman and a business woman?' The 'correct' answer is: 'He follows through; she doesn't know when to quit'.

We offer another – personal – example of being affected by gendered leadership stereotypes that may sound familiar to readers. As a master's degree student, Rebecca's friend and colleague, Brian, was a 6-foot 6-inch, 280-pound former football player, celebrity bodyguard and debate student. Rebecca was a 5-foot, 110-pound former undergraduate student and admissions counselor of the institution. Rebecca and Brian shared a faculty committee appointment and served as co-leaders of TAs in their department. Both Brian and Rebecca were two of the most vocal advocates for graduate students on the campus, often discussing together what they felt the university needed to do in this area.

Graduate students across the campus received an invitation to meet with the newly appointed dean of the graduate college as an opportunity to get to know the dean and to raise various concerns. Rebecca and Brian discussed beforehand what they thought should be mentioned at the meeting. Rebecca arrived at the meeting about five minutes late and did not see Brian there. She had the opportunity to present the arguments that she and Brian had outlined about the need for graduate students to have access to the same laptops that undergraduate students were using. She was the only individual at the meeting to present any concerns to the dean. She noted that she had worked as an undergraduate student, admissions counselor and graduate student during this transition to required laptops, and felt obligated and qualified to make this argument. Having been delayed, Brian arrived just minutes before the meeting was over, and after being introduced, stated the identical arguments that Rebecca had offered. As the meeting broke up, the graduate school dean came over and shook Brian's hand enthusiastically, thanking him for attending and sharing his valuable ideas. The dean barely acknowledged Rebecca – no handshake, no thank you, no acknowledgment. The graduate students received the opportunity to rent laptops at a very affordable price the next semester, but Rebecca has never forgotten how marginalized her opinions and person were in this situation.

This experience is common for women in the workplace and in other settings. Through enactment of gender stereotypes, women often are rhetorically positioned as dissenters and then marginalized or otherwise invalidated as full participants in institutional discourses. At a recent talk delivered at Northwestern University, Maria Klawe (2006), Dean of Engineering and Applied Science at Princeton University, provided an example almost identical to the one just presented. The other two authors of this chapter – and probably any woman who reads this essay – can relate similar stories about themselves and others. Every time instances such as these occur, the woman at the center of the story can lose confidence, feelings of self-efficacy, a sense of belonging and a perceived and actual ability to contribute (Klawe, 2006). It is not simply the protagonist who is affected, for every woman present at the encounter and every woman who hears about these common episodes is reminded about the gendered social order.

For it is both men and women who engage in detrimental stereotyping. Women tend to see themselves as less good at problem-solving, delegating, and upward influence – all qualities necessary for advancement (Catalyst,

2005). Moreover, the issues are not limited to stereotypes and perceptions – they become the stuff of everyday interaction. These stereotypes become unconscious rationales for why women might not obtain the career- and competency-developmental experiences, exposure to core business functions, access to informal networks, and visibility essential to others' recognition of leadership abilities (see Bell and Nkomo, 2001; Buzzanell, 1995, 2001). In other words, the mental maps for what we all consider to be appropriate for women's and men's behaviors influence what we admire and why and whom we trust to lead us.

So what happens when women pass the first hurdle and are recognized for leadership potential or advanced into leadership positions? In these cases, tokenism may curtail their effectiveness at their work. Kanter (1977) offers the notion of tokenism to designate the representational status of the few women who hold prominent positions in particular occupations. These individuals face a double bind in that their constant visibility means that they must perform well enough to deserve their privileged role (often higher performance than an untokenized individual) yet not perform so well that they are labeled troublemakers or mere aberrations from the group they are expected to represent.

The very possibility of becoming tokens can function as reasons why some women do not even join certain organizations and accept promotions. On the surface, this is rather silly. If a woman has the competence and record, then she should not think twice about taking a position for which she is well suited. We could simply advise the woman to get over it and move on.

But it isn't that easy or simple. If you have ever been in a situation where you are the only one of your sex, race, class or other group category, then trying to carry on a conversation, develop relationships, figure out how to maneuver in that business or social setting and know what is appropriate to say, do and feel is a difficult challenge. Kanter's research points out the pernicious effects of simple numbers. Tokens in a group – under roughly 20 percent of the total – receive a disproportionate share of attention, because of an exaggerated perception of differences, and are more readily stereotyped than are the dominant members. These group effects have consequences for tokens: 'Visibility tends to create *performance pressures*. . . . Contrast leads to heightening of *dominant culture boundaries*, including isolating the token. And assimilation results in the token's *role encapsulation*' (Kanter, 1977: 302, emphasis in original). One would wonder, if the very basis on which people develop workplace relationships and career success is not present and if the woman must prove herself again and again in every new situation, why would one voluntarily place oneself in that situation?

Why indeed. As a result of tokenism and its complex web of expectations, women can be deflected from even desiring leadership roles. The authors know a woman who was the only female computer programmer working for a division of Western Electric in the early 1970s. She was asked to join the management program. She turned down the opportunity, as she tells it, in large part because she felt she was only being offered the chance because of her sex and could not imagine succeeding, assuming that everyone else would share her perceptions of and challenge her qualifications. She knew what her male colleagues thought of the systematic promotion of women into leadership roles, and she did not want to tackle the difficulties her token status would create for her. This particular example is decades old, but we have heard comments just in the past month bemoaning that 'they just want to offer the position to her because she's a woman and they need a woman in the role'.

When women do enter high visibility positions, they may be reminded on a daily basis or at opportune times that they do not belong. Although she clearly desired and deserved her faculty appointment, Brenda J. Allen, a black female faculty member and well-regarded leader in the discipline of organizational communication, describes her disappointment and anger at practices that tried to relegate her to subordinate societal statuses. People assumed that she researched race issues, would stick up primarily for members of her own race and gender in conflicts, could sing Negro spirituals, and was a 'two-fer' hired to meet two quotas. Knowing Brenda, these assumptions sound funny to us. But her qualifications did not help her feelings of aloneness and self-questioning in a primarily white and male institution (see Allen, 2000). As yet another example, Patrice remembers a former colleague's assertion that Patrice was selected to become a manager instead of him only because she was female. Given her educational background and supervisory experience, Patrice thought that there were other qualities besides her femaleness that prompted her selection. Many years later, she still remembers her surprise and disappointment at his comments. While these types of comments and (self- and other-) expectations of tokenism did not deter Brenda or Patrice, they do nag at other women who face decisions about entry or promotion into male enclaves.

Finally, with regard to organizational structures and positions, there have been few changes at the top organizational levels, demonstrating that gender inequity exists in the very structures of power despite all the initiatives aimed at correcting the statistics. These initiatives recommend networking opportunities, additional training and other practices designed to create a level playing field for women and men. But what most initiatives do is perpetuate the idea that the women are deficient and that initiatives must correct these 'deficits'. In focusing on what women lack, these initiatives unconsciously and ironically reinforce the idea that women have to play the same game and by the same rules as men. They don't question whether the game is worth playing and whether there might be other ways to play the game. In other words, the organizational cultures remain the same.

And most organizational cultures by all assessments are not female-, or actually people-, friendly. Many corporate cultures require long hours, single-minded devotion to career ascent, geographic mobility, continuous learning and off-site training or degree programs, professional demeanor, prioritization of work over all else in life and networking with those who have use-value. If anyone wants more in life – perhaps sustained and deep connections with children, family members, friends and neighbors, community, church or spirituality, volunteering or leisure activities – this culture is not conducive to these desires. As a result, this kind of corporate culture is exclusionary and narrow-minded. Women and increasing numbers of men are finding that they want more out of life than work – they want to develop connection, wholeness, and community – and report that they are willing to take a cut in pay or refuse an assignment to achieve their goals.

In short, stereotyping, tokenism, structural barriers (for example glass and concrete ceilings and walls) and exclusionary corporate cultures can curtail other's (and their own) recognition and advancement of women's abilities and accomplishments. Simply adding women and expecting change in the landscape of top officership and high-potential employee groups has not and cannot happen. What is required is fundamental change. And radical change requires dissent.

THE PRODUCTIVE CAPACITY OF DISSENT

Patrice has co-advised an engineering design team through the service-learning program at Purdue called EPICS (Engineering Projects in Community Service) since the Summer of 2000. The men and women on this team, called the Anita Borg Institute for Women and Technology (ABIWT), work toward fulfilling the charge of the late Anita Borg, to pull girls and women into technology – not simply as users – but as people who conceive of and design technologies of use to themselves and others. Patrice's team designs hardware and software with girls aged 9–13 in mind. The idea is to create technologies and related experiences that can build confidence in girls' abilities to contribute to, major in, and have careers in STEM areas (science, technology, engineering and math). This team has worked on some incredibly cool ideas – personalized laptop shells/covers that have secret compartments, different colors and shapes, and spaces for friends' photos; bracelets that light up when in close proximity with friends' bracelets, change colors, and have accessories like charms and skins and that come in educational kits and can be (re)designed by girls; and games in which girls use competencies developed through mini-lessons in engineering fields to have fun and solve problems that they and their local communities face (for example, decorating their clubhouse using chemical engineering).

Readers may ask what this example has to do with dissent. Well, dissent can be conceptualized as an ongoing challenge to conventional gender and leadership thinking, as well as a refusal to accept or participate in the principles on which the ways things are normally done in organizational contexts and in society as a whole are based (Wikipedia, 2005). In the example of ABIWT, team members refuse to accept the low participation of girls and women in STEM disciplines and occupations. They also refuse to accept engineering education that has no real-life component, that does not give back to the community, that does not pull together multidisciplinary skills in a team-based setting, and that does not focus on users' specifications and needs.

In short, ABIWT and the entire EPICS program is revolutionary. Its numerous awards, including the Gordon Prize from the National Academy of Engineering for outstanding contributions to engineering education, and its institutionalization in the structure of a Big Ten university over the last decade (and now in its national and international versions) attest to its sustainability and innovativeness. What is most intriguing and relevant to this essay is that, at its very core, ABIWT and EPICS provide tangible evidence of the processes and opportunities that constitute productive dissent.

Not only does dissent challenge the status quo and resist any practice that does not create what dissenters believe would be a better world, but it also has two important and intertwined aspects. First, by definition, dissenters are members of the groups to which they are opposed. They situate themselves in adversarial positions within the group – by their talk, their actions, their feelings, their very being – and they refuse to conform to the principles about which they are in opposition. Thus, they can be mechanisms for change from within on many different levels – from conversations to institutional and global structures. Second, they also bear the burden of proof against change. If things work, why change them? If the candidate looks and acts like a leader, why take a chance on someone who does things differently? If engineering education in the Big Ten has managed to produce leaders in engineering fields and corporations, why mess with the curriculum?

The answers to these questions are simple. There are human resources, talents, ideas and ways of doing tasks and organizing processes that are underdeveloped or missed if one does not challenge the exclusionary nature of organizational life. But the process of dissent is tricky. If women do not voice objection to the way things are done in a fashion that retains the fundamental interests of their organizations and of their organizational relationships, then they would no longer be members, (actual or potential) leaders or dissenters. They also could not obtain the buy-in from other organizational members and, particularly, from organizational leaders who want to capitalize on the advantages that difference can bring.

As a result, women (and their supporters) need to navigate their situations carefully. They calculate each and every potential opportunity to dissent in terms of whether these are appropriate times and places to position themselves (and others) as different and as oppositional. To do otherwise would make them appear so different that their message and their potential contributions would be lost.

For example, Barbara Waugh (2001) switched from not-for-profit directorship work so that she could try to transform a major corporation (Hewlett Packard) from within. She influenced funding for societal change. She developed innovative processes such as small seed grants for intriguing but previously discouraged ideas. She planned miniconferences to bring people together to develop new ideas for handling ecological and social problems. She created readers' theatre presentations to engage audience members in diversity issues. And she amplified positive deviance at every step – as she puts it, 'finding and then amplifying people inside the organization who already embody and are living out the "desired" future state – or want to' (pp. 30–1). These people whose ideas were being amplified are not the recognized leaders because those leaders have ascended the corporate ladder by being rewarded for making things the way they are. Instead, they are the people who work at the corners of the organization and quietly engage in change.

So Barbara Waugh's primary strategy is identifying the problem, locating those who deviate from the status quo in desirable ways, recruiting them as coconspirators, and finding ways for them to carry their message to others. Is this easy? No. Waugh recounts numerous times when she awakened in the middle of the night wondering why she is doing what she is doing and questioning whether she would have a job in the morning. But the key is that she is and wants to be an organizational member, she believes in the corporate mission (HP, in her case), and she wants to draw on every resource she can muster to make the world better. She is both leader and follower; she encourages a vision of change and supports others' efforts to construct their own visions. Her coconspirators in dissent also are both leaders and followers with the difference between them and other organizational members being that they choose to capitalize on dissent.

CAPITALIZING ON DISSENT

One story often told to research team members studying women dairy farmers in India is about Sushila Devi from the village of Radhapura who had one final module on testing for milk fat before she could become secretary for her organization (Papa *et al.*, 2000). In the course of this training, the chemical reaction from ingredients caused the glass tube to explode and spray acid in Sushila's eyes.

Dr Satsangi, Sushila's trainer and a local veterinarian, flushed out Sushila's eyes and rushed her to the local hospital, then headed in his vehicle toward her home. The story continues:

> When Satsangi stopped his jeep in front of Sushila's home she said, 'Why have you brought me home?' Satsangi responded, 'I have brought you home so you can rest. You need to rest because of your injury.' Sushila protested, 'Don't leave me here; take me back to the training site.' Surprised, Satsangi replied, 'Why do you want to go there?' Sushila explained, 'I want to complete the fat testing of milk'. Shocked by Sushila's statement, Satsangi asked, 'Why do you want to complete the testing; you have been badly injured and you need to rest?' Sushila answered: 'My husband and the other men in this village have told all of us (women DCS [Dairy Cooperative Society] members) that women can do nothing. They say that running the DCS is their job. Women will get hurt if they try to test the milk. If I don't complete my testing today, we won't be able to keep the women's center open, and the cooperative will close. I must complete testing the milk to show that women can do this job and that we can make this cooperative work'. (Papa *et al.*, 2000: 112–13; see also Papa *et al.*, 2006)

And so Sushila did return to the training site and the women did make this dairy cooperative work.

It takes commitment and a comprehensive program devoted to gender transformation to capitalize on productive dissent that can recognize women's everyday acts of leadership and that can propel them into visible leadership roles. It should go without saying that the ways of changing gender hierarchies, composition and networking require top leadership commitment in the forms of codesigning, modeling, rewarding and remaining vigilant that individual and collaborative acts of dissent are done. Top leadership support also is necessary because dissent against gender inequity must be an iterative process in which leadership, along with leadership training and followership, is scrutinized continuously for effectiveness.

In this section, we follow the format of previously discussed problems that women face in organizational venues – stereotyping, tokenism, structures that act as barriers against recognition of their abilities and leadership acts, and exclusionary organizational cultures – and offer some moments or possibilities for change.

Moments of Dissent Against Gender Stereotypes

Jeffrey Murray talks about a 'rhetoric of disruption' that is designed to overcome and disrupt assumptions and stereotypes that would otherwise deface and discount the word of an Other (Murray, 2003). He notes the need for such alternatives when facing difficult situations where one wants to solicit 'a response from someone who is effectively deaf to one's appeals' (p. 261). This kind of disruption might involve confrontation as when, for instance, an organizational member relies on a problematic sex stereotype as an unstated decision premise (for example, women want to be protected; married or cohabitating women can't relocate for their jobs or go on extended and international assignments; women with young children aren't reliable). Another possible action would be to ask male colleagues to rearticulate, whenever a woman's good idea is not followed through in discussion, the same idea soon afterward (Klawe, 2006). Upon congratulations he would receive for his excellent idea, he could then mention that it should be good – it was *her* idea!

These persuasive moments – or moments of dissent against gender stereotypes – can disrupt taken-for-granted assumptions, but they cannot accomplish positive change in isolation. Murray argues that one should 'continually expose those preconceptions to the challenge of conversation' and specifically outlines a 'rhetoric of supplication' as necessary for facilitating the disruptive moments (p. 261). He is talking about a culture where people respect and are willing to listen to one another – contexts in which dissent may be heard and heeded. Herein are a role and a call to action for all members of an organization that go beyond just listening to differing perspectives on women's participation and leadership in the workforce or other organizations. As this entire book suggests, making room for dissent is good leadership. Entertaining challenges to traditional notions of even the concept, gender and practice of leadership itself is part of that room.

Dissent against Tokenism

If tokenism relies on only one person or a few individuals to be in a particular role, then working against the isolation of anyone who is different in some way from others in the workplace is helpful. In EPICS no engineering team would have only one woman scheduled into that particular lab. But creating pockets of women is only part of the answer; developing critical mass is better, and combining these (numerical) representational strategies with a questioning of all practices, processes and outcomes that are not women- or people-friendly is even better.

For instance, Anita Borg founded several networking groups, in part because of a bathroom conversation with a few women at a technology conference in which their presence was noticeably different from the majority of attendees (see http://www.anitaborg.org). These women did not return to the conference. Instead, their casual bathroom conversation evolved into the Systers network, the Grace Hopper Conference, a virtual development center for students working on technological designs, and other women-and-technology initiatives. It was the late Anita Borg's vision for and commitment to change that mattered. She found ways to bring women together, let them feel part of a majority (for the first time for many of these women in technological careers), encourage their networking with others – particularly their sharing of problems and best practices – and pool their interests in recognizing each other's contributions toward women's greater participation in all aspects of technology that capitalized on dissent.

To continue an earlier example, when her male colleague suggested to Patrice that her selection into the prestigious executive training program at her company was solely because she was female, she actually considered comparing their academic and professional records. Instead, she expressed her sympathy that he was not selected. She simply was too surprised by his comments to rebound successfully. Even today, she would not have pointed out the deficiencies in his background and experiences. But she would have analyzed the situation with him and provided some points for discussion that might have compelled him to think a bit differently. She might have enabled him to develop more as a person and become more open-minded.

Finally, it may be the spontaneous questioning about assumptions regarding one's own and others' values, behaviors, thinking and modeling of different ways to do things that provide others with the impetus and ability to see women and leadership differently. Lotte Bailyn describes a group of managers who considered themselves to be family-friendly and sensitive to women's household responsibilities (Bailyn, 1993: 116). As a result, when a female colleague had to leave a meeting at 5 p.m. to pick up her children, the other managers, all male, said not to worry and that they understood her situation. They planned to continue the meeting without her and to update her on their decisions the next day. Only one manager realized that the meeting should have stopped. In essence, the message was that her contributions to the meeting were less important than everyone else's contributions. Therefore, her input was unnecessary. Clearly, this one man's ability to question his own and others' good-intentioned response challenged all meeting participants and those who read this anecdote to think and do gender differently. The benefits are not accrued simply for those participants but can amplify throughout organizational systems, that is, throughout corporate cultures.

Dissent that Changes Corporate Culture

Rather than taking a deficit approach that tries to fix problematic (individual or group) behavior and backgrounds, we advocate change in the entire system. As noted earlier, corporate cultures can be so entrenched in traditional ways of doing things and rewarding those who comply that they can't see how or why they should change – until they start losing top talent, until a lawsuit charging sex discrimination or harassment hits, or until media publicity, websites and blogs about the company turn unfavorable. The issue is that leaders need to change the culture before there is a crisis.

We note a few ways to do this. One is to tweak the promotion and reward system. As a first step, human resources and managers need to review systematically and routinely all assignments and employee performance ratings to uncover sex stereotypes that produce negative evaluations for gender-incongruous behaviors and that reinforce traditional leadership patterns and developmental techniques (Catalyst, 2005; Hymowitz, 2005).

As a second step, a more revolutionary one, leadership should reward dissent. Although not an example of promoting female leaders from within, a telecom company Patrice consulted with advanced technical personnel to the highest corporate levels by skipping a few rungs on the engineering ladder. This move showed not only commitment to changing the culture that previously had prized managerial over technical expertise but also spoke to leadership's devotion to innovation and power-sharing. Taking a note from this example, lack of technical expertise, line expertise or long standing organizational tenure should not automatically discount women from being promoted. We recall Barbara Waugh's social movement work, not-for-profit directorships, and liberal arts – including divinity – degrees. Somehow her lack of technical expertise and her background in feminine and alternative work did not stop HP from hiring and promoting her. She now has worked for and with HP for a couple of decades. Clearly someone saw her potential and gave her a location from which HP could capitalize on her creativity and commitments.

Similarly, we note that rewards for behind-the-scenes work can bring attention to the leadership that women exhibit in all sorts of capacities. Women often speak out primarily in small and informal groups. They make sure that there are community gatherings and celebrations for life and career events. They foreground their expertise when the situation demands their overt leadership (and literally step aside when others' positions prevail or offer support when others take center stage). They monitor the quality of life progress of their institutions. We admit that these activities may not seem like leadership in the traditional sense of the term, but we argue that the inclusion and promotion of women in organizational systems must recognize the different ways in which many women, and communal men, build competencies and exercise leadership.

It is with pleasure that we note that our alma mater, Purdue University, celebrates the accomplishments of women who not only do behind-the-scenes work but also elevate women's status on campus in diverse and often unnoticed ways. These members of the Council on the Status of Women (CSW) explicitly reject exclusionary policies, practices, initiatives, hiring and so on. CSW operates both within Purdue (because all CSW affiliates are members of the institution) and outside (because CSW has no formal place in the hierarchy). Yet the power that this group of women (and some men) wield is considerable. This group awards a plaque for contributions to women on campus to one individual per year who epitomizes the kinds of leadership we describe here.

Furthermore, Purdue provides small monetary awards for those who serve the engagement (or service and outreach) aspect of the university strategic plan by traveling off-site to share their expertise. Purdue also has instituted an all-university Outstanding Graduate Faculty Mentorship Award. Its first recipient was named during the Spring 2006 semester. It recognizes traditional, reverse, virtual, speed, peer and spontaneous mentoring activities, many of which would be under the radar of collective awareness but that contribute to the vitality of a graduate program and a faculty devoted to cutting-edge discovery.

From disrupting stereotypical responses to changing corporate cultures, leadership in top institutions is recognizing women and more feminine or communal contributions to the organization and the broader community. In this way top leaders can capitalize on dissent and celebrate those who are different and those who lead in different ways.

CLOSING THOUGHTS

Much has been written about women and leadership, particularly about sex differences in leadership behaviors, expectations and outcomes (see Carli and Eagly, 2001; Eagly and Johannsen-Schmidt, 2001; Eagly and Johnson, 1990; Eagly *et al.*, 1992, 1995) and on gendered styles and values in leadership (see Helgesen, 1990; Rosener, 1990). Yet we argue that the very inclusion of women challenges the nature of leadership itself and the practices routinely associated with leadership manifestation and development.

In this chapter we describe the difficulties women face in having their competencies and different enactments of leadership recognized. Interspersed throughout the chapter are examples of women (and men) who use dissent productively to capitalize on difference-similarity dialectic tensions and elevate the status of women in organizational life. We advocate for a comprehensive program that appreciates the malleable nature of leadership. As a social construction, leadership is created through language choices, everyday interactions and structures that acknowledge some but evaluate others as lacking in leadership potential or fulfillment. In this latter group are many, but not all, women. Women typically are neither praised nor encouraged to be ambitious and aspire to top leadership positions (Fels, 2004). Instead, women often see themselves as people devoid of essential leadership characteristics (Catalyst, 2005; Hymowitz, 2005), perceptions that are reinforced when cultures reward others for overt acts of leadership and miss the behind-the-scenes and power-with leadership forms that many women display.

We argue that the only way for corporate and other leaders to capitalize on the resources of women is to engage in and encourage dissent. Without fundamental change in habitual mental processing through organizing cultures, transformation of organizations to be more inclusive and to promote women's interests will not happen. It is through productive dissent – that which aligns itself with principles of equality and actively refuses to accept the status quo – that organizational processes, manifestations and consequences can be changed.

REFERENCES

Allen, Barbara (2000), ' "Learning the ropes": a black feminist standpoint analysis', in Patrice M. Buzzanell (ed.), *Rethinking Organizational and Managerial Communication from Feminist Perspectives*, Thousand Oaks, CA: Sage, pp. 177–208.

Bailyn, Lotte (1993), *Breaking the Mold: Women, Men, and Time in the New Corporate World*, New York: The Free Press.

Bell, E. L. J. and S. M. Nkomo (2001), *Our Separate Ways: Black and White Women and the Struggle for Professional Identity*, Boston, MA: Harvard University Press.

Buzzanell, Patrice M. (1995), 'Reframing the glass ceiling as a socially constructed process: implications for understanding and change', *Communication Monographs*, **62**, 327–54.

Buzzanell, Patrice M. (2001), 'Gendered practices in the contemporary workplace: a critique of what often constitutes front page news in the *Wall Street Journal*', *Management Communication Quarterly*, **14**, 518–38.

Carli, L. L. and Alice Eagly (2001), 'Gender, hierarchy, and leadership: an introduction', *Journal of Social Issues*, **57**, 629–36.

Catalyst (2005), *Women 'Take Care'; Men 'Take Charge': Stereotyping of US Business Leaders Exposed*, New York: Catalyst Foundation.

Eagly, Alice H. and M. C. Johannsen-Schmidt (2001), 'The leadership styles of women and men', *Journal of Social Issues*, **57**, 781–97.

Eagly, Alice H. and B. T. Johnson (1990), 'Gender and leadership style: a meta-analysis', *Psychological Bulletin*, **108**, 233–56.

Eagly, Alice H., S. J. Karau and M. G. Makhijani (1995), 'Gender and the effectiveness of leaders: a meta-analysis', *Psychological Bulletin*, **117**, 125–45.

Eagly, Alice H., M. G. Makhijani and B.G. Klonsky (1992), 'Gender and the evaluation of leaders: a meta-analysis', *Psychological Bulletin*, **111**, 3–22.

Fels, A. (2004), 'Do women lack ambition?' *Harvard Business Review*, **82** (4), 50–60.

Helgesen, S. (1990), *The Female Advantage: Women's Ways of Leadership*, New York: Doubleday.

Hopper, Robert (2002), *Gendering Talk*, East Lansing, MI: Michigan State University Press.

Hymowitz, C. (2005), 'Too many women fall for stereotypes of selves, study says', *Wall Street Journal*, 24 October, B1.

Kanter, Rosabeth Moss (1977), *Men and Women of the Corporation*, New York: Basic Books.

Klawe, M. M. (2006), 'Gender, lies and video games: the truth about females and computing', presentation at Northwestern University, 23 February, Evanston, IL.

Kouzes, J. M. and B. Z. Posner (1993), *Credibility: How Leaders Gain and Lose It, Why People Demand It*, San Francisco, CA: Jossey-Bass.

Life Magazine (1997), 'The 100 people who made the millennium', **20** (10), accessed 13 October, 2005 at www.life.com/Life/millennium/people/01.html.

Murray, Jeffrey (2003), 'The face of dialogue: Emmanuel Levinas and rhetorics of disruption and supplication', *Southern Communication Journal*, **68**, 250–66.

Papa, M. J., A. Singhal, D. V. Ghanekar and W. H. Papa (2000), 'Organizing for social change through cooperative action: the [dis]empowering dimensions of women's communication', *Communication Theory*, **10**, 90–123.

Papa, M.J., A. Singhal and W. H. Papa (2006), *Organizing for Social Change: A Dialectic Journey from Theory to Praxis*, London and Thousand Oaks, CA: Sage.

Rosener, Judith B. (1990), 'Ways women lead', *Harvard Business Review*, **68**, 119–25.

Waugh, Barbara (2001), *The Soul in the Computer*, Maui, HI: Inner Ocean Publishing.

Wikipedia (2005), 'Definition of dissent: Wikipedia, the free encyclopedia', accessed 13 October, 2005 at http://en.wikipedia.org/wiki/Dissent.

8. Resistance, dissent and leadership in practice

Gail T. Fairhurst and Heather Zoller

INTRODUCTION

Laurie Graham's (1995) participant ethnography of an Indiana Subaru-Isuzu plant, a Japanese 'transplant', reveals an organization in the process of instituting team-based systems and other forms of participative management. Although not the focus of her research, Graham's case study is used here to highlight the complex relationship between leadership and dissent.

In this chapter, we draw out the lessons to be learned as we unpack the complexity of this relationship. However, rather than take a traditional focus and examine leadership as the management of dissent, we turn the scheme on its head to examine dissent as a form of leadership. Our intent is to show a more emergent view of leadership and that 'dissent leaders' are more than just the most outspoken members of a group. By examining the practice of dissent in this way we also hope to provide insight for organizational leaders all along the organizational hierarchy, from employees to supervisors, managers and executives. Based on an earlier analysis of this case (Zoller and Fairhurst, 2007), we examine dissent as leadership and the tensions and emotions that must be managed in the inevitable conflicts.

THE CASE OF SUBARU-ISUZU

In *On the Line at Subaru-Isuzu* Laurie Graham's (1995) purpose was to investigate the degree to which control shifts to employees in team-based participative management systems. Graham began working at the plant just as it was gearing up for production. Her study illustrates how management maintains control of employees in a workplace despite employee participation and team-based production. However, she also notes that as employees moved from training to production, they experienced contradictions in company policy and tensions based on cultural issues and expectations from previous work experience. As a result, employees engaged in numerous forms of resistance to managerial demands, including direct dissent. We describe several examples as a means of illustrating what can be learned by viewing dissent in terms of leadership.

In the first example, the company started a new policy of running the manufacturing line up to the end of the shift. Previously, the line stopped five minutes before the end of the shift, giving team members time to put away their tools and organize their workstations. The new policy essentially required team members to clean their stations during unpaid time. Graham provides evidence that at this point, the teams generally identified with company goals and pushed one another to meet their production quotas. However, in response to this new policy, individuals complained, using anonymous feedback forms provided by the company. When Graham's team leader explicitly asked people to stay after their shift to put away their tools, individuals began to express direct dissent as a group, saying things like, 'this is the kind of bullshit that brings in a union' (p. 122), or 'this place is getting too Japanese around here; pretty soon they will be asking us to donate our Saturdays'. One worker asserted that he was 'not a volunteer' (p. 122), and others cited dedication to organizational values, saying that they used the last five minutes of their shift to organize for the next day to keep the team running efficiently.

Graham explains that the next day the line ran until the end of shift. When she did not hear the end of shift buzzer and kept working, a team-mate who was walking by told her to stop. Graham says that later, 'I overheard our team leader ask another team member a question concerning work. He replied, "Look, it's after 3:00. I don't know" and he walked on by. From that day on, whenever the line ran up to quitting time, all of us on the team dropped whatever we were doing and immediately walked out, leaving the team leader to lock up the tools and clean the area' (p. 122).

That same month, team complaints arose over mandatory overtime issues. On a particular day, team members were told first they would be required to work overtime, and then that they would work a regular eight-hour shift after all. At the end of the shift, the line continued to move after the eight-hour shift buzzer. Graham describes that in reaction, 'nearly everyone on the car side put on a coat and walked out', although leaving the line while it is moving is a cause for firing 'and everybody knew it' (p. 123). Graham characterizes spontaneous acts of resistance such as this one as the most effective because they suggested to management that the issue was so important that individuals were willing to 'go it alone' without knowing how others would respond.

The third example of employee resistance/dissent also revolves around overtime issues. This time, the 'Trim and Final' section learned only on the day in question that they would be required to work overtime. The team leader asked members individually if they could stay. Graham and another female teammate could not. According to existing company rules, employees could not be required to work unless the overtime was announced during the previous workday. However, her team leader told them that Human Resources instructed her that they would receive an 'unexcused absence' if they left (the implications of this were unclear). In response to this statement, a third member of the team refused to work the overtime. When the manager of car production became involved, he told them: ' "Look, here at SIA we are trying to be different. If this was any other place, I wouldn't bother to talk to you. I'd just tell the group leader to tell you to work or else. I don't want to get into a position where I am talking discipline with an employee, because I know you are a good worker. I've seen your work" ' (p. 124). Graham says, 'I replied that this was not an emergency, so how could he discipline me? He said, "anyone who leaves the line while it is moving is in jeopardy of being fired" ' (p. 124).

Graham warned her teammates to expect this intimidation, and she found one in tears (although still planning to leave). However, at this point, the team leader announced that she also was leaving in protest. The car-side manager warned the team leader that her job was in jeopardy. Graham describes the response: 'The women held their ground. Finally, when faced with the intended departure of four team members, and the fact that this would shut down the line, management backed down. I suggested to the manager that if he agreed that no one would get an unexcused absence for leaving . . . both the team leader and the other protestor would agree to stay.' She added that, 'our resistance to overtime was seen as a rejection of the company's philosophy of forced cooperation' by team members (pp. 124–5).

Unfortunately, the passage of time did little to alleviate conflicts between management and workers around the issue of overtime and team-based decision-making, based on the second author's experience with this same organization some five years later (Zoller, 2003). While numerous case studies have documented the contradictions and tensions that emerge when management seeks organizational change, Graham's case study is noteworthy for its leadership dynamics. In the paragraphs that follow we chart the emergence of leadership along with the management of dissent.

LESSONS LEARNED

An understanding of the dynamics of this case suggest five key lessons:

(1) Culture must be viewed complexly;
(2) leadership is a language game;

(3)   where there is power, there is resistance in organizations;
(4)   individual acts of resistance often evolve seamlessly into overt dissent; and
(5)   resolution of differences usually requires a dialectical management of tensions and emotions.

In the following sections we explore each of these lessons for leadership generated from resistance and dissent.

Lesson 1: Culture Must be Viewed Complexly

Ever since the early 1980s, organizational culture has been a topic of concern to organizational members. While books such as *In Search of Excellence* (Peters and Waterman, 1982) and *Gaining Control of the Corporate Culture* (Kilmann *et al.*, 1985) are no longer the rage, the culture concept has remained as a focus for organizational interventions. The most obvious are the mission and philosophy statements (hereafter, mission statements) posted on websites, walls and in a variety of company texts. Management also frequently references them at company events.

The mission statement often suggests a view of culture that is monolithic and shared, such that every member of the organization aligns with its values as they work to achieve organizational goals. While it is generally understood that not everyone does this and that subcultures form, management often underestimates the degree to which disagreement (leading to dissent) and ambiguity (leading to ambivalence) work against managerial goals. For example, in organizational change initiatives company visions are still promulgated as lay-ons in some cases, despite research that suggests employee buy-in requires that management risk evolution of the vision so that it becomes a product of multiple and evolving, consensus-building conversations (Fairhurst, 1993; Fairhurst *et al.*, 1997; Tsoukas and Chia, 2002). Real buy-in for part of the vision is better than no buy-in at all, the latter being a likely outcome when one views visioning as a whole-cloth transfer of ideas.

To understand the change process is to address with employees their specific problems and predicaments with the change initiatives, possible futures and specific role expectations, among other things. Although many of these conversations would qualify as mundane, all are necessary to help employees see the fit between the hoped-for changes and their jobs. However, even when these conversations take place, management must also take care that the mechanisms used to embed the changes within the culture are consistent with one another. On this point, Schein (1985) argued that leaders must attend to five powerful primary mechanisms for embedding culture. They are:

(1) What leaders pay attention to, measure and control;
(2) leaders' reactions to critical incidents and organizational crises;
(3) deliberate role modeling, teaching and coaching by leaders;
(4) criteria for allocation of rewards and status; and
(5) criteria for recruitment, selection, promotion, retirement and excommunication (pp. 224–5).

He also proposed five secondary articulation and reinforcement mechanisms for leaders. These mechanisms are:

(1) The organization's design and structure;
(2) organizational systems and procedures;
(3) design of physical space, facades and buildings;
(4) stories, legends, myths and parables about important events and people; and
(5) formal statements of organizational philosophy, creeds and charters (p. 237).

When minor inconsistencies exist between these mechanisms, employees are likely to adapt to them. When larger inconsistencies exist, individuals will take note and experience a range of emotions, including disappointment, hurt, ambivalence, depression or anger – making the opportunity ripe for individual acts of resistance and more collective forms of dissent. This scenario appears in Graham's case study. Consider her journal recordings just two months apart regarding Team Leader 2, which shape the context for the workers' acts of resistance we described earlier:

September 20, 1989:
The team leaders are very enthusiastic about the team concept. The team leaders from Teams 1, 2, and 3 each take their jobs very seriously . . . I was repairing a ceiling wire harness in Team 2's area today. Ike from Team 2 pointed out to me that a clip was missing so I found one and taped it to the harness. While I was working on the harness, the team leader from Team 2 came up to me and gave me a short lecture on how this is the way we work best as a team – 'picking up someone else's mistake and letting them know it before it hits the end of the line and you are held accountable'. I got basically the same lecture from the team leader on Team 3 . . . All the team leaders are so patronizing and paternalistic. I think it must be the way they are taught to handle us in their Frontline sessions (monthly training for team leaders) (p. 116).

November 20, 1989:
The team leader from Team 2 told John and me that he is really depressed with how things are going. He said, 'I thought this place would be different with its team concept and all, but management is just trying to work people to death' (p. 116).

The disillusionment of Team Leader 2 is palpable. It echoes the sentiments associated with the five-minute extra running time in which employees were expected to work past their shifts without pay, and the apparent ad hoc decision making over mandatory overtime issues that produced both spontaneous acts of resistance and collective forms of dissent.

Leaders of organizations and leaders of dissent groups thus must understand that cultures can be influenced but they are never controlled. Relatedly, cultures are rarely monolithic and shared; instead, they continuously divide and fragment. Sometimes this division forms into recognizable subgroups, other times coalitions are only issue specific (Martin, 2002). But the process is ultimately an influence game, one in which individuals emerge to carry the day or maybe just the moment. To better understand the means by which cultures evolve, consider leadership as a language game.

Lesson 2: Leadership is a Language Game

Lou Pondy (1978) coined this catchphrase when referring to Wittgenstein's (1953) notion of 'language game'. For Wittgenstein, language reflexively articulates and constructs the terms, meanings, and objects to which it lays claim. A language game thus refers to the rules that we follow in our use of language. We use language games for acts large and small – ordering food, managing impressions, signaling disagreement, leading dissent and so forth. Pondy (1978) regarded leadership as a language game because leaders' effectiveness lies in their 'ability to make activity meaningful' for others; leaders 'give others a sense of understanding what they are doing' (pp. 94–5). As Pondy wrote, 'If in addition, the leader can put (the meaning of behavior) into words, then the meaning of what the group is doing becomes a social fact . . . This dual capacity . . . to make sense of things and put them into language meaningful to large numbers of people gives the person who has it enormous leverage' (pp. 94–5).

What the Pondy quote suggests is that leaders may not be able to control events, but they can control the context under which events are understood. Such logic has become part of the conventional wisdom of a 'management of meaning' view of leadership (Bryman, 1996; Fairhurst and Sarr, 1996; Reicher *et al.*, 2005; Smircich and Morgan, 1982), which often distinguishes leadership from management (Hickman, 1990; Kotter, 1990; Zaleznik, 1977). Leaders answer employees' 'why' questions, usually by referencing aspects of the mission statement (vision, mission and values). They possess a heightened sensitivity to language and seem to intuitively understand that individuals are constantly in search of meaning in increasingly turbulent work environments. By contrast, managers often are more concerned with 'how' questions given their focus on technique or process.

They may be less concerned with the big picture and more concerned with the task at hand.

The leader-manager distinction is also useful when capitalizing on more colloquial uses of the term 'leadership'. As Miller and Rose (1990) suggest, it is not 'an individual quality to be obtained by careful selection procedures', but about 'the *effectiveness* of an individual in a specific role within a specific group united for a particular purpose' (p. 22, emphasis added).

This is not unlike Robinson's (2001) more task focused definition in which, 'Leadership is exercised when ideas expressed in talk or action *are recognized by others* as capable of progressing tasks or problems which are important to them' (p. 93, emphasis added).

The utility of these definitions suggest that: (a) Leadership is a process of influence and meaning management among individuals that advances a task; (b) neither 'task' nor 'leadership' is associated with a specific organizational role such as 'supervisor' or 'manager'; (c) leadership as the management of meaning is not necessarily performed by one individual all or most of the time; and (d) leadership is attributional, thus lies in the eye of the beholder. While we explore the full leadership dynamics below, Graham's case study highlights the shifting and distributed nature of leadership among dissenting organizational members. From anonymous feedback forms and team gatherings that air out members' complaints on the five minutes extra running time to spontaneous acts of resistance and collective dissent on overtime; from a team leader who is challenged on the former issue but joins the resistance on the latter; and from Graham herself who remains an observer until the overtime issue draws her into managing a conflict – no one leader consistently emerges. Despite this, it would be a mistake to conclude that leadership was lacking as Lesson 3 shows in detail.

Lesson 3: Where There is Power, There is Resistance in Organizations

The exercise of power in organizations never achieves total control. Indeed, as Foucault (1995) advised, attempts at control inevitably breed corresponding attempts at resistance. It is the reason that company grapevines flourish the most in organizations with the tightest control of information. The key is not to attempt stamping out control or resistance, but to understand how control and resistance co-mingle and with what consequences in any given setting.

With this mindset, leadership aimed at achieving managerial control may be met by varying forms of leadership aimed at subverting or contesting that control. Which of these are interpreted as being in the best interests of the organization depends in part upon how those involved manage the meaning of their actions, as well as the cultural norms and values through which organizational members interpret those actions. Retrospectively, dissenters may become organizational heroes who changed key decision-making paths for an organization (and thus attributed leadership qualities). Organizational leaders who quash certain forms of dissent later may be blamed for a failure to allow for change; for example, managers at Apple Computer in the 1980s have been accused of cruelly dismissing all forms of dissent aimed at altering their high differentiation/high cost/low sales approach, which is now seen as a cause of their subsequent precipitous market drop compared with the IBM PC.

Organizations that proceed with the assumption that culture control is achievable face a number of potentially serious dissent-related problems. These include a lack of attention to the two-way process of communication surrounding organizational policies and norms, which results in failure to solicit and attend to member interpretations of managerial actions. Such organizations may take surface level cooperation to signal a lack of employee dissent and resistance. This may allow resistance to bubble through the organization in subtle forms, potentially erupting into overt forms of anger and dissent such as sabotage or whistle blowing. Ignoring latent resistance also risks missing important insights into organizational goals and decision-making that employees could be contributing.

Management's turning a blind eye to dissent also aids potential dissent leaders by highlighting that managerial control attempts are more vulnerable to attack than they might otherwise think. Those lower in the hierarchy often are more than capable of discerning contradictions between what management says and does, the emotions such contradictions generate, and appropriate resistance strategies. For example, management's attempts at control through participation can be met with enjoinders for actual participation, and tried and true 'family' metaphors can be emotionally exploited for themes of caring and fairness. In each example from Graham's study, we see management instituting practices that seem to contradict official written policies. In doing so, they attempt to assert managerial prerogative to establish rules and norms as they wish. Despite the fact that most workers at the plant considered themselves well-paid and lucky to have their positions, these managerial moves produced responses from covert resistance in the form of complaining to outright dissent in the form of the refusal to comply with overtime expectations – along with a corresponding set of emotions that fuel the growth of individual resistance and more collective forms of dissent.

Even when management may have been unaware of employee feelings and actions, management's attempts to assert control by running the line until the end of the shift were met with resistance as employees left the team leader to organize the team area at the end of the shift. And when the car manager directly attempted to assert traditional coercive control in response to a refusal to comply, saying, 'Look, here at SIA we are trying to be different. If this was any other place, I wouldn't bother to talk to you. I'd just tell the group leader to tell you to work or else. I don't want to get into a position where I am talking discipline with an employee, because I know you are a good worker. I've seen your work'. Graham questioned this authority. 'I replied that this was not an emergency, so how could he discipline me?' Rather than end the matter, his response, 'anyone who leaves the line while it is moving is in jeopardy of being fired' caused the team leader to join in the dissent, also refusing to work the overtime. This was a propitious moment for the now collective cause of dissent.

Employees invoked the contradiction between the team-based, participative management system they learned in training and the more traditional bureaucratic control they began encountering on the floor to resist these new demands and create some level of autonomy over their working conditions. Moreover, the resistance came to focus on the establishment of potential meanings of both practices and policy statements. Policies regarding end-of-work and overtime procedures thus were not instituted unilaterally by management but essentially negotiated between moves by managers and subtle and overt forms of dissent by workers. The expectations of management for extra work did not create control, but rather created cohesion among employees in ways contrary to the team cohesion management had promoted. During training only a short time before these events, management focused on dedication to the company and to the team in ways that would encourage 'self-motivated' compliance with job demands. Where, then, does leadership lie? It seems less apparent in the authority game of those trying to maximize organizational productivity amidst mixed messages and more apparent among those seeking to define the limits on managerial control.

Lesson 4: Individual Acts of Resistance Often Evolve Seamlessly into Overt Dissent

Organizational leaders who ignore Lesson 3 by underestimating the relationship between power and resistance may soon discover Lesson 4 for themselves. Dissent leaders (internal or external to the organization), on the other hand, can use this insight to understand that even organizational members in vulnerable positions can help to foment collective dissatisfaction and attempts at change through more subtle and covert measures.

In Graham's study we see how individual acts of resistance interweave with more overt and collective forms of dissent. Individuals expressed resistance to end-of-shift timing and overtime requirements through anonymous feedback, and then through individual complaints made in the team setting.

There we see these comments build upon one another. It was the support for employee arguments and emotions in Graham's team meeting that provided the background for overt dissent on the part of the employee who refused the direct request of his team leader to stay and clean up his area, and individual acts of dissent such as this provided the stage for the collective act of walking out after the eight-hour buzzer. Although the act of walking away from the line may have been spontaneous in that it was not planned formally, Graham makes clear that the seeds of such action were sewn from previous individual acts and collective discussion. Group discussion about the unfairness of overtime policies helped to construct the reality they so chose and, in turn, the reaction to that line moving after the buzzer. This example illustrates that there is no clear line between individual, hidden forms of resistance and more overt forms of collective dissent.

Furthermore, we see in this interweaving of collective discussion and individual action the creation of a kind of emotional scaffolding (Tronick *et al.*, 1998) for what they were feeling and collective agreement that managerial demands were unfair, unreasonable and inconsistent with the team concept. Gleaned from the observations of mother-infant interactions and extrapolated to the therapeutic relationships, emotional scaffolding occurs when one member of a relationship, such as a caregiver or therapist, provides emotional support to another that also helps to regulate or channel such emotion. Importantly, this scaffolding is premised on the mutual regulation of emotion over time. Based on Fairhurst's (2007) extension of this argument for leadership, Graham's team meetings are ideal settings for emotional support and channeling amidst a rapid fire give-and-take. When team members' comments build on one another to arrive at the conclusion 'management is being unfair', this is as much a widely supported emotional reaction as it is a rational judgment. It also follows that when individual acts of resistance grow into collective forms of dissent, reason alone will not have brought it about.

The lesson here for leaders charged with managing dissent may be quite common. Genuine attention to employee experiences and their reaction to managerial actions would allow leaders to diagnose problems, affirm emotions and create dialogue. This dialogue can lead to changes in the substance and direction of organizational policy in ways that may reduce tensions with employees, enhance member identification with the organization and improve working conditions. Conversely, organizational leaders should understand that ignoring employee emotions may heighten tensions and adversely affect employee work strain, which is a psychological, physiological or behavioral response to work stress (Cote, 2005).

Yet, the lessons for dissent leaders may be a little more complex. Organizational members, no matter their place within the hierarchy, are differentially vulnerable to organizational consequences and differentially willing to risk sanction in any given situation. Dissent leaders who wish to foment change do not have to rely solely on those willing or able to take risks, but can rely on covert forms of resistance and individual discussion of complaints to fortify and support more direct efforts at dissent. For example, Graham herself may have been more willing to risk a citation in her file because working at the plant was not her long-term goal. Yet, the willingness of others to stand with her in protest may result not only from a sense of safety in numbers, but also from the collective sense that capricious overtime demands were unfair, a sense which undoubtedly developed from individual, covert actions and collective sensemaking conversations. Thus dissent leaders who may be agitating for changes such as enforcement of right-to-know laws, improved occupational safety standards or better family leave policies do not have to rely solely on those willing and able to call directly for the change. Individual and collective, hidden and overt forms of dissent can work seamlessly together, especially if dissent leaders consider the ways in which emotion and reason work together.

The astute dissent leader is thus wise to the emotions of the moment and their temporal flow. Her ability to affirm the emotions that potential dissenters are feeling and provide for them the kind of support that channels such emotions into collective action is crucial to the sensemaking process. 'Management of meaning' is as much 'management of feeling'.

Lesson 5: Resolution of Differences Usually Requires a Dialectical Management of Tensions

The achievement of coordination in organizations, then, comes not through simple control but through balancing a number of concerns. Leadership aimed at creating this balance, regardless of the formal role in the organization, involves managing inherent tensions that may include autonomy and control, open and fixed meanings, and stability and change. Each tension forms a dialectic in which too much of one pole creates a need to balance it with the other. Each tension also may also be fraught with emotion that must likewise be managed.

Regarding autonomy and control, Graham's case study thus far illustrates that organizing is about balancing this tension. Dissent leadership prototypically involves pushing the boundaries of existing control to create autonomous spaces, usually to promote the team's adaptability to work circumstances. However, there are always limits to this autonomy, including the need for predictability and coordinated action in organizations, as well as the need for dissent leaders to create lasting change. That is, employees who may want to transform a particular practice need to see that change enshrined in related organizational practices, such as those who want new overtime protections or improved health and safety practices. And, as Foucault argued so often, the ability to control reaches its zenith in social norms. Additionally, managerial and dissent leaders must equally confront the emotions at both ends of the control spectrum, including the diminished self-esteem over the loss of control and the arrogance that often accompanies excessive control. The emotions generated at these extremes may be the impetus for change, or they may put at risk the productive management of the autonomy-control tension.

Similarly, Graham's research illustrates how organizational members throughout the hierarchy manage both the openness and fixedness of meaning. Resolving differences among organizational members involves willingness to challenge taken-for-granted meanings and feelings in an organization, and openness to discussion around the point at which agreements should be fixed in things like official policies, handbooks or evaluations. Graham's case study complicates the notion that dissenters challenge existing organizational meanings and managers manage dissent by holding on to fixed organizational meanings. Dissenters may well be in a position of challenging strategies of management that attempt to capitalize on ambiguity or re-interpret dominant understandings of organizational practices. Yet in Graham's case we see that our dissenters not only draw from stabilized organizational policy, but actively construct new roles of authority and space for negotiation through their collective efforts. Thus, fixed and open meanings are not the property of a group called 'management' or a group called 'employees' but are negotiated by both. Leadership here also depends upon where the emotional intelligence lies to exploit emotional ties that can fix meaning or render the need for fluidity and change.

Finally, viewing dissent as a form of leadership helps organizations to think in more productive terms around the need for stability versus change. In many management advice books the cultural leader is depicted as someone who promotes stability by seeking clarity, collectivity-wide consensus and consistency in the culture (Martin, 2002). Shared meaning is seen as instrumental to organizing, and the leader's job is to promote a stable, shared meaning system. However, neither management nor employees have a lock on the desire for maintaining or disrupting existing organizational norms. Leading dissent may involve altering or defending the status quo. The consequences of unhealthy levels of consensus in organizations where dissent is discouraged are well known. Charles Redding (1973) actually suggested that organizations hire a person in charge of 'anti-bureaucratization' whose job it would be to yell 'bullshit' anytime they see unproductive behavior in the name of 'this is the way we do things around here'. Argyres and Mui (1999) provide the positive example of General Electric, which extensively evaluated its managers in terms of their openness to dissent and critical feedback, and their willingness to engage with that feedback in productive ways.

In these examples and others, we must ask how the emotions associated with the change are being managed. Emotions can run the gamut from ambivalence to anxiety to exhilaration to rage, and their temporal form is likely to evolve over time. Emotions can be used strategically as 'control moves' either to promote or resist change (Rafaeli and Sutton, 1987). As mentioned, emotions can also be the source of role strain and lowered productivity. It is for these reasons that the concept of emotional intelligence for leaders has become so popular in the business press (Goleman, 1995; Goleman *et al.*, 2002; Weisinger, 1998). For many it is easy to dismiss as 'getting in touch with one's feminine side', but for the cause of dissent or the management of dissent to promote or resist change, leaders ignore emotions and their ebb and flow at their peril.

The three tensions of autonomy-control, openness-fixedness of meanings, and stability-change are complex simultaneities in organizational life, as are the emotions they are likely to generate. However, they represent much of the complexity of the leadership role. We believe that the implications of this more emergent view of leadership are as relevant for those who must manage dissent as for those who wage it.

REFERENCES

Argyres, N. and V. L. Mui (1999), 'A political-economic approach to organizational dissent: a working paper', accessed 1 June, 2007 at www.isnie.org/ISNIE99/Papers/mui.pdf.

Bryman, A. (1996), 'Leadership in organizations', in Stewart R. Clegg, C. Hardy and W. R. Nord (eds), *Handbook of Organization Studies*, London: Sage, pp. 276–92.

Buzzanell, Patrice M. (1996), 'Book review of *The Art of Framing: Managing the Language of Leadership* by G. T. Fairhurst and R. A. Sarr', *Management Communication Quarterly*, **10**, 243–54.

Cote, S. (2005), 'A social interaction model of the effects of emotion regulation on work strain', *Academy of Management Review*, **30**, 509–30.

Fairhurst, Gail T. (1993), 'Echoes of the vision: when the rest of the organization talks total quality', *Management Communication Quarterly*, **6**, 331–71.

Fairhurst, Gail T. (2007), *Discursive Leadership: In Conversation with Leadership Psychology*, Thousand Oaks, CA: Sage.

Fairhurst, Gail T., J. Jordan and K. Neuwirth (1997), 'Why are we here? Managing the meaning of an organizational mission statement', *Journal of Applied Communication Research*, **25**, 243–63.

Fairhurst, Gail T. and R. A. Sarr (1996), *The Art of Framing: Managing the Language of Leadership*, San Francisco, CA: Jossey-Bass.

Foucault, Michel (1995), *Discipline and Punish*, New York: Vintage/Random House.

Goleman, Daniel (1995), *Emotional Intelligence*, New York: Bantam.

Goleman, Daniel, Richard Boyatzis and Annie McKee (2002), *Primal Leadership: Realizing the Power of Emotional Intelligence*, Boston, MA: Harvard Business School Press.

Graham, Laurie (1995), *On the Line at Subaru-Isuzu: The Japanese and the American Worker*, Ithaca, NY: Cornell University Press.

Hickman, C. R. (1990), *Mind of a Manager, Soul of a Leader*, New York: John Wiley.

Kilmann, R., M. Saxton and R. A. Serpa (1985), *Gaining Control of the Corporate Culture*, San Francisco, CA: Jossey-Bass.

Kotter, John P. (1990), *A Force for Change: How Leadership Differs from Management*, New York: Free Press.

Martin, Joanne (2002), *Organizational Culture: Mapping the Terrain*, Thousand Oaks, CA: Sage.

Miller, P. and N. Rose (1990), 'Governing economic life', *Economy and Society*, **27**, 1–31.

Peters, Tom and Robert Waterman (1982), *In Search of Excellence: Lessons from America's Best-run Companies*, New York: Harper & Row.

Pondy, Louis R. (1978), 'Leadership is a language game', in J. M. W. McCall and M. M. Lombardo (eds), *Leadership: Where Else Can We Go?*, Durham, NC: Duke University Press, pp. 88–99.

Rafaeli, A. and R. I. Sutton (1987), 'Expression of emotion as part of the work role', *Academy of Management Review*, **12**, 23–37.

Redding, W. Charles (1973), *Communication Within the Organization*, Lafayette, IN: Purdue Research Foundation.

Reicher, Stephen, S. Alexander Haslam and Nick Hopkins (2005), 'Social identity and the dynamics of leadership: leaders and followers as collaborative agents in the transformation of social reality', *The Leadership Quarterly*, **16** (4), 547–68.

Robinson, V. M. J. (2001), 'Embedding leadership in task performance', in K. Wong and C. W. Evers (eds), *Leadershp for Quality Schooling*, London: Routledge/Falmer, pp. 90–102.

Schein, E. (1985), *Organizational Culture and Leadership*, San Francisco, CA: Jossey-Bass.

Smircich, Linda and Gareth Morgan (1982), 'Leadership: the management of meaning', *Journal of Applied Behavioral Science*, **18**, 257–73.

Tronick, E. Z., N. Bruschweiler-Stern, A. M. Harrison, K. Lyons-Ruth, A.C. Morgan, J. P. Nahum, L. Sander and D. N. Stern (1998), 'Dyadically expanded states of consciousness and the process of therapeutic change', *Infant Mental Health Journal*, **19**, 290–9.

Tsoukas, H. and R. Chia (2002), 'On organizational becoming: rethinking organizational change', *Organization Science*, **13**, 567–82.

Weisinger, H. (1998), *Emotional Intelligence at Work: The Untapped Edge for Success*, San Francisco, CA: Jossey-Bass.

Wittgenstein, Ludwig (1953), *Philosophical Investigations*, Oxford: Blackwell.

Zaleznik, Abraham (1977), 'Managers and leaders: are they different?' *Harvard Business Review*, **55**, 67–78.

Zoller, Heather M. (2003), 'Health on the line: discipline and consent in employee discourse about occupational health and safety', *Journal of Applied Communications Research*, **31** (2), 118–39.

Zoller, Heather M. and Gail T. Fairhurst (2007), 'Resistance leadership: the overlooked potential in critical organization and leadership studies', *Human Relations*, **60** (9), 1331–60.

9. Press professionalization, corporate rationalization and the management of dissent

David S. Allen

INTRODUCTION

The press has long been understood as a liberating and democratizing instrument for society's dissenting voices. News reports often carry the most dramatic and extreme expressions of dissent, and dissenters strive to create events that will gain media attention in recognition of the influence of news reporting on public opinion. However, it is well established that certain voices, be they dissenting or not, have an easier time gaining access to mainstream news reports than other voices. And even when dissenting voices do gain access, the way the media frames those voices influences the potential impact they have.

This chapter argues that two connected movements help citizens understand how the press functions to manage dissent within society: press professionalization and corporate rationalization. Rather than being a way of insuring diversity, professionalization has become a way of instituting sameness while allowing corporate values such as efficiency, profitability, popularity and individualism to be transferred from the economic sector of society to the public sphere. This process, referred to as corporate rationalization, establishes an elite, technocratic press that is more concerned with social control than allowing people to have access to dissenting voices. In doing so, professionalization tends to separate the press from the public rather than making the press a vital part of public life. In discussing the press, I refer generally to mainstream news production and distribution. Recent developments in the alternative press and new media hold promise of countering the dynamics and problems discussed in this chapter.

PROFESSIONALIZATION AND THE GLOBAL PRESS

For many, professionalization is an unquestionable and unquestioned goal. It suggests that a group has taken control of its area of work, establishing rules and standards concerning practices and behaviors, for the good of both the profession and the public. For some, professionalization also suggests that groups monitor the behavior and actions of their members through the establishment of codes of ethics. Recent scholarship highlights the ambiguities of the term 'professionalism' and its place in contemporary societies (see Cheney and Ashcraft, 2007). Nonetheless, in practical terms, professionalism is widely accepted to embody the dual functions of legitimation and regimentation.

While the goal of professionalization might be accepted, there seems to be little agreement on whether the press, either in the United States or globally, has achieved professional status. Slavko Splichal and Colin Sparks, for example, have argued that progress can be seen in the press professionalization movement due to a global growth in education, autonomy, ethics and specialist knowledge of journalists. Other studies also provide support for a growing sense of professionalism among the world's journalists. Some scholars, however, like David Weaver, observe that while many similarities exist among the world's journalists, many differences also remain. Weaver reports differences across countries on just about every measure of professionalization. He notes that most journalists agree on the importance of getting information to the public quickly and that there is some agreement on providing access for public expression of ideas. Other than that, Weaver (1998) argues it is 'more important to discover who journalists are, where they come from (including their educational experiences) and what they think about their roles, their methods and their publics than to try to classify them firmly as professionals or not' (p. 478).

While such studies of individual journalists have produced little agreement, other observers have argued that the impact of the global professionalization of the news media can be seen in the product that is created and the ideology that guides journalists. Lisbeth Clausen's (2004) study of news in Denmark and Japan found the use of '[s]imilar formats, framing processes and presentation styles across nations' (p. 41). Anandam P. Kavoori's study of news broadcasts in four countries noted that 'some differences in how each event narrativized by the different stations, the sweeping similarities stood out' (1999: 395). Kavoori found the stations shared a narrative structure that presented the 'other' world as a violent, unstable world.

The expansion of press professionalization across cultures is best understood, in the words of Peter Golding, as the 'transfer of ideology' (1979: 291).

That is, press professionalization does more than simply tell practicing journalists how they ought to behave, something some might refer to as simply occupational standards. It also reveals something about the society in which that press exists. Press professionalization tells citizens why the press is important and why what it elects to cover is valuable (and by exclusion, what it chooses to ignore is not valuable). In turn, it also tells us something about the citizens and institutions that the press are expected to cover.

The notion that there is a growing sense of global press professionalization is reflected in the work of Chris A. Paterson, who found a great deal of similarity among how television news frames international events. Acknowledging that much of this is due to the small number of providers of international video, he also found evidence of the influence of professional or occupational norms. As Paterson writes:

> The perception of single, valid, and globally appropriate view of news is so pervasive among international television news agency workers and among broadcast journalists worldwide that cultural relevance matters little in global television news distribution. . . . [A]s long as the pictures of the world's news arrive each day from people with *the* shared understanding of news, its means of production and distribution are irrelevant technicalities. (Paterson, 2003: 350)

This is not to say that the global transfer of professional ideology is all-powerful, as reflected in the studies of individual journalists. International news has both globalizing and domesticating elements (Clausen, 2004). The elements are often combined to create local meaning for international stories.

The studies suggest that while the views of individual journalists do not reflect the idea that journalists share all professional values, there is growing evidence of the standardization (or at the least routinization) of the way news is produced and presented. The larger question, however, is what that growing sense of professionalization means for citizens and the information that they receive. To understand that, we need to take a step back and examine the roots of the process of professionalization, how professionalization has been accomplished by the American press, and how that process has impacted public life and the control of dissent.

CORPORATIONS, RATIONALIZATION AND PROFESSIONALIZATION

Professionalization as a process cannot be separated from the political economy in which it was created. And the corporation, which is first and foremost an economic structure, has important connections to the professionalization movement. The corporate form is linked to notions about the role of bureaucracies in democratic life, the importance of efficient means of production, a certain definition of individualism, the fragmentation of the public and the importance of social control. And professionalization of many different occupations aids the corporations in its ability to accomplish those tasks (Allen, 2005).

But even more than that, a fundamental principle associated with the corporate form is, as R. Jeffrey Lustig (1982) has noted, the inversion of democratic principles. Whereas democratic theorists have long sought ways to harness private, corporate power for the public good, corporate representatives argue for the public good associated with strong private interests.

It would be wrong, however, to see corporations simply as an economic structure. Equally wrong would be arguing that restructuring democracy will solve the corporate problem. As Martin Sklar has noted, the corporation is best seen as a 'social movement' that changes the assumptions and guiding ideals central to a democracy (Sklar, 1988: 13). While the corporation is an economic structure, it reaches far beyond that arena and affects other areas of public life. Much as the efficiency movement associated with Taylorism and mass production of Fordism moved outside of the business world, so, too, has the ideology of corporations, bringing with it an emphasis on efficiency, control, short-turn profitability and winning as opposed to understanding.

Formal Rationalization

While Max Weber put forward at least four versions of rationalization, his idea of formal rationalization best describes the problem this chapter attempts to address. For Weber, society's development led to an increase in bureaucratic structures. And while Weber perceived there was a good side to the development of formal rules, he feared the realization of total control by bureaucratic discipline. Known as the Weberian paradox, the increasing rationalization of society freed citizens from ties to the limits of traditional society, but exposed people to increasingly controlling bureaucratic structures.

Formal rationality, according to Stephen Kalberg, 'relates to spheres of life and a structure of domination that acquired specific and delineated boundaries only with industrialization' (Kalberg, 1980: 1158). Formal rationalization encompasses the means-end calculations that have become fundamental to modern-day capitalism, nicely captured in the phrase of sociologist George Ritzer (2000), 'the McDonaldization' of society. This means-end calculation has negative consequences for the practice of democracy. For one, it eliminates the personal element and thus moves ethical considerations to the margins. Ethics is seen increasingly as some-thing that is subjective – something that cannot be calculated and cannot be controlled. Policy and business questions are reduced to questions of profitability and efficiency. The tradeoff is that while increased rationality tends to dehumanize society, it also leads to increased efficiency, a more predictable output, a greater ability to calculate or quantify parts of society, and a greater control over people, often through the use of technology. In addition, dissent is relegated to the irrational and aberrant. Weber, of course, feared the domination of rules and formal structures would lead to an 'iron cage' from which citizens would be unable to escape.

The Professions as Form of Rationalization

Professionalization, then, is best seen as a form of rationalization. And the history of the rise of the professions demonstrates that connection. At the beginning of the nineteenth century, there were three recognized profes-sions: divinity and its related university teaching, law and medicine. By the end of the century, however, professional associations had greatly expanded. But while professional associations themselves were growing, the study of professions would not begin until the twentieth century. That early work on the professions tended to focus on two main areas – the 'natural' development of professions and the typologies of a true profes-sion. More recently, sociologists have turned from trying to identify the common traits of a profession and instead have focused on what functions professions play in society. They began to recognize that professional growth was not so much a natural progression, but an attempt to accumu-late power. As Andrew Abbott describes in his assessment of these studies, '[e]thics codes came late in professionalization not because they were a cul-mination of natural growth, but because they served the function of exclud-ing outsiders, a function that became important only after the professional community had been generated and consolidated' (Abbott, 1988: 5).

The rise of professionalism in the United States is linked to its capitalis-tic roots. Professionalism, at its core, is an attempt by an occupation to obtain monopolistic control over an area of work, often with the sanction of the political and economic elites in society who sanction that attempt. This process can be seen in the Progressive Era (1890–1920) as an attempt by professionals to transfer a corporate model to the management of public affairs in America (Larson, 1977). Efficiency becomes the goal, with science being the means used to achieve that efficiency. But more importantly, science serves to separate the credentialed policymaker from class interests. The result of the Progressive Era was the rise of the bureaucracy, which in its own way becomes a new profession, but also feeds and supports new and old professions by providing 'models, sponsorship, equipment, and resources' (Larson, 1977: 145). This internal support allies professionals not with their clients, in accord with the traditional view, but rather with their colleagues or the political economy.

As such, the importance of professionalism can be seen in the passivity it has created within the body politic. Individuals began to regard professional judgments, often supported by scientific data, as unquestionable. The power granted to professions to handle the 'dangers to the public' clear the way for the ordinary citizen 'to go about the absorbing business of making a living' (Bledstein, 1976: 105). Burton Bledstein finds a suitable example of this in modern journalism, where reporters and editors gain attention 'by exaggerating the importance of the daily news, especially its apocalyptic and menacing overtones' (p. 101). As he writes:

> Professionals not only lived in an irrational world, they cultivated that irrationality by uncovering abnormality and perversity everywhere: in diseased bodies, criminal minds, political conspiracies, threats to the national security. An irrational world, an amoral one in a state of constant crisis, made the professional person who possessed his special knowledge indispensable to the victimized client, who was reduced to a condition of desperate trust. (p. 102)

There are many connections, then, between professionalization and corporate rationalization. First of all, professions and corporations share many of the same values: efficiency, expertise and profitability. And second, professionalization becomes not only a way for corporations to dominate an area of work, but a way for corporations to move beyond the economic sector. Operating behind a professional cover of public service and impartiality, professionals (sharing many values with corporations) pass on ideology to other parts of society. Along with that ideology come many assumptions about the public sphere and how best to structure and manage democracy. That transmission becomes particularly important when the institution is the press which, ideally, is a vital part of the public sphere. But professionalization has moved the press away from the public sphere.

US PRESS PROFESSIONALIZATION AND CORPORATE RATIONALIZATION

Operating with perhaps the broadest political freedom in the world, the American press continues to present a very narrow range of ideas and opinions. Watching the nightly network television news and quickly changing channels to observe what stories are being covered, a citizen will find not only that the networks often are covering the same stories, but often the stories are presented in exactly the same order. The question that comes from such observations is: how can completely independent news programs, operating free of political control, come to exactly the same conclusions night after night about what constitutes news? Recognizing that news is a human creation – something that is made, rather than simply discovered – that lack of diversity becomes an even more complex problem. The professionalization process (which brings with it routine practices and norms of conduct) helps us understand not only the lack of diversity, but also what press professionalization means for public life and the control of dissenting ideas.

A common point of departure for those trying to understand press professionalization is the development of the penny press, the movement often identified as changing the face of American journalism from one based on partisan politics to one based on the interests of the commercial marketplace. More often than not, the focus is on the rise of the penny press as it occurred in New York City in the 1830s. In these studies, evidence of professionalization can be found in the penny press's increased reliance on the methodology of objectivity as well as other precursors to so-called modern journalism. For example, Dan Schiller (1979) argues that objectivity was combined with commercialism to give the press a new political function: the surveillance of the public good. As Schiller writes, '[I]n one jump the newspaper moved from the self-interested concerns of partisan political warfare to the apparently omniscient status of protecting the people as a whole' (p. 47).

However, it is best to view the development of journalistic techniques often associated with the professionalization process as not arriving on the scene in a sudden, cataclysmic burst, but rather as a slow development over a lengthy period of time. Changes in the American press are best understood not by looking at the innovations of a few entrepreneurs in one city but rather 'shifts in the social and cultural environment' (Nerone, 1987: 401). These shifts can, in reality, be traced back to the American Revolution and the rise of partisan politics and a market economy, something that becomes clear if historians look at the 'typical' rather than 'the notorious or dramatic' (Nerone, 1987: 401).

The penny press, in the eyes of some, rather than recognizing and embodying professionalism, is better seen as the beginning of the move towards professionalism. In this regard, Michael Schudson (1978) sees the rise of objectivity as a professional methodology coming into play after World War I. The result was that while science played a central role up to World War I, objectivity did not become the press's chief methodology until after the war.

Evidence of professionalization can be found in other areas as well. In trying to change its image, journalism turned to another established institution, the university. The creation of journalism schools in the early 1900s gave the press an opportunity to shape and refine itself. As Joseph Pulitzer, whose endowment created one of the first schools, wrote: 'It is not too much to say that the press is the only great organized force which is actively and as a body upholding the standard of civic righteousness' (quoted in Birkhead, 1982: 259). The professionalization movement was ideological, attempting to convince its workers and the public of its new professional mission, though the structure of the industry and its function were essentially left unchanged (Birkhead, 1984: 11–12).

Today we see many reminders that the press professionalization process is a work in progress rather than a finished product. Debates about whether journalists ought to enjoy the same protections as the traditional professions and be able to protect their sources dominated the news in the summer of 2005. And perhaps more importantly, the press continues to struggle with understanding the influence of new technology not only on its product but on its profession. Bloggers trumpet their power to present a challenge to 'mainstream media' while those within the profession rush to find ways to turn blogs into a legitimate form of the new profession. And while this is a serious threat to the status of professional journalism, it is not the first challenge nor will it be the last. In the 1960s a challenge arose from a literary form of journalism, known as the New Journalism, that questioned the base assumptions about objective reporting. The 1990s saw the rise of civic or public journalism that promoted conversation and community connectedness. Each, in their own way, to use a 'Star Trek' phrase, has been assimilated. Perhaps more than anything, press professionalization is constantly engaged in the process of paradigm repair, finding ways to protect and defend the professional press from attacks outside occupational boundaries.

In the end, understanding press professionalization is less about understanding when and why it started, but rather about understanding how it serves as a tool of social control both inside and outside these occupational boundaries.

Rationalization of the US Press: Internal Structures

As American journalists developed a sense of what it meant to be a professional, they developed formal methods for reporting and writing the news. Jürgen Habermas (1989) has identified some of these changes in connection with the decline of the public sphere. Professionalization changed journalism from being a literary practice to a journalistic activity with accepted styles and formats. With the institutionalization of writing, journalism became a technical activity, and journalists increasingly became specialists, as work rules and codes of ethics were instituted. People who wrote for newspapers were no longer strictly members of the public, they were members of a profession. They became their own class of workers with emerging professional standards. The result was that the press ceased to be a voice of the public sphere.

Among those professional standards was objectivity. It was embraced as a methodology professional journalists use for turning everyday occurrences into news. Objectivity becomes a 'strategic ritual' that journalists use to turn facts into truth (Tuchman, 1978). The methodology of objectivity – presenting conflicting possibilities, use of supporting evidence, use of direct quotes and constructing the story in an appropriate sequence – helps disguise the fact that the journalistic story presents a constructed reality. The result is that stories that appear value-free are filled with choices, such as who to interview and what events to cover. Objectivity has become such an accepted ideology that even as journalists discover the limits of the methodology for reporting the news, the public insists on its journalists living up to that goal.

Just as important is the concept of journalistic routines. Faced with daily deadlines, journalists seek to expose themselves to the most reliable flow of material that they can find. For journalists, that secure, reliable and efficient source of material is government, and most news organizations organize their 'beats' around the structure of government. For example, it is not a coincidence that Sunday is known in the United States as a slow news day. Of course it is not because things don't happen on Sunday, but rather because it is the day that government is closed.

The consequence of this organizational strategy is that the role news plays in a democratic society is greatly restricted. The need for a reliable source of material means the government will always be 'news'; people outside of government will have a more difficult time attracting the attention of the news media. But perhaps more importantly this means that government sources filter the news that journalists report. Or, in an apt phrase, the world comes to the journalist 'bureaucratically organized' (Fishman, 1988: 44).

This routinization of the news, where journalists report more on what government tells them and less on what they witness, has changed the role of the reporter. Professional communicators not only link the elites of society with general audiences, but also link the different communities that comprise the audience. The message the professional communicators produce is marked not by that person's thoughts and beliefs, but rather 'operates under the constraints or demands imposed on one side by the ultimate audience and, on the other side, by the ultimate source' (Carey, 1969: 28). In that way, the news is shaped less by individual action and more by the constraints placed on, and the information provided to, the journalist. Professionalization of the press brings corporate values to the public through its routinization of the news process and valuing the scientific methodology of objectivity – a methodology that serves to reinforce dominant values within society.

Professionalization of the press has consequences not just for the reporter and the production of news, but it also influences what role the citizen plays in public affairs. And while professionalization, with its emphasis on routines and efficiency, has created a sameness about the news, it has also served to disempower citizens by framing them as an informed, but inactive, public.

Creating a Watchdog Press: External Constraints

Corporate rationalization has influenced democracy not only by changing the methodology of journalism, but also by how it changed the way institutions relate to citizens in society. The Progressives, so vital to the establishment of the American professional culture, put forward a paternalistic view of the citizenry. This view is reflected in the developing professional ideology of the press as a watchdog on government.

While the Progressives and their followers embraced the watchdog function, it was not an invention of the Progressive Era. Elements of the watchdog function of the press can be traced to the earliest years of the country. The earliest printers argued that the press ought to check governmental power. Even in pre-Revolutionary times, printers of weekly publications increasingly realized that their stories required some investigative work, thorough enough not to alienate readers (Smith, 1988). Attempting to attract readers by promising to unearth new information, the printers took on what T. C. Leonard called 'the role of stewards to the community' (Leonard, 1986: 56).

That stewardship would greatly increase in the nineteenth century. The change can be directly traced to the penny press. Coming during the Jacksonian age, the rise of the middle class is seen as being of utmost importance to the development of the penny press. But perhaps more important was the democratization of all walks of life during this period, generated by the rise of consumerism and the notion of equality across social classes. And the penny press became the public's representative of that egalitarian ideal. The press was far more than the voice of the middle class, however. The penny press instead becomes the defender of the public order (Schiller, 1981: 10), giving citizens equal access to knowledge and changing the public sphere.

The press takes on a more paternalistic role during the Progressive Era, when journalists quickened their separation from the public sphere. In

Walter Lippmann's (1920) classic *Liberty and the News*, he issued a call for the professionalization of the newspaper industry to correct the information being collected by 'anonymous and untrained and prejudiced witnesses'. He wrote that 'there is everywhere an increasingly angry disillusionment with the press' and warned journalists that if they do not control themselves, 'the next generation will attempt to bring the publishing business under greater social control' (p. 75). Lippmann's call for professionalization of the press was shared by others in the industry. However, it was unique in that the press did not have to be saved from big business but rather from itself.

Lippmann's call, however, also brought with it a new view of the press's role in society. Whereas public opinion had originally been linked with the middle class in nineteenth-century America, by the early twentieth century public opinion had no claim to representing the middle class and therefore was not rational. Public opinion was no longer viewed as the voice of the middle class. As Schudson writes: 'The professional classes now took public opinion to be irrational and therefore something to study, direct, manipulate, and control. The professions developed a proprietary attitude toward "reason" and a paternalistic attitude toward the public' (1978: 129).

The desire to control and manage the public while remaining separate from it is mirrored in the development of the public relations industry, an industry with deep ties to journalism. Yet, much of journalism's professionalization movement is the attempt to separate itself from that industry – to demonstrate to citizens that the press is the public's true representative. This was done by imitating science and creating a formal method that emphasized facts over values.

This desire to lead citizens to truth rather than allowing them to discover it for themselves is central to the establishment of the watchdog role of the press. In his study of the history of political reporting in America, Thomas Leonard notes that the Progressive Era presents a paradox: at the same time that muckraking journalism grew – a movement intended to excite citizens about public life – political participation declined. Progressivism and the journalism of that period undermined 'the ritual' of political participation, turning people away from parties to which they commonly turned for 'indoctrination, social pressure, and, if need be, the payoff' (Leonard, 1986: 198). Some journals of the day deplored mass democracy, and their message found elites who were willing to listen. Muckrakers saw it as wrong to use politics to protect 'parochial interests', and hoped to create a new citizen by getting rid of 'ethnic and religious loyalties' (p. 202). The end result was one that today is all too familiar:

> A profession that loved politics increasingly followed reporting conventions that made the public turn away. Gains in drawing attention to politics were often a

loss in comprehension about how the political system worked. That easy ver-
nacular of politics had broken down because the stories that the press now told,
meant less to those listening. (Leonard, 1986: 223)

While some have viewed the watchdog concept as dangerous to a free
press (for example, see Gleason, 1990), it is often viewed as a way to insure
the realization of a good society. One of the clearest accounts of this
version can be found in what has been called the social responsibility theory
of the press, a theory that can be traced to the work of the 1947
Commission on Freedom of the Press. In social responsibility theory, the
press finds a foundational principle to institutionalize the watchdog
concept as a way to address the problems of modern democracy. Following
in the steps of Progressive reformers, social responsibility theory puts its
faith in educated, enlightened individuals to lead society. The development
of that elite can be achieved through the professionalization of journalism,
with journalists educating demand.

This view of society and its elite is evident in the writings of members of
the Commission on Freedom of the Press. William E. Hocking, perhaps the
philosophical guiding force of the commission, notes that liberalism was
built on certain apparently erroneous assumptions: '(T)hat man by nature
knows what he wants, and consistently wants the right. The fact that we
appear to face today – and one that closely concerns the responsibilities of
the press – is that men do not know what they want in any socially reliable
way' (quoted in McIntyre, 1987: 148).

A more recent articulation of these ideas can be found in Vincent Blasi's
'checking value' theory of the First Amendment. For Blasi, the core
meaning of the First Amendment for eighteenth-century theorists was the
role-free expression 'performs in checking the abuse of official power' (Blasi,
1977: 528). The rise of big government has necessitated 'well-organized,
well-financed, professional critics' to counter government (p. 541).

In the end, the watchdog concept undervalues the role of the public
sphere. Taking what is portrayed as a more realistic perspective, advocates
of a watchdog press are only too willing to put the press in a privileged position in an attempt to check government. But the cost of granting the press
institutional status is to remove it from the public sphere. The press moves
closer to state authority, to the elites in society, toward a position of representing the governors rather than the governed.

The result is that today's journalism relies on a formal methodology and
routines to increase its ability to manage public life, all central elements of
the watchdog function of the press and corporate rationalization. This is
reflected in how the press covers dissenting voices in society. Numerous
studies of how the press covers protest groups demonstrate that the more

these groups are believed to be a threat to the status quo, the more likely they are to receive negative coverage (Gitlin, 1980). These 'threats' can be seen not only in the type of issues being covered, but also the size of the groups, the actions of the groups and the way that members of the dissenting groups dress or act (McLeod and Hertog, 1992; Shoemaker, 1984).

While today's press justifies its existence and its place in society through the public, arguing that it brings fruition to the public's right to know, professional standards have served to limit how groups are covered and how those groups are presented to the public. More than anything, press professionalization has served to legitimize an institution that serves as a form of social control in the public sphere. But as noted earlier, the implications of press professionalization go far beyond the boundaries of the occupation of journalism: it also helps create a particular kind of public.

The Press and an Inactive, Spectator Public

The watchdog concept of the press is often linked with another so-called right, the public's right to know, a concept that has little if any Constitutional legitimacy. Over the years, state and federal governments have adopted legislation that gives the press and public access to information, but the US Supreme Court has never suggested that citizens have a Constitutional right to know. However, in a number of instances courts have been willing to grant special privileges to the press as an aid to public information (Allen, 1995). As a result, press rights are often equated with the public's right to know.

The popularization of the right to know originated with journalists, and the executive editor of the Associated Press, Kent Cooper, is often credited with originating the term. In a 1956 book Cooper wrote that journalists have adopted the phrase 'as a slogan in the cause of conserving and broadening the right which has commonly been called "press freedom"'. The press's ties to the concept were furthered when the American Society of Newspaper Editors commissioned Harold Cross to study the issue. However, Cross's study trumpets not so much a public right but rather a press right. He suggests that newspapers fight for the public's right to know because it is through newspapers that the public will benefit. Cross (1953) argues that while justifications for denying access to information to the general public can be defended, those justifications cannot hold for the news media:

> The newspaper does not act out of mere or idle curiosity. It is not in the competition with the fee status of records custodians. . . . In a manner of speaking, when made by a newspaper, application of the right to inspect tends to circumvent, or

at least dilute, the fear that if one citizen or other person be granted such right the rest of the community will march in upon the records, not as single spies but in battalions. (p. 123)

Several things are important to note about Cross's words. First of all, acting out of curiosity is cast as a bad thing. A citizenry seeking information simply to enlighten itself is not something to be protected, while people or institutions acting for instrumental reasons are to be valued. And second, the inquiring public is envisioned not as citizens, but as spies. A public interest in obtaining information is seen as a threat to the stability of government. As such, the press can help subvert that threat by being the professional collector of information and protecting government from hordes of citizens.

Today the public's right to know is used to justify the existence of numerous press privileges. At the forefront is the idea of journalist's privilege, a professional power that allows journalists to withhold information under certain circumstances. The push for this privilege, which is closely connected to journalism's professionalization process, is an attempt to receive governmental recognition that the press is an inactive public's official representative. However, the idea of journalists' privilege raises the same problems as professionalization in general.

A recent example is the case involving *New York Times* reporter Judith Miller and former CIA operative Valerie Plame whose identity was outed by a leak from the Bush Administration. Miller was jailed for 85 days for refusing to identify her source for her stories about Plame. She was released only after her source, Vice President Dick Cheney's chief of staff, I. Lewis 'Scooter' Libby, released her from her promise of confidentiality. Many journalists defended Miller and used her in their calls for federal legislation that would give journalists a professional right to protect their sources. However, as even journalists recognized, basing the right to withhold information from the public on a right of the public to know is a difficult argument to sustain. Would it have been better for citizens to know that Miller's source was Libby? Or was the public better served by giving Miller the power to make that determination for her readers?

The Miller case illustrates how professionalization shapes both the internal practices and external effects of the press. Professional practices emphasize the watchdog nature of the press, which calls on the press to make elites the focus of its attention. Dissenting voices are news only when they confront or are confronted by the elites in society. At the same time, the press purports to act as a stand-in for an inactive public, making decisions about what the public needs to know and what it does not need to know. The press pretends to provide citizens with a complete story that does not need to be interpreted or taken apart. The role for citizens is to passively receive the information and not ask too many questions. There is little room for disagreement or dissent, even in situations where stories spark questions. Stories are told in prescribed frame that protect the existing political structure. Ultimately then, as Miller's actions raised too many ethical red flags, the profession cut its ties with her. She lost her job and was widely criticized as a rogue individual. The Miller story, in the end, was less about sources of information and more about a profession attempting to preserve it credibility.

The Public Sphere and Corporate Rationalization

While the world's press adopts professional norms and practices, the important question facing journalism is not whether journalists are professionals, but rather what the professionalization process means for democracy, dissent and news. Professionalization is best seen as a way of separating the press from the public sphere and linking it ever more closely to the values and missions of the corporation. The professional press is less and less of the public sphere and more and more uses the public to justify special rights and privileges within society.

The professionalization movement turns questions of public policy into technical questions that only specially trained elites are able to address. Checking government's actions, and the subsequent information provided to the public about those actions, becomes a job for the trained journalist. Issues impacting the press are not seen as public issues, but rather as professional, technical issues. The press presents stories not as something to be acted on, but rather as events that have already been completed (see Hallin, 1985). From a technical systems perspective, the important questions for the professional press are means-ends questions oriented toward efficiency. An active public sphere is not driven by such means-end questions. Instead, the rationality that grounds the public sphere is a communicative one based on the desire for understanding. Ideas need to develop legitimacy to survive and legitimacy is achieved through providing good reasons why one alternative is superior to another. The goal is not more information, but the creation of what G. Thomas Goodnight has called a 'deliberative rhetoric' – argumentation that allows individuals to test and create social knowledge to 'uncover, assess, and resolve problems' (1982: 214).

Many in today's news media seem uninterested in aiding that discursive goal, unless it fits nicely within the confines of increased profit margins. The rhetoric that media managers use today to justify what they do increasingly emphasizes profitability and efficiency over public service. While there was debate about whether earlier media managers lived up to claims that they 'were afflicting the comfortable and comforting the afflicted' or serving as a watchdog on government, few disagreed that these were admirable goals. Today, media managers have mostly abandoned those clichés, preferring a more realistic and instrumental set of goals. For example, when John Hogan, the president and chief executive of Clear Channel's radio division (which owns some 1200 radio stations), was asked by *New York Times* writers to explain his division's apparent conservative political agenda, he termed such claims as 'laughable'. *The Times* report went on to explain the corporate ideology that drives Clear Channel: 'Clear Channel, he (Hogan) said, is purely a company that builds audiences through entertainment so that advertisers can sell goods and services to them. "We're in the business of having the largest possible audience," Mr Hogan said, not "the most politically unified audience" ' (Schwartz and Fabrikant, 2003: 1).

Clear Channel should be praised for candor, but it should concern citizens who rely on the news media that profitability and serving markets are their primary concerns. The idea of corporate rationalization is validated by the fact that media managers no longer feel the need to rely on claims of public service or aiding democracy to justify what they do. Today's press seems increasingly driven by a corporately rationalized value system.

RESISTING CORPORATION RATIONALIZATION: THE PRESS AS LEADER

There are few easy ways out of the problem described in this chapter. It cannot be accomplished simply by changing the ownership structure of the press, although it might be a step in the right direction. Nor can we legislate our way out of the problem. The establishment press needs to rethink its view of the public and take a leading role in creating an active public, valuing the public creation of meaning, promoting the use of public space and protecting expressive association. Of the four, the idea of creating an active public has been most closely examined by the American press. The press needs to come to terms with what it means by the public and the role the public plays in society. It needs to move beyond the view that the public is comprised of individuals who share few similarities, all waging battles to push through their individual agendas. Individual and collective dissenting voices should not be viewed as being destructive of a public, but as helping to broaden the perspective of the public. Avenues and techniques that will allow the formation of an active public need to be developed so that the public's deliberative potential might be realized. No longer would the profession's highest calling simply be the production of information or serving as a check on government. In this vision the goal becomes the establishment of ways and means to activate and involve the public.

While promoting a notion of an active public is central to the realization of discourse democracy, it is not enough. The press also needs to understand that it plays an important leadership role in the creation of public meaning. It needs to understand the sociology of the news and how news not only aids in the establishment of meaning, but also limits the creation of meaning. Just as law abhors ambiguity, so it appears does journalism. Rather than providing the raw material that enables citizens to figure out what events mean in their life, journalism too often attempts to provide a single authoritative narrative of an event. This, of course, helps to ensure the power and influence of its voice within the community. It also can serve to distance the press from a community, such as when the press's interpretation differs significantly from public interpretations. But more importantly, it silences dissenting voices that are not seen as being important to that narrative. Allowing dissent is a way to change the story of public life. Today, journalism often retells a story through its own lens that is, as I have noted, heavily influenced by corporate values. In short, the press needs to break free of its routinized, rationalized world.

In that same vein, the press can play a leadership role in the protection of public space. Public space is more than parks and streets; it includes other venues for interaction that have been traditionally opened for public use, both real and virtual. Media outlets that justify their existence through their democratic mission fall into that category. While US courts today disagree, preferring to emphasize property rights, a newspaper or broadcast outlet is as much a public forum as any city park and ought to be viewed in that manner. Admittedly this raises many questions, especially of corporate property rights, which cannot be addressed adequately here. Nonetheless, new models for creating and protecting public space are emerging on the Internet and other alternative broadcast media. Protecting public space requires the press to do more than simply open itself up to citizens, however. It also requires the press to be strong advocates in monitoring how public space is used and governed. The press ought to not only encourage the use of public space, including private places that have been generally open to the public, but also serve as sentinels to make sure that public space is used for more openly deliberative purposes.

And finally, the press needs to play an active leadership role in protecting expressive association. In important ways the first three categories – promoting active citizens, valuing public meaning, and protecting public space – help achieve expressive association, but more is needed. The press needs to understand that the importance of association is not simply to make an individual's voice louder, but rather that it allows others to share ideas. The press needs to understand that within any association there are valid disagreements. Reporting about associations should display those differences not to hurt the solidarity of associations or to demonstrate some discord within the organization, but rather to increase the range of views that come into the public sphere. Relying on facile political labels, the hallmarks of most political commentary today, and turning issues into simplified competitions between good and bad or right and wrong are entertaining, efficient and easy ways to explain our political world. Unfortunately, that approach often fails to capture the complexity of public issues. It is in that complexity where we often can find beliefs and values that serve to cross the lines of association and enrich public deliberation.

In the end, the mainstream press's mission in creating an active public is difficult and eclectic. It must be at once partisan and yet open to differing views; it needs to be at once a watchdog that protects public life but not elitist and exclusive (see Baker, 2002). More fundamentally, the press as leader must break free from its routinized, rationalized corporate logic. In effect, to lead in these vitally important areas of public life the press must become a dissenting enterprise within its own practice, redefining how it functions and what its identity is. Evidence is accumulating from the new media that the inclusion of dissenting voices and opinions is desired by active citizens: the press as leader will be wise to heed that trend, both for its own sustainability and for the vitality of public life.

REFERENCES

Abbott, A. (1988), *The System of Professions: An Essay on the Division of Expert Labor*, Chicago, IL: University of Chicago Press.

Allen, David S. (1995), 'The Supreme Court and the creation of an (in)active public sphere', in David S. Allen and Robert Jensen (eds), *Freeing the First Amendment: Critical Perspectives on Freedom of Expression*, New York: New York University Press, pp. 93–113.

Allen, David S. (2005), *Democracy, Inc.: The Press and Law in the Corporate Rationalization of the Public Sphere*, Urbana, IL: University of Illinois Press.

Baker, C. E. (2002), *Media, Markets, and Democracy*, Cambridge: Cambridge University Press.

Birkhead, D. (1982), 'Presenting the press: journalism and the professional project', unpublished doctoral dissertation, University of Iowa.

Birkhead, D. (1984), 'The power in the image: professionalism and the "communications revolution"', *American Journalism*, **1** (2), 1–14.

Blasi, Vincent (1977), 'The checking value in First Amendment theory', *American Bar Foundation Research Journal*, **3**, 521–649.

Bledstein, Burton J. (1976), *The Culture of Professionalism: The Middle Class and the Development of Higher Education in America*, New York: W. W. Norton.

Carey, James W. (1969), 'The communications revolution and the professional communicator', in *The Sociology of Mass Media Communicators: The Sociological Review Monograph 13*, P. Halmos (ed.), London: Blackwell, pp. 23–38.

Cheney, George and Karen Lee Ashcraft (2007), 'Considering "the professional" in communication studies: implications for theory and research within and beyond the boundaries of organizational communication', *Communication Theory*, **17** (2), 146–75.

Clausen, Lisbeth (2004), 'Localizing the global: "domestication" processes in international news production,' *Media, Culture & Society*, **26**, 25–44.

Cooper, Kent (1956), *The Right To Know*, New York: Farrar, Straus and Cudahy.

Cross, Harold L. (1953), *The People's Right to Know*, New York: Columbia University Press.

Fishman, Michael (1988), *Manufacturing the News*, Austin, TX: University of Texas Press.

Gitlin, Todd (1980), *The Whole World is Watching: Mass Media and the Making and Unmaking of the New Left*, Berkeley, CA: University of California Press.

Gleason, T. (1990), *The Watchdog Concept: The Press and the Courts in Nineteenth-Century America*, Ames, IA: Iowa State University.

Golding, Peter (1979), 'Media professionalism in the Third World and the transfer of an ideology', in J. Curran, Michael Gurevitch and J. Woollacott (eds), *Mass Communication and Society*, Beverly Hills, CA: Sage, pp. 290–308.

Goodnight, G. Thomas (1982), 'The personal, technical, and the public spheres of argument: a speculative inquiry into the art of public deliberations', *Journal of the American Forensic Association*, **18**, 214–27.

Habermas, Jürgen (1989), *The Structural Transformation of the Public Sphere*, translated by T. Burger, Cambridge, MA: MIT Press.

Hallin, D. C. (1985), 'The American news media: a critical theory perspective', in *Critical Theory and Public Life*, J. Forester (ed.), Cambridge, MA: MIT Press, pp. 121–46.

Hocking, W. E. (1947), *Freedom of the Press: A Framework of Principle*, Chicago, IL: University of Chicago Press.

Kalberg, Stephen (1980), 'Max Weber's types of rationality: cornerstones for the analysis of rationalization processes in history', *American Journal of Sociology*, **85**, 1145–79.

Kavoori, Anandam P. (1999), 'Discursive texts, reflexive audiences: global trends in television news texts and audience reception', *Journal of Broadcasting & Electronic Media*, **43**, 386–98.

Larson, M. S. (1977), *The Rise of Professionalism: A Sociological Analysis*, Berkeley, CA: University of California Press.

Leonard, Thomas C. (1986), *The Power of the Press: The Birth of American Political Reporting*, New York: Oxford University Press.

Lippmann, Walter (1920), *Liberty and the News*, New York: Harcourt, Brace & Howe.

Lustig, R. J. (1982), *Corporate Liberalism: The Origins of Modern American Political Theory, 1890–1920*, Berkeley, CA: University of California Press.

McIntyre, J. S. (1987), 'Repositioning a landmark: The Hutchins Commission and freedom of the press', *Critical Studies in Mass Communication*, **4**, 136–60.

McLeod, Doug M. and James K. Hertog (1992), 'The manufacture of public opinion by reporters: informal cues for public perceptions of protest groups', *Discourse and Society*, **3**, 259–75.

van Natta, Don Jr, Adam Liptak and Clifford J. Levy (2005), 'The Miller case: a notebook, a cause, a jail cell and a deal', *New York Times*, 16 October, accessed at www.nytimes.com/2005/10/16/national/16leak.html.

Nerone, J. C. (1987), 'The mythology of the penny press', *Critical Studies in Mass Communication*, **4**, 376–404.

Paterson, Chris A. (2003), 'The transference of frames in global television', in *Framing Public Life: Perspectives on Media and Our Understanding of the Social World*, S. D. Reese, Oscar H. Gandy, Jr., and A. E. Grant (eds), Mahwah, NJ: Lawrence Erlbaum, pp. 337–53.

Patterson, T. E. (1993), 'Irony of the free press: professional journalism and news diversity', paper presented to the annual meeting of the American Political Science Association, 3–6 September, 1992, Chicago, IL.

Ritzer, George (2000), *McDonaldization of Society: New Century Edition*, Thousand Oaks, CA: Pine Forge Press.

Schiller, Dan (1979), 'An historical approach to objectivity and professionalism in American news reporting', *Journal of Communications*, **29**, 46–57.

Schiller, Dan (1981), *Objectivity and the News: A Social History of American Newspapers*, Philadelphia, PA: University of Pennsylvania Press.

Schudson, Michael (1978), *Discovering the News: A Social History of American Newspapers*, New York: Basic Books.

Schwartz, J. and G. Fabrikant (2003), 'War puts radio giant on the defensive', *The New York Times*, 31 March, C 1.

Shoemaker, Pamela (1984), 'Media treatment of deviant political groups', *Journalism Quarterly*, **61**, 66–75.

Sklar, Martin J. (1988), *The Corporate Reconstruction of American Capitalism, 1890–1916: The Market, the Law, and Politics*, New York: Cambridge University Press.

Smith, J. A. (1988), *Printers and Press Freedoms: The Ideology of Early American Journalists*, New York: Oxford University Press.

Tuchman, Gaye (1978), *Making News: A Study in the Construction of Reality*, New York: Free Press.

Weaver, David (1998), *The Global Journalist: News People Around the World*, Cresskill, NJ: Hampton Press.

10. The sanctity of dissent

Paul Toscano

INTRODUCTION

This chapter originally appeared in a book that justified dissent within the Church of Jesus Christ of Latter-day Saints (Toscano, 1995). My arguments, however, apply not only to ecclesiastical settings but to institutions and organizations of the academy, of industry, of commerce and finance, and of the military (except, perhaps, when in actual combat). I have made some minor editorial changes to the original chapter to give my arguments a more general scope and application. However, for the most part I continue to illustrate my points with references to LDS Church doctrine, history and practice, leaving the generalization of specific examples to the reader.

My purpose was to explain to the LDS community why dissent should be embraced as holy – that is, as inspired and ordained of God and necessary to the spiritual well being of the church and its members. Here, I expand that purpose to include the broader contexts just described.

To dissent is to differ in sentiment or opinion, to disagree with the philosophy, methods or goals of others, especially the majority. It is to withhold one's assent. Dissent is almost always disruptive. It can be dangerous, even violent. There exist forms of dissent as acceptable as casting a ballot, as provocative as crossing a boundary, as intolerable as terrorism or hate crimes. Moreover, the purposes of dissent may range from the sublimely noble to the utterly contemptible. Clearly, a community need not endure every manifestation of dissent.

Nevertheless, dissent in its essence is holy. Jesus himself was a dissenter, and this fact alone hallows dissent. 'Think not', he said, 'that I am come to send peace on earth: I came not to send peace, but a sword' (Matt. 10:34).[1] The sword is asserted here not as a metaphor for physical violence, but as the cruciform symbol of opposition. The cutting edge of contrary opinion can divide a complacent community, challenging its received wisdom and settled opinions. Actual physical confrontation, thought sometimes to be necessary, is not essential. The essence of dissent – that is, dissent stripped of any specific form or context – is the fundamental right to disagree and to express that disagreement. In this chapter, when I speak of dissent, I mean this essential freedom of opposition. In the first part of this chapter, I will discuss ten reasons why I believe dissent is sacred; later I will show how dissent is further sanctified by the adoption of certain means and objections.

HOW DISSENT IS SACRED

Dissent is holy because without it there can be no consent. Consent is a voluntary meeting of the minds. It is the agreement of free individuals who share a perception of what is mutually beneficial or at least acceptable to them. Consent is meaningful only where dissent is permitted and protected. Consent draws its power from the possibility of dissent. Unless the consenting parties are free to dissent, their consent is without substance and pointless. Thus if dissent is proscribed, assent is illusory. Like a fascist election, it is a counterfeit, a fraud – because behind it there is no true accord. To eliminate dissent, then, is to curtail personal freedom, to forbid individuals from voicing their true opinions. It is to silence both their hopes and their fears. It is to force people to accept what they might deem unacceptable, even harmful. By eliminating dissent, a community takes from its members the power to resist or contradict. The suppression of dissent dilutes the capacity for independent reassessment of facts and theories. It neutralizes opposition. It abridges an individual's ability to tacitly assent, to actively agree, to change one's mind, to protest, to object, or to cry out in pain. Such a system is a prison in which every act of kindness may be an exploitation and every act of love, a rape.

Dissent is holy because it is the backbone of individual freedom, the freedom from arbitrary compulsion. Any proscription of dissent is an attack on this hallowed principle. Leaders make such attacks at all levels of various institutions – religious and otherwise. A prevailing view of many religious authorities is that we are free only to choose what is good. 'After all', the argument goes, 'the commandments are clear. There are church leaders to guide us. Why be free when you can be right.'

Goodness, however, does not result from obedience, even obedience to someone good. It results from spiritual transformation, a change of heart, a rebirth. Goodness is personal spiritual maturity. We cannot mature spiritually if we are under compulsion, if we are required to yield to others the responsibility for our words and deeds. Goodness results from turning our hearts to God, from listening to the voice of God within our hearts; within the hearts of our family and friends; within the hearts of all the concerned members of our communities. We cannot be free and slavishly follow a prescribed catechism. We cannot be organization men and women. We must work out our own salvation, not with smugness and certainty, but 'with fear and trembling' (Philip. 2.12).

Dissent is holy because it is a recurring theme of the Old Testament. Adam and Eve dissented in Eden as a necessary step toward spiritual growth. Abraham argued with God over the fate of Sodom. David disputed with Saul. Elijah with the priests of Baal. Children are encouraged to dissent when they are enjoined to 'leave father and mother' (Gen. 2:24); adults, whenever they are encouraged to exercise independent judgment and personal initiative.

Jesus intended for us to dissent. The New Testament presents him as declaring:

> I am come to set a man at variance against his father, and the daughter against her mother, and the daughter-in-law against her mother-in-law. A man's foes shall be they of his own household. He that loveth father or mother more than me is not worthy of me: and he that loveth son or daughter more than me is not worthy of me. And he that taketh not his cross, and followeth after me, is not worthy of me. (Matt. 10:35-38)

Hard words from the Prince of Peace. They mean that essential to Christian salvation is the sacred freedom to dissent from the wisdom of the group – the family, the church, the state – in order to be true to the wisdom of God. Easy to say. That is why so many find it easier simply to assent, even when assent is cajoled or coerced. Many such are fond of saying of the church or nation to their dissenting brothers and sisters: 'Love it or leave it'.

The same is true in Islam. Though the Holy Qur'an:

> recognizes revelation as a source of knowledge higher than reason, at the same time, it accepts that the truth of the principles established by revelation may be judged by reason. Hence, the Qur'an repeatedly appeals to reason and denounces those who do not use their reasoning faculty. While the sources of Islamic Shari'a (Cannon law and jurisprudence) is the Holy Qur'an and the Hadith (the sayings of the Prophet), the Hadith expressly recognizes the exercise of judgment in deriving decisions on issues where there is no direction from the scriptures. (Ghazanfar, personal correspondence)

Many people cannot accept the possibility that their religious or even secular authorities can be wrong, might be headed toward idolatry, heresy, or even treason. But they can. There are many instances of such betrayals in history.

A church – like any institution – can be no purer than its members. It can sin. It can commit crimes. It can also be corrected and improved, not just by its leaders, but by its members who take responsibility for its health, spirituality, and well-being. In defense of dissent, Brigham Young once said:

> Now when I was an elder I was as willing to correct an error in the brethren as I am now. But the people do not see it so. Now if you should be with the 12 [apostles] or any body [of leaders] you would have right to correct an error as well as with a member but you could not correct them by cutting them off from the church because they are over you in the priesthood. (*Wilford Woodruff's Journal*, 2 June, 1857, LDS Archives)

The scriptures of the Church of Jesus Christ of Latter-day Saints urge every member to cry repentance to his or her generation. What is such a cry but the voice of dissent?

Dissent is holy because it is the root of personal responsibility and spiritual maturation. Without dissent, self-determination is not possible. Only those who are free to disagree with the prevailing views of the group can learn full implications of their personal views. Only those free to dissent can fully take part in the decision-making processes that shape their lives and destinies. Only they, by participating in the governing decisions of the group, can experience spiritual and intellectual development. For this reason, dissent is an indispensable component of every moral organization dedicated to the empowerment or salvation of the individual. A system that punishes dissent thwarts personal growth, perpetuates childishness and promotes arrested adolescence. It will come, eventually, to value compliance and obedience above the personal sanctity of its members. In such a system, individuals will be valued only if they repress their personal insights, spiritual or otherwise, in the interests of conformity. Those who do not or cannot comply will be scapegoated or marginalized. Such a system will urge or even compel its members to live by principles they do not truly value and to submit to values they do not truly accept. Inevitably such a system will become joyless and unforgiving in its denial of the truth. It will become evil.

Dissent is holy because it is essential to continuing personal revelation. The most vital role of revelation is to initiate change, correction, reproof, not to reinforce the status quo. To eliminate dissent, then, is to risk silencing the 'still small voice' of the Holy Spirit speaking to us the discourse of dissent. Though Mormonism is based on the concept of continuing revelation, the church does not accept God as dissenter, despite his incarnation as a rebellious Rabbi. The argument against the sanctity of dissent goes like this: The church is not a democracy. It is a theocracy. It is governed by God through his chosen leaders. When we sustain them, we give our consent, we agree to obey our leaders because they have been chosen by God and are inspired to know what is best for us.

This view contradicts the weight of scripture and religious experience. Prophets do not always speak as prophets. Prophecy is a spiritual gift, not an office. Contact with God is uncertain at best, even for the best of us.

Jesus said, 'The wind bloweth where it listeth and thou hearest the sound thereof, but canst not tell whence it cometh and whither it goeth; so is everyone that is born of the spirit' (John 3:8).

Salvation and spirituality are like the wind – real but uncertain, powerful but outside human control. It is improper for a church to insist that its authorized leaders may be relied upon with certainty. This assertion wrongly suggests that members may rely upon the church and leaders for salvation. But the church is the source of salvation. The church is what needs to be saved. Salvation is God's work, not our work. In scripture God states emphatically, 'This is my work and my glory – to bring to pass the immortality and eternal life of [men and women]' (Moses 1:39).

Unfortunately, life-after-death and salvation seem fairly mysterious and even doubtful to many of us. We long for certainty, for security, for safety not only with regard to the hereafter but to the here-and-now. The institutions of church and state are all too willing to assume (or at least to pretend to assume) the burden of providing these. Individuals are encouraged to exercise their own judgment in voluntarily affiliating themselves with the organization, but thereafter are encouraged to lay aside independent judgment and follow their leaders. Their personal involvement is then limited to confirming the decisions of those in charge and to obey even when leaders are wrong. Such an outlook contravenes the First Commandment: 'I am the Lord thy God . . . thou shalt have no other gods before me' (Ex. 20:2–3). Neither the church nor any other institution, no matter how beneficial, has the power to heal, forgive, redeem, resurrect, exalt or transform. Institutions may play a role in all these, to encourage change and forgiveness, to lessen fear, foster faith, raise hope and promote charity. But institutions can do this only if they permit dissent. An organization (or even an individual) that prohibits dissent will in time relegate itself to the profane business of hawking self-improvement schemes that motivated short-term material gains at the expense of long-term growth and maturation. A church that does this will limit its mission to the production of respectable members who make good employees rather than saints, and fine family members rather than true disciples.

A church without dissent is to religion what fast-food is to haute cuisine. Preachments will inevitably focus on safety from the 'thousand natural shocks that flesh is heir to' (*Hamlet*, III, I, 62–3), safety from the very experiences of life that we have been placed on earth to encounter as essential to the attainment of wisdom and compassion. By quashing dissent, an institution discourages its members from relying on their inner spiritual strength and creativity and to rely upon the unreliable judgment of others.

Dissent is holy because it is an antidote to idolatry, the essence of which is to mistake the part for the whole, to see as simple what is complex. The truth of any matter is whole and dynamic, while symbols, texts, ritual, formulas, myths and plans are, in comparison, incomplete and static. When the corporate world fixes the attention of individuals on these lesser constructs rather than the greater, it begins to distance them from authenticity. When this happens, the voice of truth is muted in the institution, but continues to speak a discourse of dissent through the institution's loyal critics. The prohibition on dissent thus facilities idolatry, by stimulating the adulation of rules, traditions, conventional wisdom, authority and power rather than encouraging respect for honesty, creativity and merit. Idolatry is often the invention of well-meaning persons attempting to preserve some semblance of faith. It is often promoted in the name of spiritual certitude or purity. But the authentic life is not one of certainty, security or safety. No fixed patterns or formulas were meant to work for everyone. The spiritual journey is tailor-made for the individual taking it. It is through the instrumentality of dissent that idolatry is contradicted, the personal dimension restored, and the right of each individual to follow the dictates of his or her own conscience preserved.

Dissent is holy because it gives sight to the blind. A system that proscribes dissent blinds itself. There are many kinds of sight: foresight, insight and hindsight. Perhaps the most valuable is ironic sight. Usually, we think of irony as sarcasm, but it has a broader literary meaning: irony is the technique of seeing or communicating two or more meanings in a single utterance – often by seeming self-contradiction. Ironic vision is the vision that sees simultaneously the natural and the supernatural, theoretical and practical, spiritual and material, spiritual and physical, sacred and profane, cosmic and mundane. Irony sees in a symbol, event or experience various levels of meaning at once; it sees ourselves as others see us. It allows us to escape the prison of our egos and view our lives and relationships from new and differing perspectives. To see ourselves as we are seen by those who employ us and whom we employ, by those who depend on us and on whom we depend, by those who teach and learn from us, who lead and follow us, who love and hate us. To see from these shifting perspectives is probably one of the most maturing experiences any individual can have. This may be the greatest, if not least valued, of all attributes.

Any system that proscribes dissent, that requires its members to accept the party line on all important questions contrary to their true feelings, robs its members of ironic visions. Introspection will become more and more difficult. Individuals will find themselves increasingly unable to see the world, their organization, themselves or their relationships from the vantage point of other members or of non-members of their group. To use another LDS-specific example, without ironic vision in the church, individual Mormons will not be inclined to ask important questions: How is the LDS church in its second century like the Christian church in its second century? How is the current leadership and membership of the church responsible for the continued practice of polygamy by Mormon fundamentalists? How do others view us when we brag about our living leaders and then show them the actual enfeebled and incapacitated condition of our church president? What does the church look and feel like from the point of view of a conservative? A widow? A survivalist? A bishop? A divorcee? A teenager? A homosexual? An apostle? An apostle's wife? In the absence of dissent, members will have little impetus to ask: What are the church's problems? What causes those problems? What must be done to eliminate those problems? The Old Testament proverb states: 'Where there is no vision, the people perish' (Prov. 29:18). Dissent is crucial to this very vision.

Dissent is holy because it can also heal institutional blindness. In the New Testament, Jesus accuses the Pharisees of blindness as if it were a sin (Matt. 23). I used to be confused by this enunciation. Why should Jesus treat blindness as a sin? Blindness is a sin when it is self-inflicted by those who do not wish to see the sins they have committed or enabled, who do not wish to see their own pain and suffering, or the pain and suffering they have caused others. This type of blindness is denial. It is the ultimate mechanism of control to which abusers retreat when their abuses are exposed. Self-inflicted blindness may be institutionalized. Institutions do this by punishing truth-telling and rewarding the denial or repression of truth. This cannot happen in an institution, unless there exist individual leaders willing to enforce such punishments and rewards.

How are such accomplices identified and empowered in an institution? First, the leadership must be stratified into descending classes of power. Then rules, spoken and unspoken, must be developed to govern each of these levels of leadership and, more importantly, an individual's advancement from one of these groups to another. If an individual is to move into a higher stratum of leadership – with its increased power, privileges, and tenure – she must demonstrate not only obedience to all policies and procedures, but to all the nuances of political correctness and be expert in recognizing and submitting to the personal views of the top brass. To advance one must anticipate how superiors will respond in any given situation. Second-to becomes the pass key to promotion. Only those truly in tune will ascend to the inner circles of leadership with all their benefits and rewards. The system ensures that only those juniors who have become replicas of their seniors will participate in the most important decisions of the leadership elite.

This is precisely the system that was employed by Soviet premier Leonid Brezhnev to ensure the stability of communism in the Soviet Union. For this reason, I refer to this system in Mormonism as the Brezhnevization of the church. Its problem, however, is that it not only screens out the undesirables, it also screens out the capable and creative. In the Soviet Union, the leadership became incapable of responding to the need of the people or of the group. Self-interest, corruption and incompetence crippled the country. The leadership responded to criticism by becoming ever-more rigid and authoritarian. Finally, compelled by desperate circumstances, the leadership had no other choice than to make concessions. This was like putting a crack in an already weakened and swollen dam. The internal pressures caused a breach and a flood that no amount of renewed authoritarianism could avert or contain. The problem with rewarding consent and punishing dissent is that it causes self-inflicted blindness that deprives the institution of vision, ironic or otherwise. Dissent is holy because it is, perhaps, the only corrective to institutional blindness, the only means of giving to its blind members insight, foresight, and hindsight into perspectives to which their minds would otherwise be closed. Dissent is holy because, even if the blind refuse to see, its purpose is to prepare against the hour of disaster, when the blind lead the blind into a ditch.

Dissent is holy because it is the foundation of peace. Though the principal reason for the elimination of dissent is to avoid discord and disruption, the elimination of dissent does not promote peace. Instead, the absence of dissent is evidence of unspoken turmoil bidden by repression, suppression or oppression. Yes, dissent is noisy. And some feel dissent should be silenced in the interest of tranquility. But tranquility is not peace. Silence is not peace. In fact, silence when imposed by the strong on the weak is one of the most efficient mechanisms of control. The first act of physical, sexual or spiritual abusers is to silence their victims. Real peace is based on freedom, authenticity and love. These cannot flower in the inhospitable climate of suppression and repression. We should not listen to those who cry 'peace, peace', when there is no peace – when peace is merely a euphemism for subjugation. We must avoid confusing peace with its counterfeits: politeness, pseudo-community, feigned love and the comfortable familiarity of the status quo.

Dissent is holy because it safeguards the community from self-destruction. To eliminate dissent is to doom the organization. Unless the discourse of dissent is permitted, protected, and encouraged, an organization has no way to test the adequacy of its decision to meet the problems of the group. It has no way to assure itself that its policies accord with spiritual truth, with natural reality, or with the needs of its members. Only by allowing dissent to be expressed and to accumulate support on the basis of merit alone can a group be assured that its decisions are made in light of the experience of all its concerned members rather than the limited experience of its leadership enclave. Of course, there are problems with democratic governance. The majority almost never has the technical knowledge possessed by an expert minority; and the wisdom of the majority is by no means infallible. This is precisely the point. What is necessary to protect the community from both the wrongheadedness of the elite is a courageous and loyal opposition. When the wisdom of the many and the prudence of the few fail, an organization is most likely to find the vitality and vision to survive in the voices of its dissenting members.

MEANS AND OBJECTIVES FOR SANCTIFYING DISSENT

Let me now discuss briefly seven means and objectives that can add to the sanctity of dissent: dissent is hallowed when its objective is the eradication of evil. Many do not believe in evil. Or if we do, we see it as only illusory or superficial. Many do not believe in evil people, evil groups or evil systems. This view informed England prior to World War II. Many Britons believed Hitler was not evil, merely misunderstood, and that it was possible to make peace with him. This view obtained even after the Anschluss of Austria, the attack on Czechoslovakia, and the invasion of Poland. For those who do not believe in evil, there seems little justification for dissent. The holiest dissent, with all its discord and cantankerousness, is asserted to oppose evil, to expose evil, to resist evil. I believe in the reality of evil.[2]

For me, evil is something quite specific. It is the persistent or systematic abuse of power by the strong to the detriment of the weak. Evil in this sense can corrupt individuals and institutions. The church is not exempt. Within an ecclesiastical structure, evil can and does manifest itself as spiritual abuse, which I have defined and discussed in other places (see Toscano, 1995).

Evil must not be confused with one's personal sins. I am not here calling for personal perfection in leaders or in members of institutions. I understand that everyone is susceptible to foolishness, bad judgment, contrariness, selfishness and sin. These are not the issue. They should not be confused with the systematic abuse of power, which is a sin of relationship. Leaders who abuse power do so not merely because they are imperfect, but because they hold a false concept of authority that is shared to some degree by their community. When leaders commit power abuses, they do so because their followers – often powerful followers – enable them to do so.

Let me emphasize that it is dangerous to permanently stigmatize any person or institution as evil. This, too, is an abuse. Notwithstanding this caveat, it is critical to see that the heart of darkness, the soul of evil, is the deliberate perpetuation and exploitation of powerlessness by the strong of the weak, sometimes with the complicity of the weak. The antidote to such unhallowed control is the sanctity of dissent.

Dissent is further sanctified when its substance is truth. Truth telling is the holiest discourse of dissent. But truth telling is hard. We do not deal in truth directly. We deal in shifting perceptions of truth. Our knowledge, whether attained by study or by faith, whether sacred or secular, is incomplete, limited, inaccurate and flawed. We see through a glass, darkly. Different people see the same events and hear the same words differently. Intentions are often misunderstood. The same facts give rise to differing conclusions depending upon one's assumptions, convictions, intentions and expectations. Each of us is flawed and often disposed to manage or mismanage the truth in our own interest. In the hands of controlling people, truth becomes a terrible weapon.

For all these reasons, authentic truth tellers must first search their own hearts for and rid themselves of any inclination to be self-serving, or to perpetuate or exploit the weak, even if the weak seem to serve it, even if the weak have the outward appearance of being strong. Truth telling requires us to face and admit our own weaknesses, shortcomings and sins. As truth tellers we must be willing to reveal our own lack of knowledge, flawed logic, faulty intuitions, misunderstandings, inexperience, fears, doubts, fantasies, false hopes, egotistical dreams and uninformed or unsettled opinions. We must be willing to confess the abuses we have perpetrated or enabled and to acknowledge how we have been controlled, compelled and dominated by others. We must make these disclosures at the proper level of abstraction. It will not do for us to reveal the abuses of others with great specificity and then tolerate our own with great generality.

In other words, we must not only be forthright but evenhanded, not only factually accurate but intellectually honest. Our motives and agendas must be clear. We cannot allow ourselves to hide our hurt, our pain, our anger behind facades of composure and value-neutral rhetoric. Disinformation and nondisclosure merely postpone the moment of truth. If we wish to tell the truth, we must be willing to make fools of ourselves, rather than to cover our sins, gratify our pride and deflect humiliation. Our stories must be without melodrama, without romantic excess, without flawless characters, without deceptions. We must accept that, as truth tellers, we will often appear politically incorrect and less astute than our opponents.

Our dissent is further sanctified when we take seriously the views of others. Dissent, if it is to be effective, must follow the golden rule. It must treat others as it would be treated. It must listen, even when its opposition is unpleasant, confused, discordant and controlling. We cannot be like those in the free speech movement of the 1960s who, in the interest of the cause of free speech, suppressed the speech of their opponents. Listening is not easy. There is always the temptation to stop listening, to be defensive, to protect ourselves, to anticipate rejection by rejecting others first. Dissent does not allow us to withdraw from others. Dissent is to criticize, not to trivialize. Although dissent may sometimes be polemical, it must never be dishonest. True dissent is not possible if we associate only with those who are like us, who comfort us, who tell us what we want to hear. We cannot truly dissent if we cease to hear our loyal opposition. Dissent is holiest when it treats the views of others as it wishes its own views to be treated.

Dissent is further sanctified when it promotes genuine community. By telling truth and listening to others, we come to terms with our own experiences of abuse and the experiences of others; we break down facades; we take responsibility for our personal and our community shadows. Through dissent we provide each other with the common bread of authenticity and the common cup of charity. However, to take responsibility is not to take blame. No person can assume culpability for the freely chosen beliefs, acts and words of others. Those who do will invariably try to impose righteousness to avoid this vicarious guilt. Too many leaders, church leaders in particular, think this way. But leaders are not responsible for the wrongs of members; nor can members avoid personal responsibility by blindly following leaders. We are, however, all responsible for the well-being of the institutions to which we belong.

Such responsible dissent possesses the power to awaken consciousness, raise awareness, create paradigms, alter opinions, heal wounds and bring wholeness and holiness to our community. But it must be remembered that dissent raises the stakes. It is by nature confrontational. Even when carefully and artfully advanced, truth telling and dissent are usually not well received. One of the recurring mistakes of my life has been my silly belief that I would somehow endear myself to others by telling them what I believe to be the truth. Jesus, however, did not say that the truth would makes us well-liked. He said that 'the truth shall make you free' (John 8:32). What he did not say was that it would first make many madder than hell.

But this is just another reason why dissent is holy: it fosters accountability. To tell the truth is to call to account, to call to repent. This is unpleasant business. It invites reciprocity. It invites calls to repentance to be leveled in return. When this happens, we must listen to each other. If we do not, we risk entering a vicious cycle of mutual distrust and backbiting that will postpone hearing. Confrontation is often necessary to break this vicious cycle, especially if abusive individuals respond to calls to account with denial, with self-inflicted blindness. In such instances, confrontation is to dissenters what a scalpel is to a surgeon – it inflicts the wounds that heal.

Nevertheless, hurt feelings may be lessened if our call is not petty, trivial or mean-spirited – if the discourse of dissent is not directed against personal short-comings, petty sins and pet peeves but in favor of liberty and love and against the perpetuation or exploitation of powerlessness.

Dissent is sanctified when it is sacrificial, tactful, hopeful, charitable, clear, courageous and grace-filled. Jesus cautioned us to be as wise as serpents and as harmless as doves. Those church members who dissent vocally or publicly must be prepared for criticism and censure, for accusations of impurity, impiety and impropriety, for charges of disloyalty and even heresy. They must be prepared to lose their membership in the group. Let there be no mistake, these are highly punitive actions that, if not administered with the utmost care and the utmost consideration for fairness and due process, can become acts of abuse and even violence. Nevertheless, when these abuses come, dissent is made holier if abused dissenters do not become heartless, reckless or cruel; if they face abuse without returning abuse; if they remain fair and forthright in the face of denial; if they rely on the inner strength when abandoned by family, friends, co-workers, neighbors, fellow members and when threatened with the loss of jobs, careers and financial security. Clearly, dissent is not for everyone, nor is it necessary that everyone dissent. It is a spiritual vocation. Not all are called. But those who are will probably not find peace or fulfillment in any other way.

There is one more reason I believe dissent to be holy. It is, perhaps, the most important of all. I will make my point with a story: in 1412, there was born to French peasants of Domremy-la-Purcell, a girl – Jeanne to the French, Joan to us. When she was 12, she began to see and hear in vision St Michael, St Catherine and St Margaret. In 1429, during the Hundred Years' War, just when the English were about to capture Orleans, Joan was exhorted by these heavenly beings to save France. She presented herself to the king, and a board of theologians approved her claims. At the age of 17 and with no experience of combat, she – clad in armor, mounted on a charger and holding aloft a white banner emblazoned with the fleur-de-lis (the symbol of God's grace) – led the French in battle after battle to a stunning and decisive victory against the English. At the dauphin's coronation she held the place of honor beside him. Later, King Charles withdrew his support for further campaigns, but Joan continued, engaging the English at Compiegne, near Paris. There, captured by Burgundian soldiers, she was sold to the English, who turned her over to an ecclesiastical court at Rouen to be tried for heresy and sorcery. She underwent 14 months of interrogation. She was accused of consorting with demons, of wearing a man's apparel and of insubordination, but her most seditious crime, her most heinous sin, was that she believed that she was directly responsible to God and not to the Catholic church. She penitently confessed herself a sinner and was sentenced to life imprisonment rather than to death. But once in prison she set aside the counsels of the church and, in direct response to the revelations of God, resumed wearing men's clothes. For this she was condemned as a relapsed heretic and, on the 30th day of May 1431, in the Old Market Square of Rouen, Joan of Arc was burned at the stake. Twenty-five years later, the church retried her case and proclaimed her innocent. In 1920 she was canonized St Joan by Pope Benedict XV. Dissent is holy because it requires us to be ultimately responsible not to any earthly power but to God directly.

Earlier, I said that the sword is the cruciform symbol of dissent against cruelty, corruption, unhallowed control, against denial, false peace and forced silence. Jesus spoke the discourse of divine dissent against such evils in history. The spirit of all the great religions continues in the present to speak the same discourse in the hearts of many. Those who hear that voice, the voice of one crying in the wilderness, must give up all hope of banal material success, must take up – not the sword – but the cross and, like St Joan, find sanctuary in the sanctity of dissent.

Let me close with the same caution with which I opened: my arguments for understanding dissent as sanctified and the ways of dissent as hallowed are not confined to religious people or institutions of faith. The spirituality of everyday work, life and career argues that a nonreligious spiritual longing and motivation animates the working, academic, professional, family and civic lives of many who would not classify themselves as religious. Consequently, my words are intended both to penetrate the hearts of individuals and enfold the structures of institutions, whether religious or secular, private or public, with the call to find sanctuary in the sanctity of dissent.

NOTES

1. All citations of Biblical sources are from the King James version. Other citations are from the Book of Mormon, published by the Church of Jesus Christ of Latter Day Saints, 1972.
2. For an excellent set of essays on evil, see *The Hedgehog Review*, **2**, (2), Summer 2000. Especially useful are Jennifer Geddes's review of recent books on evil and the issue's annotated bibliography.

REFERENCES

Kenney, S. G. (1981–4), *Wilford Woodruff's Journal*, 9 vols, Midvale, UT: Signature Books.
Toscano, Paul (1995), *The Sanctity of Dissent*, Salt Lake City, UT: Signature Books.

11. Elevating dissent and transcending fear-based culture at war and at work

George Cheney and Daniel J. Lair

While I was fearing it, it came,
But came with less of fear,
Because that fearing it so long
Had almost made it dear.
(Dickinson, 1960: 558)

INTRODUCTION: TRYING TO CONNECT SOME DOTS

For us this chapter is both something we feel compelled to write and something about which we feel vexed and uncertain. We are drawn to the set of issues indicated in the title above because of what we have been noticing for some years about life in the US: that in a society that publicly values individual expression, active democratic participation and diversity of opinion, there is a great deal of fear about entertaining views outside whatever functions as, or is defined as, the mainstream set of positions at the time (see Lapham, 2004). This is as true at work as it is in politics and in the popular media. But 'fear' really doesn't capture the entire range of sentiments around us: alongside that emotion there seem to be feelings of apathy, alienation, resignation and retreat (Westen, 2007). In fact, these are the sentiments and stances that have been apparent to us and to others in a great many conversations in recent years, and in particularly since September 11, 2001.

Of course, many scholars and pundits bemoan the apparently shrinking public sphere, especially in terms of the lack of vibrancy of political discussions, even as they themselves in many instances bow to the conversion of news and opinion into entertainment. Think, for example, of the double entendre CNN Headline News uses to promote its overly energetic and earnest news commentary host Glen Beck: 'Glen's Got Issues'. Today, these trends are simply reinforced by the increased concentration of ownership of mainstream media. The lament about lack of engagement, or even sustained concentration, by those we used to call 'citizens' is especially true in the public, political sphere, although we wish to make connections here to the worlds of work and consumption as well. In fact, we would argue that work and consumption cannot any longer be divorced from a comprehensive analysis of political and democratic life. As Bruce Barry (2007) observes, so much of what passes for our public sphere today really is the world of work; thus, it makes sense to consider what is happening at work as well as in the explicitly political realm when we discuss dissent. As he puts it succinctly, 'Work is, in other words, where civic discourse happens for many people' (p. 24). Moreover, we find that the presumably apolitical nature of work and consumption is itself an important issue, particularly in an era when the citizen-as-consumer metaphor is increasingly pervasive (for example, Cohen, 2003).

None of this is to deny that many segments of our society are engaged civically in other ways: not only with their families and neighborhoods but also across geographic, class and racial borders. In this regard, 2008 Democratic presidential candidate Barack Obama's website (www.barackobama.com) encourages young people, especially, to write in with their stories of 'making a positive difference'. But when it comes to public debate and dialogue on issues of national and global importance, one can spend a day walking the streets of most major US cities and hear scarcely a mention of war, genocide, poverty, disease, the environment, the displacement of peoples or other issues of that magnitude. This silence of the citizenry is deafening, even as consumer activity continues undeterred (Peters, 2007). In the face of this lack of democratic vitality, few observers seem to be able to do anything other than throw up their hands.

Of course, any analysis of the breadth suggested here must take into account a host of factors, must be longitudinal to afford sound comparisons and must offer mountains of rigorously obtained empirical evidence. We should take into account the changes in the institutions of government, business, the media and social movement organizations in the past three decades or so. Also we should consider the many informal ways in which social capital (Putnam, 2000) has diminished in some areas but also, perhaps, increased in other arenas. Finally, we would need to consider the evolution of nationalism, in both its aggressive and defensive expressions, within the US and across the globe. We do not expect to accomplish that ambitious project in this chapter. However, what we would like to do here is to take the roles of dissent in politics and work life as starting points, widen the scope of discussion even further to include our roles as producers and consumers, draw upon some current examples (some discouraging, some hopeful), and then suggest some potential avenues for reinvigorating democracy through emergent and sometimes collective leadership. At the risk of ranging a bit too broadly with this commentary, we would still hope to provoke further thought and discussion about some aspects of our democratic society that are not always understood as being of a piece. The ultimate goal we have in mind is to learn how best to foster a stronger culture of peacemaking through dialogue in the contemporary United States (see Joseph, 2007). Thus, we see the allowance for and even encouragement of dissent in a variety of forums as essential to a reconsideration of not only of what democracy means at home but to how it applies more broadly on the global scene.

CASING THE PROBLEM OF DISSENT IN THE US TODAY

'Dissent' is a term that is tossed around in conversation and in the popular media without much attention to its meaning. One citizen may speak of dissent as 'dangerous' while someone else sports a bumper sticker that says, 'Dissent is patriotic'. Accounting for such a wide range of responses, we'd like here to define dissent broadly, following Sunstein (2003), as 'the rejection of the views that most people hold' (p. 7). Dissent in this role is the counterpoint to conformity, and each term depends on the other for its meaning and center of gravity. This formulation is particularly useful because it reminds us not to position dissent at just one point along the political spectrum. Dissent is in fact a relative term: the dissenting voice goes against the popular or at least the most vocal opinion. Dissent can therefore come from the Right or the Left, and we can even imagine it emanating from the Center, precisely because a discussion is thought to be permanently polarized when someone or some group speaks out assertively from 'the middle'. Dissent is relevant wherever there can be a group and therefore a majority opinion: in a family, in a workplace, in a high court, in an academic discipline, in a military establishment and, of course, in politics.

In her collection of US protest literature from the Revolutionary War to the present, Trodd (2006) observes that dissent takes a number of different forms, including opposition but also embracing appropriation and making effective use of collective memory. While the examples of 11 reform movements mentioned by Trodd would all be defined as broadly 'political', many of the lessons from them apply to more localized contexts such as work. For example, a key strategy for labor is to take symbols advanced by capitalism writ large and by management in particular – such as 'productivity' and 'fairness' and to advocate them in particular senses.

Dissent at work often involves the ability to challenge existing policies without fear of retribution and it can be encouraged or discouraged at the level of the organization's climate. Thus, it is important at the outset to consider dissent at work on continua that run from informal to formal and individual to collective (or organized). Thus, dissent may be something quite spontaneous, as in an unplanned 'eruption' by an employee at a meeting or methodical and well timed such as the labor organizing spectacles in the film *Bread and Roses* (O'Brien, 2000), about the case of Justice for Janitors in Los Angeles. In fact, as Jeffrey Kassing's research (for example, Kassing, in press) reveals, there has been insufficient attention to how the culture of a workplace or organization can suppress, tolerate or sometimes encourage dissent – and this applies to various expressions along the dimensions mentioned above. Too often, especially in US society, we attribute dissent only to individuals, failing to see how it is that their dissenting messages or activities are generated and sometimes supported if not only instigated. Such an attribution in fact perpetuates the challenge to dissenters in the workplace and elsewhere because the dissenter may be so easily isolated and her view neutralized. In talking about dissent, of course, one must be careful not to assume that she necessarily holds the right answer, the seeming 'voice in the wilderness', when choosing to stand outside the mainstream of opinion on whatever issue. Therefore, we are reminded of the need to place oneself in the shoes of both the dissenter and the holder of the view being criticized or exposed for scrutiny.

With that said, we would like to argue that the culture of dissent in the US has become largely associated with Left-leaning politics since 1980. We choose this date because with the beginning of 'the Reagan Revolution', conservative wings of the Republican Party managed to appropriate the symbol of revolution from its previous attachment to the Left. It's as if the glue holding one pair of symbols became weak, thereby allowing a major realignment (see Mouffe, 1999). Symbols in this sense are like pieces of Velcro that get stuck together for a while and then come unstuck. Certainly, there emerged a deliberate, aggressive reframing of conservativism at this time: rather than associating itself so much with tradition and the 'conservation' of the past, the Right presented itself as the engine of change, as the path to the future, all the while carrying the idea that the true spirit of the nation was animated by a close relationship between Christian religiosity and politics. Reagan's convention acceptance addresses and inaugural addresses of 1980 and 1984 were especially effective at merging the ideas of restoration of 'The Shining City on the Hill' with 'freedom' from governmental control (in the arenas of business and social welfare); with a return to fundamental social values and mores; and for progress beyond old, tired patterns (including things as diverse as the

Cold War, the welfare state and the counterculture's questioning of the US consumption and limits to growth). In this way, traditionalism was marshaled in the service of a broader revolutionary ideal, while great leadership was popularly understood as the ability to present a positive, inspiring vision where past, present and future are woven together in a single, monochromatic rhetorical fabric. Here we are reminded of the relative character of the notions of tradition and revolution as well: traditional with respect to what? Revolutionary *vis-à-vis* which structure or set of practices? (see Shils, 1981).

What this has meant for the US Left, in both symbolism and in terms of broader ideology, is that it has been cast as a worn-out throwback to the 1960s. This rhetorical casting shows up in lots of ways: from dismissive and derisive television portrayals of protests by 'ex-hippies' to shouts of 'unpatriotic' about efforts to pull US troops out of Iraq, even when a clear majority of US opinion in fact had swung that way by late 2006. In an earlier essay, Cheney and Lair (2004) described the ways in which political dissent in wartime is cast chiefly in two roles: either as 'marginal oddity' or as a genuine threat (to freedom, unity, democracy and other embracing values and value terms). Hackett and Zhao (1994) showed how these two different yet closely interrelated themes were dominant in news coverage of protesters during the Gulf War of 1991. In the first case, the dissenter is seen as quirky and irrelevant; in the second case, as threatening or even traitorous. In the news and sometimes even in the courtrooms, there have been dismissive treatments of something as seemingly innocuous as the sporting of a T-shirt or a bumper sticker with a political message. When the act is perceived as threatening, people have sometimes been expelled from shopping malls or fired from their jobs – in both cases with the justification that the dissenting activity occurred in a private domain (Barry, 2007).

Because of these two portrayals – which we might shorthand as 'bad' or 'mad' – many peace groups are reluctant to engage in activities such as street marches, vigils in front of government buildings, the singing of Vietnam-period protest songs and similar actions. In fact, as Maney *et al.*, (2005) argue, a variety of US peace movement organizations have found the need to assert nationalism – defined here as the elevation of nation-based identity over most others – in order to try to be heard. Nationalism accepts, even takes for granted, the primacy of the nation state and asserts a particular national identity as a key 'answer' to an array of important questions such as 'why kill?' (Lasswell, 1965). Nationalism, in one form or another, is such a shaping influence in contemporary US politics that a peace group risks irrelevance or worse by ignoring it. This means that some kind of (re)appropriation of nation-based symbols and imagery is essential to persuasiveness beyond the choir.

Debates over strategy in peace groups often result in their departing from traditional tactics yet replacing them largely with individual actions such as the writing of editorials, the construction of blogs and lobbying with Congressional staffers. In this way, dissent to some degree is self-censored, and opportunities for the further development of group solidarity are lost. In fact, some observers have questioned the overall effectiveness of going down the mainstream lobbying path, wondering if the antiwar groups themselves, such as Americans Against Escalation in Iraq, have taken some of the emotional energy and sense of urgency out of their own movement (Crowley, 2007). Meanwhile, the drumbeats of war coming regularly from Fox News (see the film *Outfoxed*: Greenwald, 2004) and allied media sources are simply bolstered by the absence of countervoices and countervisions.

RECOGNIZING SIMILARITIES AND DIFFERENCES BETWEEN TODAY AND THE VIETNAM ERA

Many people who remember that time (and many who don't) are heard to say these days, 'Why is the culture of dissent, of protest, so muted with respect to the Iraq War, when polls show public opinion overwhelmingly against continued US military involvement in that country?' As a *Los Angeles Times* commentator recently put it, while echoing many others, 'Why is there no outrage?' (Paddock, 2007). The answers are multiple and complex, but let's consider a bit of background in terms of how US citizens commonly understand or remember war.

Putting the US Civil War (1861–5) aside, there are three prevailing narratives that US citizens tell about wars in which the US has been engaged. The first is the story of independence, drawing primarily on the Revolutionary War (1776–83) as the chief example, but also referencing the War of 1812 (against Great Britain), during which the national anthem, 'The Star Spangled Banner', was written. This war is consistently linked to ideographs, or master symbols with material as well as ideological force (McGee, 1980), of independence, freedom and democracy. Those master value terms, of course, are seldom defined in any discussion, and they maintain their power and mystique for vast audiences precisely because of their lack of definition. The power of the symbolism surrounding the US Revolutionary War was invoked by the Reagan Administration during the 1980s in support of the Contras who were then battling the elected Marxist government of Daniel Ortega in Nicaragua. By calling the opposition forces 'Freedom Fighters', Reagan and his advisors sought to capture the positive associations with the winning side in the US War of Independence and further suggest that the battle, now as then, was against tyranny. By contrast, many Democrats in the US Congress referred to the same opposition forces as 'Rebels', thus invoking the losing and presumably unjust side in the US Civil War.

The second major narrative employed for understanding war in the US is World War II. US involvement in World War I, while significant, came comparatively late enough in the conflict, 1917, and talk of the 'Great War' was soon eclipsed by the second global conflict, often dated in the West from the invasion of Poland by Germany on 1 September, 1939 and ending with the dropping of the second atomic bomb, on Nagasaki, on 9 August, 1945. World War II unquestionably established the US as the leading world power, both militarily and economically, just as it led directly to the so-called Cold War between the US and the Soviet Union, 1945–91 (Vidal, 2003).

Of course, World War II is often cited as 'The Good War' (Terkel, 1984), a global resistance to fascism and military dictatorship, just as it is often advanced as a case against pacifism (in philosophical as well as practical discussions), because US involvement was ultimately deemed a necessity. In recent years, the aura surrounding US sacrifice and victory during World War II has been revived and strengthened by such films as *Saving Private Ryan* (Spielberg, 1998) and *Band of Brothers* (Hanks and Spielberg, 2001), as well as books such as *The Greatest Generation* (Brokaw, 1998). In certain ways, the honor, sacrifice and triumph of World War II has never been so salient since the war itself as during the post-9/11 period.

Importantly, these popular reflections and media events have occurred during the presidential administration of George W. Bush, a presidency largely defined by the terrorist attacks of 11 September, 2001 and by the responses to those events. In fact pundits and scholars were already calling Bush a one-term president when the terrorist attacks occurred, and Bush was recast in its aftermath as a strong, decisive leader. As some writers have observed (for example, Hasian, 2005; Ivie, 2005, 2007), Bush's appropriation of World War II analogies, terms and imagery began almost immediately after the attacks on New York and Washington, DC and helped to cast the response in terms of urgent action (as opposed to opportunity for reflection, or even a pause), warfare (in contrast with police action) and a struggle 'for civilization' (rather than a targeted, strategic operation). Further, this rhetorical build-up that stressed victimage, honor and urgency also concealed the imperial ambitions and record of the US government itself (Hartnett and Stengrim, 2006).

This rhetorical and political cover culminated in the launch of the 'War on Terror' in October 2001 – first with an attack on the Taliban-controlled failed state of Afghanistan – a conflict defined as transcending nations, groups, causes, conflicts and of course any defined period of time. With the

Senate's war authorization bill of October 2002 and the Patriot Act of 2001, the Administration essentially asked for *carte blanche* to wage war against 'terrorists' in the US as well as abroad. The recent revelation that less than a handful of senators actually read these bills in their entirety is testimony to how leaders as well as many citizens were swept up by the 'globalized' – or universal – framing of US responses to 9/11.

Mainstream media coverage (including by *The New York Times*, which later apologized for its meek acceptance of the Administration's position), advertising (such as that by General Motors), and popular culture writ large (perhaps best exemplified by a series of Top 40 Country hits, many of which reinforce nationalistic themes) all fell into line, with perhaps the most dramatic and consistently adopted iconic connection being expressed by the photo-cum-figurine of the three firefighters at Ground Zero and its deliberate association with the Battle of (and monument to) Iwo Jima. At least for a time, supporters of the Iraq War, following just 17 months on the heels of the invasion of Afghanistan, could exploit rather effectively the spirit of 'The Good War'.

By the summer of 2004, however, there were cracks in the foundation of support, and the Vietnam War analogy emerged in national-level discussion. This was first apparent in a significant way in the summer of 2004, following the revelations of the photos of torture and abuse from the Abu Ghraib prison in Baghdad and when it became apparent that what had been called the 'post-war' phase was really still the war itself. At that time, also, the 'selling of the Iraq War' based on faulty premises, such as the threat of possession of weapons of mass destruction, came into full view. Now there is widespread cynicism about the persuasive case made for the war, yet the nation remains somewhat divided on what to do about current US involvement, in part because of the fear of genocide in the wake of a complete allied troop pull-out. In fact many might observe in the wake of the Democratic victory in the 2006 midterm election a greater acceptance of dissent, evidenced perhaps most strongly by the 'defection' of key Republicans, like Maine Senator Olympia Snowe, on the issue of the war. We would argue, however, that this seemingly increased tolerance is marginal at best: while more political leaders are willing to argue now that the current war policy has been a failure, those whose dissenting voices call for intense inquiries as to how we got here or to hold policymakers accountable are still generally dismissed as either 'mad', 'bad', or both. In many ways, this increased tolerance for dissent parallels an increasingly mainstream negative reaction towards the Vietnam War by the early 1970s. A recent reminder of this came in the form of the firestorm of criticism received by former Democratic Senator Mike Gravel of Alaska when he suggested in a YouTube debate (23 July, 2007) that US soldiers were 'dying in vain' in Iraq.

The Vietnam War analogy, however, is a bit more complex, in part because of the competing interpretations or narratives about the war itself. Perhaps the prevailing one has been that the war was 'a bad mistake'; that the US intervened in what was essentially a civil war; that there was insufficient homegrown support for the US and its allies in Saigon; and that a great deal of blood was spilled unnecessarily as the US assumed the position of the previous colonial power in Southeast Asia, France. The competing account is that the war was a mistake not on moral grounds but on strategic ones, arguing that the US had every right to try to contain communist expansion in that part of the world but that US policy manifested an ambivalence about military involvement that ultimately doomed US operations, led to a humiliating final pull-out in April of 1975, and ensured the triumph of the communist forces based in Hanoi. From this standpoint, 'the spectre of Vietnam' refers to the felt need to restrain US military intervention because of the fear of 'another Vietnam'. Indeed, this was the stance of Oliver North and others as they defended their illegal activity in the Iran-Contra affair in 1986. The failed case of US military and humanitarian intervention in Somalia, seared into memory by the images in the film *Black Hawk Down* (Scott, 2001), only served to reinforce the view for some that the US needed to regain its military resolve and be as strategic as possible in contemplating military ventures.

Since the evocation of the Vietnam War analogy in the case of the Iraq War, the rhetorical battle between that image and the World War II image has continued. Debates over the Vietnam War's relevance and meaning surface as frequently in congressional hearings as they do on radio and television talk shows. In a widely discussed speech to the Veterans of Foreign Wars convention in Kansas City, MO (22 August, 2007), President Bush tried to 'reinscribe' in the US collective memory what might be called in this case the revisionist history of the Vietnam War, by saying 'one unmistakable legacy of Vietnam is that the price of America's withdrawal was paid by millions of innocent citizens'.

As we move to the domain of dissent and debate about the Iraq War, however, several features of the contemporary public landscape become evident. First, unlike during the years of US involvement in Vietnam (1962–75), there is no universal military conscription. Missing is the ongoing public tension over 'who will go?' that accompanied the lottery during the years 1969–73. In the case of Iraq, uncertainty remains about deployment for some regiments and reserve members, of course, but the armed forces do remain all-voluntary, as they have been since 1973. Second, in the present case, US economic and political interests are engaged because of the wealth of Iraqi oil. This leads segments of the population that would ordinarily oppose the war to question whether the US should fully disengage. Some of the same segments of the country fear the growth of the conflict into a regional war should the US leave altogether. As we write, questions are being raised about the wisdom of building a new US embassy in Baghdad at the cost of more than US$500 billion.

Third, mainstream media control over access to the images of war is much tighter now than during Vietnam – a war which, by most descriptions, 'came right into the living room' because of the freedom with which news correspondents followed soldiers into battle. The 'test' cases for decreased media access were the invasions of Grenada (1983) and Panama (1989). By the time of the first Gulf War (or Desert Storm) in 1991, the Pentagon was well-practiced at keeping correspondents in circumscribed areas – in that case, principally, in and around Riyadh, the capital of Saudi Arabia. Today we find the constraints on access to and portrayal of the images of war so thoroughgoing that the Administration has banned the videotaping of the coffins of fallen US soldiers as they are unloaded from planes at Andrews Air Force Base in suburban Maryland. Journalists who operate with any sort of military protection are 'embedded' with the troops under the current Pentagon rules, meaning that their freedom to roam and freedom to 'view' are sharply circumscribed (Danner, personal correspondence, 2006). As a result of all these policies, the US citizen, the US television viewer, is largely 'protected' from carnage. (Meanwhile, films such as *300* (Snyder, 2006) which features abduction, torture and death are part of mainstream public fare.) All of these developments are intensified by the level of concentration of ownership in the mainstream US media (see McChesney, 2000).

Fourth, it may well be argued that university students as well as many other segments of the population are so busily engaged in their careers, families and personal lives that there is little room for engagement in the public sphere. Thus, we should acknowledge the effects of sheer increase in the pace of life: what we might call a *de facto* conservatism, taken in the traditional sense, among both politically inclined and apolitical people. That is to say, most people have little time to contemplate how to engage the public sphere let alone become part of it in any interactive way.

Fifth and finally, the dissent surrounding the Vietnam War was encouraged, in both material and symbolic terms, by a decade of dissent on issues of civil rights: a social movement which not only provided opportunities for many of the future war protesters to learn about advocacy but also fostered an anti-establishment ethos which encouraged many to ask critical questions regarding multiple issues. Dissent related to the current war has no such recent history to draw from. In fact, conformity seems to predominate now in that we may identify a growing cultural reluctance to criticize policies that are strongly associated with the idea of 'American' (Coy, personal correspondence, 2007). The equation of 'support our troops' with support for policy only strengthens the protective shell over the failed US policy in Iraq, even at a time when public support for the war is at a low ebb. While this claim is more difficult to substantiate than the others, it becomes important for consideration as we explore the cultural-political role of fear below.

PENETRATING THE FEAR-BASED CULTURE OF THE CONTEMPORARY US

First of all, what would or how could we describe US culture as fearful? After all, the US has had a stable democracy since 1865, has been an industrial giant since the 1880s, and has been clearly a superpower since 1945. In fact, since the fall of the Soviet Union in 1991, the US has been regularly described as *the* superpower, at least in terms of military and economic reach. What is seldom mentioned is that the bipolar structure of the Cold War itself may have restrained some of the imperialistic tendencies of the US government just as it perhaps contained extreme expressions of religious and ethnic nationalism we see today.

When asked about the question of fear, many observers would point to the watershed event of September 11, 2001. The terrorist attacks in New York, Washington, DC and eastern Pennsylvania (where the hijacked flight United 93 crashed) indeed represented the first major act of violence by a group of foreigners on US soil since Pearl Harbor on 7 December, 1941. This precedent in itself, of course, helped to lend support to the analogy between the US response to 9/11 and World War II. However, the mere parallel cannot substitute for careful analysis of the similarities and differences.

One of the most powerful segments of the film *Bowling for Columbine* (Moore, 2002), a film released the year after the 9/11 attacks, was not a bit on the roles of guns and bombs in the US but rather an entertaining but poignant part on fear. Director Michael Moore was walking through a poor neighborhood of East Los Angeles with psychologist Barry Glassner (1999), author of the *Culture of Fear*. With his trademark showmanship, Moore observed that both men felt quite safe in a presumably – and famously – dangerous neighborhood. With that there was a transition to a series of news stories on fear over the years – from communism to drugs to killer bees to identity theft to you name it. Glassner's thesis is not that these things deserve to be dismissed, but rather that, generally speaking, US citizens are fearing the wrong things and investing far too much energy and time in problems that pale by comparison to broader social, economic and environmental concerns. It's as if the 'Martian invaders' are always coming, explains Glassner, priming people for the selling of fear by politicians, media representatives and anyone who has the cultural stage for a moment. In fact, the readiness to externalize fear leads many US citizens ever to be looking out for enemies on the horizon. Glassner's (1999) analysis leads us to a series of propositions about fear in the contemporary United States.

First, many fears are exaggerated; in many cases, we fear the wrong things; the imagined scenario substitutes for analysis. These are in fact three interrelated points that have as their inspiration Glassner's (1999) book. The folk and political doctrine of American exceptionalism – expressed in one form as 'It can't happen here' – only reinforces this feeling, as has been in evidence since 9/11 (see the collection of essays in Scraton, 2002). At the interpersonal, day-to-day level, talk of threats and fears can exaggerate our view of real danger (as with crime on television); alternatively, excessive portrayals of violence can numb us (as with video games). It's not that we should look at a particular news report or video game or TV program; rather, we should look at many messages and their cumulative effects, over time. This is what is meant by the 'cultivation' of a skewed worldview through exposure to the media, as opposed to the assumption of direct and immediate effects of seeing a particular message containing violence or having some other feature (Gerbner, 1994).

Second, politics and policies often drum up and then 'satisfy' fears, as with states of emergency followed by the 'supplying' of security (Lasswell, 1965 [1935]). The temptation to scapegoat is one of the most powerful forces in human relations – 'We are never so unified as when we have a *goat* in common' (Burke, personal correspondence, 1987). In conditions of panic, of emergency, we may surrender all reason if we find an appealing enemy. And, this temptation to scapegoat is all the more forceful when it becomes a substitute for mortification, thus functioning as a displacement of guilt (Burke, 1969 [1950]). In every war since the US Civil War, the enemy has been portrayed as both bad and mad: that is, as evil and as irrational (Ivie, 1980). This is extraordinary, when we consider the apparent dissimilarities between and among these conflicts. The same is true for most other nations in the build up and execution of war. This kind of simplistic rhetoric paves the way for dehumanizing the other side. Once that happens, of course, there is 'no room' for dissent, as was articulated by the Bush Administration and many supporters after the invasion of Iraq in March 2003. Even in the case of World War I, which the US entered so reluctantly in 1917, many war protesters were tried for sedition.

Third, at the level of public discussion and public policy, if an emergency occurs or is created, then the leader of the country is in a good position to try to 'help' by responding to or eliminating the danger. The film *Wag the*

Dog (Levinson, 1997) portrays well how this is accomplished – in that case, through a manufactured crisis (see Lipman-Blumen, Chapter 3 this volume, and Bostdorff, 1994, on created crises). In the case of the Bush Administration, the danger of terrorism is now portrayed quite literally as 'everywhere', and the war on terrorism is seen as unending. This specter looms so large in US political discourse and consequently in the public mind that the analysis of actual odds of being killed or wounded in a terrorist attack, *vis-à-vis* other less spectacular but in reality far more threatening dangers, is obscured. Consider the fact that – assertions that we live in an age of terror notwithstanding – since the late 1960s, about as many US citizens have died from terrorist attacks as have died from such statistical oddities as lightning strikes or peanut allergies, even including the deaths of 9/11 (Mueller, 2005). So, we can have a permanent state of emergency, which can be used to justify even more executive powers and the suspension of individual rights.

In this case, too, the president comes across as the sole savior of the people who knows how to react decisively to the crisis (again, see Lasswell, 1965 [1935]). Bush is, as he has insisted more than once, 'The Decider'. In this context, 'security' is treated in a short-term military way, obscuring broader issues of peace, justice and equality that provide the foundation for lasting security (Cheney and Vogt, 2003). In fact even the role of domestic police forces is overlooked, so single-minded has been the focus on war as an instrument of restored, or at least bolstered, security.

Fourth, the tendency to scapegoat is heightened, as the body political and body social imagine all sorts of inside and outside threats. Boundary issues in the psychological as well as geographical and political senses are important for all nations. With much of the current rhetoric over both terrorism and immigration in the West, however, a sense of violation of boundaries has been intensified (see Douglas, 1996). For many citizens and leaders, the US is very much like a body that protects itself from invaders – real, potential and invented – and is unfortunately prone to see almost anything as a threat. A good example of this is Cuba, the tiny island nation of ten million people, that is regularly depicted as a menace just off the Florida coast – almost like a needle that can penetrate the skin of the nation. This psychological-geographic-political casting of Cuba was well portrayed with 1960s-era footage of 'the Cuban threat' in Michael Moore's film *Sicko* (Moore, 2007). The idea of the constant but unexamined threat was revisited as Fidel Castro's health deteriorated in July 2007, and his brother Raúl began to take the reins of power.

Fifth, even within a wartime situation, the ability of people to retreat into an apolitical consumer space is noteworthy. *The Onion*, a popular satire newspaper, captured it all well with a mock headline just three weeks after 9/11: 'A Shattered Nation Longs To Care About Stupid Bullshit Again' (2001). On the serious side, this comment was supported by Bush's remarks at a press conference on 9/12: 'Now, the American people have got to go about their business. We cannot let the terrorists achieve the objective of frightening our nation to the point where we don't – where we don't conduct business, where people don't shop' (Bush, 2001). Bush's exhortation implicitly invokes the World War II narrative here, as well, through a subtle (though likely unintentional) allusion to the efforts of the 'home front': after all, the 'Greatest Generation' included not only those who put their lives on the line on the battlefields of Europe and the Pacific, but also the efforts of the men and women back in the US, heroically working to maintain the industrial engine supporting the war effort, as well as sacrificing their 'normal' lives through the rationing of gasoline and food. Bush's call, though, offers a curious reversal of this narrative, encouraging helpless-feeling US citizens to fight the war on terror by preserving their sense of normalcy.

It's not that seeking normalcy is bad; it's missing the connection between something like lifestyle and politics – for example the connection between rampant, even ramped up, consumption and global issues. 'Normal life' is defined *as* consumption (Miles, 1998), and political engagement is not seen as part of the sphere of individual conscience, concern or activity, except to the extent in some quarters that consumption is politicized (see Kendall *et al.*, 2007). Ironically, the activities of consumption also take individuals into the realm of fear – or attempts to assuage it – in an endless pursuit of the satisfaction of goals for which consumption cannot be effective. The essential messages of all advertising are 'You're not okay'; 'Things are not good'; 'You need this stuff' (Ewen, 1976; Kilbourne, 1999). Consumption and work are connected on the issue of fear as well, with many workers trapped in what economist Schor (1992) has dubbed 'the insidious cycle of work and spend', needing their income to sustain their habits of consumption, and adjusting their habits of consumption in accordance with their income level. Trapped in a cycle of debt, fear of the loss of a job exerts a powerful force on US workers. Now combine these ideas with the prevailing use of fear in the news: consumption becomes the objective, as well as the vehicle, but also the problem for the individual.

We may in fact observe a type of 'discursive closure' (Deetz, 1992) in a circle of relationships between issues and actions. Individuals are urged to assuage societal fears which are, at a deeper level, linked to individual fears (and their unsatisfactory psychological resolution). And this is one of the primary ways in which the challenge of dissent is so much more vexing now than it was, say, during the late 1960s or early 1970s in the US. Consumption has become an entire sphere of activity, which stands alongside family, work and politics (or what's left of the last domain). Politics, for many people, is reduced to the status of a style or fashion – and this is never so clear as in many young people's characterizations of feminism as a lifestyle choice more than as a political commitment.

Consumption, though an embracing set of activities with all sorts of implications for policy, nationally and globally, is largely depoliticized (Schor, 1999), except for some pockets of socially conscious consumption. Still, consumption becomes sacralized at the level of national culture in the vaunted expression of 'the American way of life'. To the extent that dissenters, on the streets or in the workplace, obstruct consumption ('normal activity') and an ever-expanding market for all ('the American promise'), they are by definition today 'un-American' or at the very least odd. Moreover, we would argue that consumerist thinking seeps into nearly every corner of our culture, showing its influence in the ways people get 'annoyed' by political protests to the commodification of war itself. The inability of anti-war efforts to get many people to think seriously about the horrors of war and to engage war in terms of its consequences is wrapped up with cultural trends that we consider next.

ACKNOWLEDGING THE COEXISTENCE OF A POLITICS OF STYLE AND A (SECRET) FONDNESS FOR AUTHORITARIANISM AND MILITARISM

This is a complex argument that helps to explain the simultaneous existence of a culture of fear, unquestioned respect for certain kinds of authority and a style that is both apparently apolitical and *de facto* politically charged in its militaristic, often aggressive overtones. For support for these ideas and their interconnections, we turn to a fascinating and insightful essay by Thomas de Zengotita (2003) in *Harper's* magazine called 'The romance of empire and the politics of self-love'. De Zengotita was writing just three months into the Iraq War and one month after Bush's astoundingly premature 'Mission Accomplished' announcement. The author muses about when a full-throated expression of empire first came to the fore in US politics and in the popular media. (This question is different, then, from the matter of when the US *became* an empire in practical terms.) de Zengotita then sidelines this question, but explores the interconnections of images of wartime confidence in contexts as diverse as action figures and comments by some political and military leaders. While his perspective is difficult to summarize in a few sentences, de Zengotita's treatment of emotional attachments to a supremely confident (yet uninformed) president and to the sense of going to battle in a titanic struggle against 'forces of evil' bring to the fore questions about the politics of style and aggression in an age when so many of our popular stories (from films such as *Star Wars* to *Alien* to television's *24*) reinforce the glamour of violence, 'gear' and unmitigated triumph. What is kept from view or largely stylized is the carnage, adds de Zengotita, making it possible for many citizens – especially men – to crystallize and then defeat their fears through vicarious participation of what promises to be another 'Greatest Generation'. Or, so things seemed to be in mid-2003, before Abu Ghraib, before the 'insurgency', before all-out civil war, before a widely recognized disaster.

de Zengotita's (2003) essay thus adds to a powerful and important literature on the glorification of war, including J. Glenn Gray's (1959) classic *Warriors*, which explains at the level of the foxhole the exhilaration and the camaraderie of the battlefield.

Interestingly, neither President Bush nor any members of his inner circle (former Secretary of State Colin Powell was the exception) have actually participated in battle, but their confidence in leading the nation in that direction, with largely manufactured evidence of weapons of mass destruction, is undeterred and seemingly untouched by the horrors of war or its limits as an instrument of foreign policy.

A considerable proportion of battle-tested generals through history and across nations have been distressed by the ease with which new calls to war can be issued and followed by leaders. This is true with respect to the interpersonal bonds forged in battle, the emotional excitement of unity in opposition to a common enemy, and the emotionally charged national purpose that arises at times of military engagement. This is precisely why Chris Hedges (2002) entitled his popular book *War Is a Force That Gives Us Meaning*. He wanted to make clear the powerful emotional bonds that can draw together groups at time of war, especially when they are searching for unity and direction in other domains.

At least three forces are at work to effect what Christopher Coker (2004) calls 'the reenchantment of war'. First is the idea that war can be fought on a limited scale and, at least for the victor, result in contained casualties and destruction in both military and civilian spheres. Here, we might consider the considerable unease generated by the more than 3700 US military casualties in the Iraq War at the time of writing. This is a distressing figure to be sure, but one which is relatively minor compared to the allied losses in other US wars, save the first Gulf War. That these concerns exist demonstrate the strength of the contemporary expectation that wars might be fought casualty-free (at least on 'our side'). Let's call this the 'surgical strike' thesis. Second, is the way technology has created a whole new spectacle of war that is at once present and distant: as in the case of following the lights of bombers and bombs over Baghdad in the dark of night. It was, in fact, such videogame-like imagery that lay behind Baudrillard's (1995) tongue-in-cheek observation that 'the Gulf War did not take place', at least for its spectators or consumers in the Western world. Third, is the continued invocation of the mythic status of the warrior and warrior culture, which is potent on both the interpersonal and the mass-mediated levels (Ehrenreich, 1997). This is evident in the imagery of recent armed forces recruiting advertisements, which tend to downplay careerism and highlight heroism. In all three ways, war is made more than just palatable – it is actually seen as desirable.

From the standpoint of leadership as well as citizenship what is most distressing is how these trends make war less of a conscious choice for the US population than before. War itself becomes taken for granted – accepted as part of realism (Dunn, 2005) – and any war in which the US is engaged is then *de facto* consider a righteous cause. Because neither the horrors nor the repeat performances are examined as parts of a larger pattern, the circular justifications continue: 'we are at war because we have to be, and we are at war and so it is right'. As long as the glamor of it is sufficiently represented in popular culture and there is no vibrant debate over policy, it is difficult to mount credible opposition to war with the capacity to influence policy until well into a conflict – as is the case with the Iraq War. In fact, the secret – and often not-so-secret romance with war, its symbols, and its narrow construal of masculinity – afflicts other domains of society.

PARALLEL FRAMINGS OF DISSENT AT WORK AND WAR

Despite the widespread use of the war metaphor in US business, including references such as 'destroying the competition', one does not ordinarily think to draw connections between the treatment of dissent in wartime and the treatment of dissent at work. However, we believe that the parallels are more than accidental or trivial. For example, these parallels are evidenced clearly by Rice's above-discussed call for US citizens to return to work, and so on as normal in the wake of 9/11. Consider as well the manner in which the current war in Iraq can be seen as a partial result of not only a lack of effective dissent in the public sphere but also a lack of dissent in the 'private' sphere of the workplaces of the many governmental agencies that were gathering and interpreting intelligence in the years, months and weeks before the war. Only now are many of these pressures to conform coming to light, in part through 'tell-all' biographies of life inside the Bush Administration, such as the narratives of former White House advisor Richard Clarke (2004) and former Secretary of the Treasury Paul O'Neill (Suskind, 2004).

We find these parallels somewhat ironic, given that for several decades, scholars have been writing about the need to infuse democratic, participatory politics into the arena of work in the US (see for example, Pateman, 1970). Chief among the arguments in favor of this move is the idea that democratic practice ought not to be limited to the public sphere or the public sector and that employers should not then be able to rest entirely on the right of the 'at will' employment doctrine (enshrined by the US Supreme Court since the 1880s) to proscribe dissent. This idea has both formal and informal applications when it comes to work practices and is one of the most important linkages of the political reality to the domain of work: the argument that vigorous informed discussion and debate should be a feature of both arenas. Politics is spreading to the workplace, but not quite as Pateman envisioned. Rather, political discussion at work is seen as something to be regulated by employers, by appealing to court decisions in their favor and the at will employment doctrine, just as they do in arguing against unions and for employee conformance to rules of behavior (Barry, 2007).

Most notable is the right of workers to organize themselves as a union and to represent their interests collectively *vis-à-vis* ownership and management. This is not the place for an extended discussion of the state of union organizing in the US (or elsewhere), but it does bear mention that the dramatic decline in union membership from the early 1970s until very recently (with some specific labor organizing successes since 1998) has been caused in no small part by aggressive union-busting campaigns of corporations, collusion by government beginning with the Reagan Administration's firing of striking air traffic controllers in 1981, and by persistently negative cultural associations with labor bosses – combined with increasing identification by young people with 'management'. The politics of casting labor negatively on the US national scene offers a cultural foundation for employers' union-busting efforts.

Amid an array of books that have heralded a new 'participatory', 'team-oriented' and 'entrepreneurial' workplace in the past two decades, some observers have noted that in certain ways a harsher reality of work continues. This reality includes instances of authoritarian rule, the surrender of basic rights such as free speech, aggressive and sometimes brutal union-busting tactics and a type of participation that demands even more sweat equity by the worker. While there are indeed shining examples of corporate social responsibility in terms of treatment of employees (see for example, ARUP Laboratories, Patagonia, REI and other companies commonly featured in corporate social responsibility and best places to work lists), the complete picture of work today does not reveal the sharp breakpoints from past unenlightened practices that histories of management and CEOs themselves like to tout (Cloud, 2001, 2005).

In fact, as we have argued elsewhere (Cheney and Lair, 2004), the difference between the 'rhetoric' and the 'reality' of issues such as employee voice, empowerment and participation can be productively viewed in terms of the parallel rhetorical treatment of dissent in both the corporate and political arenas. Here we would highlight three broad similarities. First, we observe that in both the world of work and the world of politics, dissent is frequently cast as disruptive, subversive and potentially damaging to the dissenter. So, for example, politicians are frequently taken to task for advancing positions which diverge too far from the mainstream, as was the case on a recent Sunday morning talk show, where eight of 12 political commentators argued that Barack Obama was making a mistake by not staying 'positive' and instead directly attacked chief rival Hillary Clinton's position on the war (Matthews, 2007, 29 July). Similarly, Smith (2001) argues, given the social pressures of the meritocratic structure of the career 'ladder' in the corporate world, many workers fear negative consequences to their career for speaking up. In both cases, would-be dissenters are cast as facing significant personal costs for their disruptive behaviors.

A second rhetorical parallel between treatments of dissent in politics and work rests on the manner in which dissent is cast as necessarily anti-progress. Here the central notion is that plans already underway should not be challenged or altered in any significant manner. Consider, for example, the Bush Administration's recent and continuing calls for questioning of the Iraq war policy to cease until the 2007 troop 'surge' is given a chance to work, a pattern which has been repeated several times regarding the introduction of new plans to bring Iraq under control. Similarly, Zorn *et al.*, (1999) have noted that managerially-driven change initiatives are rarely reconsidered after they have been initiated, regardless of their reception or measurable outcomes. Here dissent, rather than being viewed as an opportunity to re-evaluate current policies while in progress, is cast instead as necessarily a 'fly in the ointment', impeding the ability of such policies to achieve their assumedly inevitable potential.

A third significant parallel is the manner in which dissent is framed as an inappropriate response to apparently new situations. Here dissent is dismissed with what Burke (1969 [1945]) would term a 'scenic warrant': dissent is simply something that is not appropriate given current circumstances. Consider the manner in which the weeks and months 'post-9/11' were cast as an entirely new era, one in which the value of security took precedence over the kinds of civil liberties which support dissent in the name of guarding against future terrorist attacks. In the world of work, the specter of the 'New Economy' functions in much the same manner, casting as obsolete the need for organized labor against the need for global competitiveness (Cloud, 2001). These rhetorical tactics represent strategies by which dissent is discouraged and contained inside of the political and work spheres. Dissenters are cast not only as nay-sayers but as people who are holding back progress toward a goal that is presumed to be above reproach.

These parallels take on a heightened currency, however, in light of a disturbing trend in which contemporary workplaces are seen suppressing dissent not only concerning internal issues regarding the workplace, but also regarding external, political issues as well. Barry (2007) chronicles several surprising – and chilling – ways in which speech has become less free in the contemporary US workplace. Barry cites two different but interrelated examples to show how broadly restrictions on free speech at work have been applied by employers and sometimes by the courts. In one 2004 case an Alabama factory worker was told to remove her John Kerry bumper sticker from her car or be fired – one of several similar instances around the US during that election (see Noah, 2004). What made this case particularly noteworthy, however, was that at the same time, the CEO was including pro-Bush commentaries in envelopes accompanying paychecks. In another case a Texas stockbroker was told by his employer to curtail his off-work political activism against affirmative action or risk dismissal. He ultimately quit his job, citing pressure not only from his employer but also from the City of Houston, with whom his employer had contracts. These cases are interesting not only because of how free speech and employer/employee rights are construed but also in terms of how the domains of work and politics are defined. They remind us even more of how blurred these spheres have become and of the need to analyze and protect options for dissent in the public sphere broadly conceived.

Importantly, Barry sees one of the severest areas of limits to civil rights in the workplace to be political expression, in addition to corporate campaigns against labor organizing. The two trends go hand in hand, Barry argues, because of the ways the courts have supported the positions of employers in recent decades: 'Limits on free speech go hand in hand with an absence of due-process rights and just-cause protections in the American workplace' (Barry, 2007: 7). What we see then are a series of parallel strategies operating across several domains, seeking to discourage dissent in the first place and, failing that, attempting to quarantine dissent in order to diminish its effectiveness. These parallel treatments of dissent across the public spheres of both the political arena and the workplace are similar not only at the level of strategy, but also in terms of their consequences for the public at large. That is, we have to wonder whether a cultural-political environment more tolerant of dissent might have helped us to avoid political and economic disasters such as the Iraq War and the wave of Enron-like scandals in the early 2000s, where dissenting whistleblowers emerged only after too much damage had been done. The challenge, then, is to find ways to promote and encourage not only acts of individual dissent, but also a greater tolerance and respect for dissent itself.

EMBRACING DISSENT AND TRANSCENDING FEAR

If fear is seen as a broad cultural pattern in the US, then wide-ranging cultural solutions cannot be ignored. In fact, a cultural approach seems essential, given that the dismissal of dissent in the political arena is largely cultural in the first place, couched in a consistent pattern of rhetorical tropes and strategies rather than directly codified into law. And in an era where 49 of the 50 states (Montana is the lone exception) adopt a policy of at will employment, often employees have no legal recourse to protect their right to dissent in the workplace. Accordingly, what we need are strategies that can raise the profile – in both quantitative and qualitative terms – of dissent in politics and in the workplace. Let's consider a few such potential strategies:

1. At the community level, hold workshops on 'thinking about the unthinkable' (Borgenicht *et al.*, 2007). That is, to the extent possible within areas of expertise, help to bring to light the processes involved in being fearful about the open discussion of a pressing social issue.
2. For the traditional media, write editorials about 'under-covered' issues and positions on issues (see for example, the *UTNE Reader*). For the alternative media, do what can be done to distribute commentaries such as 'the ten most important stories not covered last year'.
3. In terms of popular culture, support efforts to create documentaries that deal not only with specific issues that are being obscured or minimized but also that talk about processes of conformity, dissent and the suppression of dialogue and debate.
4. Within politics, support even long-shot candidates whose message has not been honed by myriad handlers and who speak frankly on issues such as the war, economy, health care and education.
5. At and around work, insist on the rights of employees to express their views, whenever you have the opportunity to speak on this matter and especially to influence managers, administrators and CEOs.
6. Do what you can to turn around the unfair characterizations of organized labor that provide tacit support for efforts at union busting that have prevailed for more than a quarter-century. In a related vein, support workers' calls for justice in your local community.

7. Be aware of how fears are exploited by some leaders and media com-
    mentators on issues as diverse as health care reform, immigration
    reform and alternative energy development.

We present this list certainly not as an exhaustive, or even a privileged,
series of strategies for promoting dissent in the political and work arenas.
While these strategies range from engaging in acts of dissent directly to
finding ways to promote others' dissent, what they share in common is a
desire to overcome or at least offer credible alternatives to the cultural and
ideological forces seeking to suppress dissent. Restoring dissent's long
democratic tradition requires considerable effort not only to dissent, but
also to promote the idea of dissent itself, from the highest levels of leadership in our major institutions to informal, localized grassroots movements.

EPILOGUE: LEADING TOWARD DEMOCRACY WITHOUT INSECURITY

The US today is perhaps exceptional for the scope and intensity of fear that
exists within its borders at the same time that many of its leaders and citizens insist on the nation's supreme status on the world stage. We are
reminded by this condition of the powerful bond between personal insecurity and nationalism, a connection that was first explored in depth between
the two world wars by Harold Lasswell (1965 [1935]). These fears exercise
constraints on creative thinking at work, on possibilities for collaboration
in communities and on transformation of international tensions. Taken
together, these fears hinder the full expression of democracy itself, inas-
much as dissenting opinions are suppressed or are not even considered.
Leadership that not only tolerates but actually encourages dissent is vitally
needed in all arenas of public life.

The trick is to harness not only public energy but also public imagination, especially in light of the sheer pace of life, the mountains of distrac-
tions and the base appeals that infuse advertising and popular culture.
When the idea of 'citizenship' seems to college students like a quaint relic
of a distant past, we know that a great deal of cultural groundwork needs
to be laid for a revival of democratic spirit. Part of that revival must come
from captivating experiences themselves: meaningful work practices,
effective political campaigns and satisfying service activities. But, when the
rush to war and blind obedience to a political leader's latest proclamation
are so seductive, there must be diverse counter-messages to deflect people
from aggressively pursuing the chimera of total security (Ivie, 2007). As
Berry and Duncan (2003) write, the official definitions of 'terrorism' and

'security' are far too restrictive, limiting people's visions not only of what is but also of what is possible.

REFERENCES

Agamben, Giorgio (2005), *State of Exception*, Chicago, IL: University of Chicago Press.

Armour, Edward B. (2003), 'US workers are being denied their right to unionize', *The Salt Lake Tribune*, 8 December, A-11.

Atleson, James (2003), ' "An injury to one": transnational labor solidarity and the rule of domestic law,' in J. A. Gross (ed.), *Workers' Rights as Human Rights*, Ithaca, NY and London: Cornell University Press, pp. 160–82.

Baudrillard, Jean (1995), *The Gulf War Did Not Take Place*, tr. by Paul Patton, Bloomington, IN: Indiana University Press.

Barry, Bruce (2007), *Speechless: The Erosion of Free Expression in the American Workplace*, San Francisco, CA: Berrett-Koehler.

Berry, Wendell and David James Duncan (2003), *Citizens Dissent: Security, Morality and Leadership in an Age of Terror*, Great Barrington, MA: The Orion Society.

Billig, Michael (1995), *Banal Nationalism*, London: Sage

Bird, Kai and Martin J. Sherwin (2006), *American Prometheus: The Triumph and Tragedy of J. Robert Oppenheimer*, New York: Knopf.

Borgenicht, Louis, George Cheney, Mary Dickson and Annette Rose (2007), 'Thinking about the unthinkable and discussing the undiscussable', March, Utah Humanities Council Grant, Salt Lake City.

Bostdorff, Denise (1994), *The Presidency and the Rhetoric of Foreign Crisis*, Columbia, SC: University of South Carolina Press.

Bovard, James (2004), 'Quarantining dissent: how the Secret Service protects Bush from free speech', *The San Francisco Chronicle*, 4 January, D-1.

Brokaw, Tom (1998), *The Greatest Generation*, New York: Random House.

Burke, Kenneth (1969 [1945]), *A Grammar of Motives*, Berkeley, CA: University of California Press.

Burke, Kenneth (1969 [1950]), *A Rhetoric of Motives*, Berkeley, CA: University of California Press.

Bush, George W. (2001), the President's news conference, 11 October, accessed 17 August, 2007 at www.presidency.ucsb.edu/ws/index.php?pid=73426.

Cheney, George (2007), 'What do we mean when we say "productivity", "participation" and "satisfaction" at work?', remarks made at the What's the Economy For, Anyway? Conference, 6 October, Washington, DC.

Cheney, George and Daniel J. Lair (2004), ' "Following" and leading dissent in US politics and labor', in Nancy S. Huber and J. Thomas Wren (eds), *Building Leadership Bridges 2004*, College Park, MD: International Leadership Association, pp. 115–29.

Cheney, George and L. D. Vogt (2003), 'On framing for progressive social change', unpublished manuscript, University of Utah Department of Communication, Salt Lake City, UT.

Clarke, Richard (2004), *Against All Enemies*, New York: Free Press.

Cloud, Dana (2001), 'Laboring under the sign of the new', *Management Communication Quarterly*, **15**, 268–78.

Cloud, Dana (2005), 'Fighting words: labor and the limits of communication at Staley, 1993–1996,' *Management Communication Quarterly*, **18**, 509–42.

CNN.com (2004), 'Man fired for heckling Bush', 21 August, accessed 20 August, 2007 at www.cnn.com/2004/US/South/08/21/heckler.fired.ap/index.html.

Cohen, Lizabeth (2003), *A Consumer's Republic: The Politics of Mass Consumption*, New York: Random House.

Coker, Christopher (2004), *The Future of War: The Re-enchantment of War in the Twenty-first Century*, Oxford, UK: Blackwell.

Crowley, Michael (2007), 'Can lobbyists stop the war?' *The New York Times Magazine*, 9 September, pp. 54–9.

Deetz, Stanley (1992), *Democracy in an Age of Corporate Colonization*, Albany, NY: SUNY Press.

De Zengotita, Thomas (2003), 'The romance of empire and the politics of self-love', *Harper's Magazine*, July, pp. 31–40.

Dickinson, Emily (1960), *The Complete Poems of Emily Dickinson*, Boston, MA: Little, Brown.

Douglas, Mary (1996), *Natural Symbols: Explorations in Cosmology*, London: Routledge.

Dunn, David J. (2005), *The First Fifty Years of Peace Research*, London: Ashgate.

Ehrenreich, Barbara (1997), *Blood Rites: Origins and History of the Passions for War*, New York: Henry Holt.

Ewen, Stuart (1976), *Captains of Consciousness*, New York: McGraw-Hill.

Gerbner, George (1994), *The Killing Screens: Media and the Culture of Violence*, Northampton, MA: Media Education Foundation.

Glassner, Barry (1999), *The Culture of Fear*, New York: Basic Books.

Gravel, Mike (2007), 'Are the troops dying in vain?', 23 July, accessed 20 August, 2007 at www.youtube.com/watch?v=Hu_bm9pmpig.

Gray, J. Glenn (1959), *Warriors: Reflections on Men in Battle*, New York: Harcourt, Brace.

Greenwald, Robert (producer) (2004), *Outfoxed*, film, Culver City, CA: Brave New Films.

Hackett, Robert A. and Yueh-zhi Zhao (1994), 'Challenging a master narrative: peace protest and opinion/editorial protest discourse in the US press during the Gulf War', *Discourse & Society*, **5** (4), 509–41.

Hanks, Tom and Steven Spielberg (executive producers) (2001), *Band of Brothers*, television series, USA: HBO.

Hartnett, Stephen John and Laura Ann Stengrim (2006), *Globalization and Empire: The US Invasion of Iraq, Free Markets, and Twilight of Democracy*, Tuscaloosa, AL: University of Alabama Press.

Hasian, Marouf (2005), *In the Name of Necessity: Military Tribunals and the Loss of American Civil Liberties*, Tuscaloosa, AL: University of Alabama Press.

Hedges, Chris (2002), *War is a Force That Gives Us Meaning*, New York: Public Affairs.

Hoaglund, Edward (2003), 'The American dissident: individualism as a matter of conscience', *Harper's*, August, pp. 33–41.

Ivie, Robert L. (1980), 'Images of savagery in American justifications for war', *Communication Monographs*, **47**, 279–94.

Ivie, Robert L. (2005), *Democracy and America's War on Terror*, Tuscaloosa, AL: University of Alabama Press.

Ivie, Robert L. (2007), *Dissent from War*, Bloomfield, CT: Kumarian Press.

Joseph, Paul (2007), *Are Americans Becoming More Peaceful?* Boulder, CO: Paradigm Publishers.

Kassing, Jeffrey W. (in press), 'A comparison of factors contributing to employees' expression of dissent', *Communication Quarterly*.

Kendall, Brenden E., Rebecca E. Gill, and George Cheney (2007), 'Consumer activism and corporate social responsibility: How strong a connection?' in Steve May, George Cheney and Juliet Roper (eds), *The Debate Over Corporate Social Responsibility*, New York: Oxford University Press, pp. 241–66.

Kilbourne, Jean (1999), *Can't Buy Me Love: How Advertising Changes the Way We Think and Feel*, New York: Simon & Schuster.

Lapham, Lewis (2004), *Gag Rule: On the Suppression of Dissent and the Stifling of Democracy*, New York: Penguin Press.

Lasswell, Harold (1965 [1935]), *World Politics and Personal Insecurity*, New York: Free Press.

Levinson, Barry (director) (1997), *Wag the Dog*, film, US: New Line Cinema.

Maney, Gregory M., Lynne M. Woehrle and Patrick G. Coy (2005), 'Harnessing and challenging hegemony: the US peace movement after 9/11', *Sociological Perspectives*, **48** (3), 357–81.

Matthews, Chris, (2007), *The Chris Matthews Show*, television transcript, 29 July, accessed 20 August at www.thechrismatthewsshow.com/html/transcript/index.php?selected=1&id=70.

McChesney, Robert (2000), *Rich Media, Poor Democracy*, New York: The New Press.

McGee, Michael (1980), 'The "ideograph": a link between rhetoric and ideology', *Quarterly Journal of Speech*, **66**, 1–16.

Miles, Steve (1998), *Consumerism as a Way of Life*, London: Sage.

Moore, Michael (director) (2002), *Bowling for Columbine*, film, US: Alliance Atlantis Communications.

Moore, Michael (director) (2007), *Sicko*, film, US: Dog Eat Dog Films.

Mouffe, Chantal (1999), 'Deliberative democracy or agonistic pluralism?' *Social Research*, **66**, 745–58.

Mueller, John (2005), 'Six rather unusual propositions about terrorism', *Terrorism and Political Violence*, **17**, 487–505.

Noah, Timothy (2004), 'Bumper sticker insubordination', *Slate*, 14 September, accessed 20 August, 2007 at www.slate.com/id/2106714.

O'Brien, Rebecca (producer) (2000), *Bread and Roses*, film, US: Lions Gate Films.

The Onion (2001), 'A Shattered Nation Longs To Care About Stupid Bullshit Again', 3 October, accessed 20 August, 2007 at www.theonion.com/content/node/28129.

Paddock, Richard C. (2007), 'Antiwar speakers on campus are lecturers, not students, this time', *The Los Angeles Times*, 5 July, accessed 20 August at www.latimes.com/news/local/la-me-protest5jul05,1,185208.story.

Pateman, Carole (1970), *Participation and Democratic Theory*, Cambridge, UK: Cambridge University Press.

Peters, Jeremy W. (2007), 'Somehow the spending does not stop', *The New York Times*, 5 July, sec. 4, 4.

Putnam, Robert (2000), *Bowling Alone*, New York: Simon & Schuster.

Robin, Corey (2004), *Fear: The History of an Idea*, New York and Oxford: Oxford University Press.

Schor, Juliet (1999), 'The new politics of consumption: why Americans want so much more than they need', *Boston Review*, **24** (3), 1–8.

Scott, Ridley (producer and director) (2001), *Black Hawk Down*, film, Los Angeles, CA: Revolution Studios.

Scraton, Phil (ed.) (2002), *Beyond September 11: An Anthology of Dissent*, Ann Arbor, MI and London: University of Michigan Press/Pluto Press.

Schor, Juliet (1992), *The Overworked American*, New York: Basic Books.

Shils, Edward (1981), *Tradition*, Chicago, IL: University of Chicago Press.

Smith, Vicki (2001), *Crossing the Great Divide: Worker Risk and Opportunity in the New Economy*, Ithaca, NY and London: Cornell University Press.

Snyder, Zach (director) (2006), *300*, film, US: Warner Brothers.

Spielberg, Steven (producer and director) (1998), *Saving Private Ryan*, film, US: Paramount.

Sunstein, Cass R. (2003), *Why Societies Need Dissent*, Cambridge, MA and London: Harvard University Press.

Suskind, Ron (2004), *The Price of Loyalty: George Bush, the White House, and the Education of Paul O'Neill*, New York: Simon & Shuster.

Terkel, Studs (1984), *The Good War*, New York: The New Press.

Trodd, Zoe (ed.) (2006), *American Protest Literature*, Cambridge, MA and London: Harvard University Press.

Vidal, Gore (2003), 'We are the patriots', *The Nation*, 2 June, pp. 11–14.

Westen, Drew (2007), *The Political Brain: The Role of Emotion in Deciding the Fate of the Nation*, New York: Public Affairs.

Zorn, Theodore E., Lars Thøger Christensen and George Cheney (1999), *Do We Really Want Constant Change?* San Francisco, CA: Berrett-Koehler.

12. Making a place for the practice of dissenting

Robyn Penman

DISSENT IN THE MODERN WORLD

It's Just Not On

We don't think much of dissent in the modern world. Indeed, it has become increasingly apparent to me that some powerful elements in our society are actively seeking to silence dissent. As I was writing this chapter, two significant political events occurred that demonstrated quite markedly our current attitude to dissent – at least the attitudes of those in power in Australia.

First, the New South Wales state government removed the requirement for unanimous jury verdicts in criminal trials. Previously in NSW jurors in criminal trials were required to reach unanimous verdicts. But on 10 November, 2005, the NSW Attorney-General declared he would change this to accept a majority verdict of 11 to 1 in criminal trials. This flew in the face of the High Court arguments and a Law Reform Commission review. Learned legal opinion had it that unanimous verdicts were justified on the grounds of historical legacies, legal principles and the rule of law.

But despite the learned legal opinion, it was clear that unanimous verdicts were not justified administratively, especially in terms of so-called inefficiencies and failures. When the change was first proposed it was claimed that up to 10 percent of criminal trials in NSW will fail because the jury is unable to reach a unanimous verdict. When I read that claim, it struck me that something was very odd and I pondered it for some time. Why is the trial a failure if the jury can't reach a unanimous verdict? What does such a view have to say about the notion of justice and reasonable doubt? What's wrong with one person saying they can't agree? Does this really determine the outcome? If so, in what way does it matter?

As I pondered the above questions, I read further arguments in favor of removing the requirement for a unanimous verdict. Many of these revolved around the demotic figure of the 'rogue' juror who gums up the system out of perversity. In these latter arguments, it is believed that the lone voice of dissent is always the loony voice, and usually that of the 'loony left'. But why should this be so? Why is the dissenting voice bad? Why can't it be the case that the single person who dissents may be right or has, at least, the right to express reasonable doubt?

What struck me most forcefully, however, was the consequence of this change to an 11 to 1 verdict requirement. With the change to majority verdicts, the role of the dissenter is further marginalized; indeed, you could almost say they have been disempowered. When you know you are the dissenting voice and it doesn't count, why dissent? Why bother to speak up with reasonable doubt if the other 11 can just override you?

The second, and even more disturbing, event that occurred as I was writing, was the proposal for a new set of anti-terrorism laws that raised the hackles of all who valued the notion of civil liberties and human rights. In newspaper reviews of the proposed legislation, it turned out that, unbeknownst to most of the citizenry of Australia, the Parliament had already passed legislation a few years ago that denied any human rights or due process to anyone even vaguely suspected of knowing anything about terrorism. In an October 2005 speech given by Malcolm Fraser, Australian Prime Minister from 1975 to 1983, he pointed out that Australia is the only democratic country that has legislated for the detention of people who the authorities do not necessarily suspect of wrong doing or even of wrong thought. In Australia, anyone can be detained merely because authorities believe they might know something that they don't even know they know. That's an extraordinary power for quelling any hint of dissent, whether known, intended or otherwise. It also reflects, quite strongly, the current political attitude to dissent – it's just not on.

In the new proposals there is also a revival of the act of sedition and a broadening of its definition; most notably, intention is no longer part of the requirement for an act to be seditious. You are acting seditiously if you support insurgency – whether intended or not – in any country where Australian troops are deployed. Such support includes, for example, voicing opposition to the war in Iraq. Had the proposed new legislation been enacted earlier, all who protested against the war in Vietnam could have been jailed. Other seditious acts involve promoting ill will and hostility amongst various groups – again, whether intended or not. And, under this provision, it would seem that even acts of satire or legitimate expressions of protest could be found to be seditious.

In essence, the proposed antiterrorism laws and the particular changes to the sedition laws are a real threat to the idea of free speech and, even more broadly, to the idea of democracy itself. If nothing else, democracy is about the right to participate in society and, if one cannot freely talk, then how can one participate?

Why is This So?

Why is it that the West can ostensibly praise the virtue of free speech and democracy and at the same time place so little value on dissent or, even worse, legislate it out of existence? Whatever happened to the International Convention on Civil and Political Rights, to which Australia is a signatory? That convention states that everyone shall have the right to freedom of expression and this right shall include the right to seek, receive and impart ideas of all kinds. I guess that's also just not on for now.

It's as if one has the right to speak but not to disagree when one does. It's as if one can pay lip service to the importance of communicating in a democratic society but not take it seriously. But, if this is so, why bother speaking? What purpose can be served by speaking, if such a limited role is placed on it? Why bother speaking if all one can do is agree?

These questions point to a fundamental set of contradictions or tensions in the modern world that arise because of some very basic beliefs about the nature of knowledge and certainty, and the nature and role of communication. Indeed, these beliefs are so well-entrenched that many people take them as real and immutable. Nevertheless, in the spirit of this chapter and this book, I hope you will not only allow me to dissent from these mainstream beliefs, but that you also will be open to where my dissenting voice may lead you.

As a way of helping you to appreciate the underpinnings to our modern disparagement of dissent, and at the same time pave the way for shucking such a view, I would like you to step back in time with me to Europe in the seventeenth century – to the beginning of the Enlightenment and the beginning of Modernity. Here I will draw on Stephen Toulmin's (1990) account of the development of modernity. He argues that, during the seventeenth century, the philosophers of the day – most notably Descartes – made a number of fundamental moves away from the foundational beliefs of the Renaissance and the humanism entailed in that era.

First, the seventeenth-century philosophers moved from an oral mode of argument for making judgments to a written form of proof that could be judged in terms of formal logic. Rhetoric as a means of questioning the conditions and the circumstances in which arguments carry conviction was dismissed as a way of assessing the rational merit of argument. Instead only written, formal logic was valid as the means for assessment. In such circumstances, the value of people arguing for and against ideas was dismissed. By extension, the role of dissent went as well. There was no place for the dissenting voice in the rationalist pursuit for truth.

Second, the seventeenth-century philosophers moved from a concern with the local, transient and particular aspects of life and language to a pre-occupation with general, abstract principles that would apply across time and place. This set of moves took modern philosophers away from partic-ular, practical problems to the search for abstract and timeless methods for deriving general solutions to universal problems. Implicit in this search for principles was the belief in the idea of certainty. If you applied the right methods, then you could be assured of the certain, right answer. This drive for certainty also militated against a role for dissent. It's just not acceptable to laud the role of dissent, when it is believed there can be one certain uni-versal answer.

Richard Bernstein (1992), in his considerations of the ethical-political horizons of modernity/postmodernity, also points to the denigration of dissent as a significant outcome of our embracing of modernity. He argues that the dominant tendency in modern Western philosophy and meta-physics has always been to privilege and valorize unity, harmony and total-ity. But in order to do this – to valorize unity, harmony and totality, and damn dissent – we have to attribute language and communication with a peculiarly limited role. Again, this may be best appreciated by returning to the seventeenth century. But this time we won't visit Descartes in France. Instead, we're going to consider a moral tale described by Davies (1987) of the struggle to redefine language in England.

Prior to the Enlightenment, the Romantics saw language as open-ended, creative and inherently imperfect. But the English 'linguistic radicals' of the early Enlightenment days found this concept abhorrent. They just couldn't cope with the idea of language as an ever-moving stream, a medium of innovation, and a source of great uncertainty. They could not build a secure, permanent body of human knowledge using rationally val-idated methods that relied on working from formal logic, applying general principles and abstract axioms, with something as uncertain as ordinary human language.

For example, in the *Leviathan* (first published in 1651), Thomas Hobbes urged that people had to purge language of all ambiguity, expel metaphor, outlaw new phrasings and reduce language to a rational system of signs. Wilkins, a compatriot of Hobbes, went even further. He argued that natural languages were just too treacherous to be tolerated – the meanings kept on changing and betraying the speaker/ listener. Wilkins wanted to destroy the very nature of language in which words referred to things other than them-selves – where words stand for things – and make the words the things themselves. I cannot conceive how anyone could make the words the things themselves, but Wilkins tried to in order to ensure understanding, eliminate contention and guarantee that the pathway to pure knowledge was achievable.

These linguistic radicals, however, were merely forerunners to the main work that sealed the fate of communication for three centuries. The main work was undertaken by John Locke. Indeed, it was Locke who coined the term communication in the way it is still popularly used today, to mean the transmission of ideas from one person to another. Prior to that appropriation, communication was restricted to the physical conveyance of matter or energy.

To understand the role Locke ascribed to communication, we need to start with his *Essay Concerning Human Understanding* (1997 [1690]). The foundational unit for Locke's treatise on understanding was the idea. But ideas are private things and humans are, according to Locke, social beings. So how do ideas get from one mind to another? They get there via signs. To be social beings, we need 'sensible and public signs' to signify the ideas in our minds. These sensible and public signs are our words. For Locke, words stood for nothing but the ideas in the mind of the person who used them. However, he wrote: 'To make words serviceable to the end of communication, it is necessary . . . that they excite, in the hearer, exactly the same idea, they stand for in the mind of the speaker' (Locke, 1997 [1690]: 426).

In order to know what the ideas of people were and to gauge the collective will, communication had to occur – but only of a particular sort. Because Locke could only conceive of understandings and opinions as coming fully formed in the minds of individuals, he saw no need for a public process for the forming of the will of the majority. There was no need to talk about or debate ideas because we already had them in our heads. As a consequence, community opinion was taken simply to be the collective majority of individual ideas.

In Locke's view of social life, conflict and incommensurability were removed from the public realm and placed in the private experiences of individuals. This was important to Locke. He wanted to ensure that the public sphere was confined to matters of science and reason, not politics and morality. He believed that, in a civil society, people reasoned through their ideas rationally, in a scientific manner; they did not, and should not, generate their ideas out of debate or other forms of public conversations. Once again, I hope you can see how dissent has been dismissed here – as anathema to reason.

The whole sense of communication developed by Locke reflects pretty well the same view of communication we operate on in everyday life today. If you ask anyone to define communication, it will inevitably involve a description based on the sending and receiving of messages – just as Locke formulated it. More formally today, this is referred to as the conduit, or transmission, view of communication. And it is this view that we have to discard here – at least for the moment – if we are to proceed to build up a view in which dissent can have a place.

On the Other Hand . . .

But before I proceed to describe a new place for dissent I think it might be important to consider – albeit briefly – why we might want to find such a place. Why might we want to discard the traditions of the past three centuries and start to valorize rather than denigrate dissent? Haven't these traditions served us well over the past 300 years? Is there any point in changing our worldview? My answer is yes. I believe there are two very good reasons for at least being open to the possibility of changing our worldview.

In the first instance, the tradition of Modernity has not served us well when it comes to the sustainability and viability of the human condition. In that tradition, the search for certainty has led us along paths in which we think and act as if we can solve the world's problems by the application of certain unassailable principles. But the end consequence of this scientific way of thinking has been the denial of the importance of diversity for long term survival.

James Scott (1998) has written a compelling and tragic account of the consequences of the application of what he calls the principles of High Modernity to human problems. In his book, subtitled 'How Certain Schemes to Improve the Human Condition Have Failed', Scott describes such grand schemes as the Great Leap Forward in China, collectivization in Russia and compulsory villagization in Tanzania, Mozambique and Ethiopia, and he shows how these are among the greatest human tragedies of the twentieth century. He also shows how these tragedies came about because of, among other things, an extreme self-confidence in scientific and technical progress.

The same general argument can be made in the world of agriculture, where we are increasingly recognizing that the practice of monoculture – which also arose out of an extreme confidence in the application of scientific techniques – is non-sustainable. Again, James Scott provides compelling accounts of monocultures which are, as a rule, more fragile and hence more vulnerable to the stress of disease and weather than are polycultures. Scott in particular considers the modernist's approach to forest planning and use. The utilitarian commercial and fiscal logic that led to geometric, monocropped, same-age forests also led to severe ecological damage. Where the formula had been applied with the greatest rigor the greatest damage was done, and it eventually became necessary to attempt to restore much of the forest's original diversity and complexity.

A very different but fundamentally important example of the denial of diversity can be found in the imposition of a standard language, usually English, across diverse cultures. Although this imposition is believed to ease so-called 'communication barriers', it also oppresses or eliminates the diversity of options for understanding. Languages are, in fact, a major source of cultural wealth for humanity, and diversity in language needs to be encouraged not minimized. If we are to enlarge our understanding of the human condition, we need to be continually searching for new expressions. Human progress depends on our capacity to create new models, metaphors and analogies and these all require new, and creative, language use.

And this brings me to my second reason for being open to a change of worldview. The traditional understanding of communication as a transmission process just does not serve us well if we want to foster creative language use, nor does it serve us well if we want to address any number of contemporary communication challenges. As the foundation director of the Communication Research Institute of Australia, I repeatedly found over a 15-year period that mainstream communication studies and understandings had little to offer when it came to resolving the practical communication problems that our member organizations brought to us. The mainstream understanding of communication as a simple transmission process focuses on the individuals – as senders or receivers – and thus pushes the notion of community aside. It focuses on the end effects – message received – and thus ignores the means. And it presumes the possibility of certainty and thus denies the open-ended creativity of communicating.

So I find there are very good reasons for putting aside the traditions of modernity and its concomitant limited view of communication. In putting these traditions aside we need to be prepared to take a great leap from where we are now to where we could be in the future. Below I take this leap and invite you to do so with me.

WHERE DISSENT HAS A PLACE IN THE POSTMODERN WORLD

To be able to foster diversity and valorize dissent, we need to step out of the modern worldview and into the postmodern. Although, in using the word 'postmodern', I am mindful of both Richard Bernstein's (1992) and Stephen Toulmin's (1990) caution about the slippery and vague nature of the term. More than a decade after their cautions the term is still as slippery but I shall use it to reflect a new mood or 'constellation' in which the paradigm for understanding is radically different from that associated with the tradition of modernity.

Central to the new postmodern constellation of beliefs is the crucial role played by language and communication. In this world, language is not subservient to knowledge, as Locke would have it; rather it is the means whereby knowledge is created. Our knowledge of the world is created out of our communication about it.

The recognition that knowledge is created in the human realm, in our communication, is one shared by the pragmatic philosophy tradition founded by John Dewey (1981) and the newer arguments of the social constructionists (for example, Pearce, 1995; Penman, 2000; Shotter, 1993), among others. Both traditions reject the traditional assumption of knowledge as representations of well-formed objectivity existing in an external world. Instead, it is assumed that knowledge does not have an objective, immutable base in the 'real' world – it is not out there to be found or discovered. Instead, knowledge is created by us, in our conversations. For contemporary pragmatic philosophers such as Richard Rorty, conversation is 'the ultimate context in which knowledge is to be understood' (Rorty, 1980: 389).

This 'relocation' of knowledge requires a profound shift in our understanding of the world. Perhaps the most significant challenge that arises from this shift it what it means for a notion of truth. In the postmodern realm we can't accommodate the commonsense or correspondence notion of truth – that a statement or claim is true if it conforms with the facts or agrees with an independent reality. In the postmodern realm there is no independent reality with which any claim can agree. So what are we to do about truth?

In considering the above question, Richard Campbell (1992) said that '[w]hether we can work out a different conception of truth, or whether we have to give up on truth altogether seems to me to be one of the profound philosophical challenges of our time' (1992: 6). I would agree. I also believe that the way in which we approach a new understanding of truth has direct implications for our take on dissent. Here I want to briefly outline the argument for a different, and useful, view of truth developed by Campbell.

He proposed that instead of taking the conventional notion of truth (as reflecting an immutable reality) we locate the notion of truth firmly in action, particularly in linguistic practice. By a series of rigorously developed steps, Campbell leads us in an exploration of what it can mean to locate truth firmly in action. Among those steps are a number of critical points.

First, he turned the abstract notion of truth into an adverb, and wrote about 'acting truly': 'if we are to act truly, our approach to entities in the world must maintain an open attitude, so that we let them show themselves as they are' (Campbell, 1992: 425). There is a twofold openness required: we need to be open in our pointing to how things are in talk, and things need to be revealing something of how they are. When we turn to communicating, acting truly calls for a reciprocal openness between participants, allowing things to be revealing. This is not an easy task. All too often in everyday communicating, we have a tendency to quickly impose interpretations – to make rapid decisions about what is going on or what was said. To remain open requires us to hold off our too-quick interpretations and to allow for other possibilities to emerge.

Second, in acting truly we are at the same time committed to the continual possibility of revision in the light of a more adequate understanding. This acknowledges the very temporal and context-bound nature of all communicating and provides for the transitory nature of what we understand. Truth is not an uncompromisable, universal fact; rather, it is a contextually bound, local phenomenon. However, as Campbell pointed out, recognizing the socially constructed and therefore changeable nature of our search for understanding is no justification for regarding questions of truth as irrelevant. As he wrote: 'Socially constructed realities may not be timeless or impervious to political action, but they are real nevertheless' (1992: 430).

Third, Campbell argued 'Being true is an achievement attained when the commitments expressed in making the statement, or in performing the deed, are fulfilled' (p. 436). For Campbell, being true is being faithful. Campbell noted that this notion of being true as faithful returns us to a much earlier conception of truth shown in the Old English root of the word, meaning 'good faith'. Indeed, there was a similar understanding in ancient Greece (before Plato purged it). Truth, in the Homeric sense, required such things as fidelity, loyalty, constancy and allegiance. When we apply this notion to communicating, being true is acting faithfully into our social situations. It is acting with integrity and insight toward others and the reality – however socially constructed – of the situation.

To sum up Campbell's argument: 'The truth, therefore, is not to be found . . . in trying to construct an impersonal and timeless account of reality which flies in the face of our own humanity. It is rather to be achieved in the quality and authenticity of our faithful life-activities' (1992: 438). Campbell has very much turned the notion of truth around with his philosophical investigations. He has transformed it into an activity (a verb) that is ongoing and essentially moral in character, for to evaluate activities as true requires us to ask questions about faithfulness, integrity, authenticity and the like. This can be nothing else but an ongoing open inquiry that occurs in our communicating.

Where Communicating is Reconstructed

This brings me to the next step we have to make in order to give dissent a place of value. We have to reconsider our understanding of the process of communicating. If this is the process where we can act truly, in good faith, and where dissent can have a role, then it behoves us to consider its nature in the postmodern realm seriously.

There is no little irony in the fact that what I now propose to do is to build up a picture of the practice of dissenting based on my previous conceptual work on communication (Penman, 2000) that, in itself, dissents from the status quo. Here I will draw on that account to briefly describe another way of construing communication and to explore the practice of dissenting as one form of communicating.

As a starting point – and one radically different from Locke – we need to imagine that the basic human reality is not individual people or their ideas, but people in conversation. This is in marked contrast from the Cartesian position, where the person is first and foremost an isolated thinker employing reason to objectively derive knowledge. This is captured in Descarte's famous Latin motto, *cogito ergo sum* (I think, therefore I am). In contrast, Heidegger argued that we are first and foremost a situated interpreter, understander or 'sense maker' engaged in everyday coping, and as a situated interpreter we are irreducibly relational not individual, social not psychological. For Heidegger, the primary human reality was being in the world – being engaged with others in language (Stewart, 1995).

When we start with ourselves as being-in-language, our focus moves to how we make sense *in* communicating – not *out* of it. In joinly acting together in communicating we create a wonderfully uncertain and often mysterious process – something readily recognized by the Romanticist before the advent of the Linguistic Purists in the Enlightenment. The most amazing thing about this mysterious and uncertain process, though, is that somehow we usually manage to go on. But how?

Given that our understanding of the world is generated in communicating, and that this is a process occurring over time, it makes sense that the temporal context plays a major role in our understanding. What we determine to be knowledge and how we interpret communicative action is a function of the historical context in which the process takes place. As the context changes, so too does our understanding. Just as important, without the context, we cannot make sense of communicative action.

This very temporality of understanding means it is not possible to have a stable knowledge base. Nevertheless, it is still possible to say, at any point in time, that 'Now I understand'. But, what does it mean to say this, to say we know for the moment? This was one of the central questions of Wittgenstein's extensive investigations into the philosophy of language. He argued that we understood when we were able to simply keep going on with each other: '[T]ry not to think of understanding as a "mental process" at all'; instead, simply ask 'in what kind of circumstances do we say "now I can go on"?' (1953: 154).

Trying to imagine this notion of understanding can be very difficult. We have developed such an entrenched set of intramental terms that locate meaning and understanding in ideas inside the heads of people, it can be difficult to relocate meaning outside in the momentary understandings between people. Sometimes I find it helps to imagine a good conversation as something akin to a good dance. Although in this instance it can only be a particular kind of dance: one whose performance relies on the coordinated action between partners. With each step that the partners take in coordination with each other, the dance moves forward. Each partner is able to go on with the other when each moves in ways that enable such progress. That the dance goes on shows that moments of understanding have occurred.

However, the understanding achieved is only momentary. The meanings generated in communicating are never complete or even capable of being finished. In continually bringing about a new state of affairs, joint participations and the implicated meanings are always emergent and never finished. This last point is important. There is no possibility that meaning can be complete, if only. . . . On the contrary, meanings are essentially unfinishable.

The very constitutive nature of communicating, along with its vagueness and indeterminacy, guarantees that there is a great deal of diversity to communicating, or at least in our interpretations of it. Then when you realize there is no empirical base to any interpretation – there is no world out there outside of our communicating about it – the possibilities are endless.

And Putting Dissent in its Place

Underlying this construction of communicating as a wonderful, messy, diverse and essentially open-ended process is the recognition that disorder and chaos are at the base of social life. Once we come to this realization, then dissent starts to make more sense. Indeed, within this view, dissent is an inevitable aspect of life in which communicating is involved. But, more importantly for the argument here, it is also a process to be valued. Within a modern worldview, you may accept that dissent cannot be avoided, at all times and at all costs, but within that same worldview dissent is not to be encouraged. Here – from a postmodern frame – on the other hand, dissent is to be valued and encouraged.

By dissenting, or accepting dissent, we keep ourselves continually open to alternative possibilities and to new directions. Richard Rorty argued that this openness in human conversation is so important that it should be the moral task of any social philosopher or critic to defend it. Rorty has also argued that it is far more important to keep the argument going than to finish it, and I would agree with him – to some extent. Yes, it is important to keep the conversation going, to avoid premature closure, to consider dissenting views and to recognize that understandings are never complete and inviolate. But, on the other hand, I would want to be careful not to fall into the nihilistic trap of the deconstructionists (for example, Derrida, 1977). From their perspective, all attempts at discovering underlying order must inevitably fail and therefore there is no point in attempting such a search. While I agree there is no point in searching for an underlying order, there could be every point in imposing order onto chaos in some instances, at some times. This means that yes, dissent does have a place, and a very important one, but not all dissent is necessarily good all of the time. There could well be good reasons for confining dissent or for choosing some form of dissent over others.

At this point, I cannot help but recall a recent event in Australia that well illustrates the need to make judgments about dissent, and most importantly, shows that some dissent is still bad even when viewed from a postmodern perspective. With the 'war on terror' we are all are being cajoled into keeping an eye out for 'the terrorist next door'. This so-called war has, of course, generated an increasing fear of the other, the foreigner in our midst and especially the foreigner from the Middle East. As I was writing (nearing the end of 2005), this fear erupted at one beautiful beachside suburb in Sydney into a horrible tribal war. While there were many contributions to this violent outburst, the final straw was the gathering of thousands of Australian youth (mainly male and all white) to protest against the 'Lebs' (Lebanese) coming to the beach. This started as a peaceful rally to demonstrate the superiority of white Australia (that's blunt, but it was how it was) and then turned into an ugly running brawl that continued for days and over different locations.

These Australian youth were expressing a dissenting view from the ostensibly mainstream stance of multiculturalism. That they wanted to dissent is acceptable, but their mode of doing so is not – indeed, it was nothing short of reprehensible. This points directly to the need to consider the mode or practice of expressing dissent.

DISSENTING WELL

The Importance of Understanding the Practice

So far, I have built up a picture, using the postmodern worldview, of dissent being a natural or ordinary aspect of everyday life. It is an inevitable outcome of the very nature of communicating – in which disorder and uncertainty reign supreme. But in order to appreciate the positive role that can be played by dissent, we need to turn to a consideration of the practice of dissenting.

It helps here if we talk about dissenting and not dissent – in the same way and for the same reason that I have been using communicating and not communication, and acting truly and not truth. When we talk about dissenting, or communicating, in the verb (or gerund) form we are bringing the process to the fore. Rather than treating dissent or communication as a 'thing' – noun-form – we are saying that it is an act in progress, it is something we do, and it is something we do jointly with others.

This emphasis on doing and experiencing is very much at the heart of the arguments of John Dewey and the pragmatic philosophers who followed him. Dewey (1981) argued that it was critical to take everyday human experience seriously and to do this we need to value what is in process, not what is presumed finished or ended. In arguing thus, Dewey strove to redress the imbalance of the Cartesian school that relegated experience to a secondary and almost irrelevant place in the scheme of things.

Dewey urged us to ask: What do we experience about things we do and about happenings in our world? For Dewey, and for me here, it is this point of experience that is our empirical reality. What we experience as we act into our world is the primary point of any reality we can know. This observation is especially important when it comes to considering communicating and the dissenting form of it. We cannot even attempt to understand what it is to participate – to act jointly with others – if we do not return to our experience of it. Experience leads us directly to embodied persons in the real, everyday world and it is our lived experience in communicating that is the fount of our practical knowledge.

Acting in Good Faith

Because we are working within the new constellation of postmodernism, we have no recourse to an independent or external form of evaluation when it comes to making judgments about the process of dissenting. We cannot say that an act of dissent was good because it did something outside the process of communicating; rather, we can only say it's good from within the process of communicating itself. In other words, any judgment or evaluation that we make about a practice of dissenting relies on the quality of the practice of communicating itself.

To help here, let's return to one of Richard Campbell's arguments about truth. He said: 'If we are to act truly, our approach to entities in the world must maintain an open attitude, so that we let them show themselves as they are' (1992: 425). What Campbell is pointing to is the need to respect, and act in good faith toward, the inherent aspects of the process we are dealing with. Here, we are dealing with communicating. So, to develop criteria that act in good faith means to evaluate the process of communicating in terms of the extent to which its features are recognized or denied. In other words, I am proposing a principle of self-affirmation: good communicating affirms all the characteristics of itself – it is true to itself. On the other hand, bad communicating renders aspects of the process invisible, or denies their existence. Bad communicating does not reflect good faith with the process.

The best example I can think of to illustrate this point here is the view of communication as a conduit or transmission process – where communication is described as the simple act of sending and receiving messages. You might still want to think that that's the right view, because however else could it be? And, if you do, then, from within my framework, you are confining a very complex process to a simple act of passing on messages. This transmission view renders many aspects of the communicating process invisible, or denies their existence, and thus is a form of bad communicating.

In what I have discussed so far about the practice of communicating in a postmodern world, we can identify four key characteristics of communicating that would require open affirmation for the process to be classed as good: constitutiveness, contextuality, diversity and incompleteness. Dissenting well comes about when there is open affirmation of these same features during the practice of dissenting. Let's have a closer look at what this can mean.

When I talk about communicating being constitutive, I am talking about the way in which we construct our understanding in our communicating, not independently of it. We don't make sense of something and then engage in communication with others about it; the sense is made in the act of communicating itself – even if it is only communicating with ourself. This assertion inexorably follows from the starting point I discussed earlier – where we need to take the basic human reality as people in conversation, or being-in-language.

Given that we constitute our understandings in communicating, meaning is neither fixed or invariant; rather it is constantly changing with our every act of participation. A poor communicating practice, and a poor dissenting one, would be where the rightness of a point or argument was asserted on the grounds of an objective reality. What springs to mind here are arguments between different religious groups where each asserts the correctness of their faith on the grounds of 'God's' word – usually written and usually taken as inviolate.

The second important feature of communicating is the pivotal role played by context. We understand things by using the context in which communicating takes place. Context provides the frame for meaning generation. The context, however, is no more stable than the communication process itself. So, the meaning given to any particular communicative action or episode must be seen as subject to infinite revision. The understanding of an action at any particular point in time and in any given structural context is subject to constant revision as the retrospective and emergent contexts change with the process itself.

When the meaning of an action or set of words is taken to be immutable over time and/or space, then this critical feature of contextuality is denied. As Richard Campbell expressed it, this denial of context is a denial of our historicity that flies in the face of our own humanity. In contrast, if we are to act truly and respect the communicating process for what it is or could be, we must be committed to the continual possibility of revising our understandings. Realizing that the same action can take on new meanings in different contexts means that we recognize the transitory nature of our understanding.

The third feature we need to be sensitive to is the diversity to communicating, or to our interpretations of it. There can be as many different interpretations of acts or utterances that we as participants are capable of generating. Most importantly, there is no necessarily single, right interpretation – although you'd probably think so if you've ever overheard a marital argument (not your own, of course) that's gone from bad to worse on the basis that each partner's different claim to interpretation is the only correct one. Those sorts of arguments are clear examples of bad communicating.

Better descriptions or interpretations need to recognize that there are no objective, outside grounds on which to make a claim that one interpretation is better than another. It's not possible to say that this interpretation is better than that one because it is more real. In other words, we cannot resort to fact and, instead, must inevitably return to value. We may wish to say that this interpretation is better than another, but we can only do so on non-factual grounds, such as moral or esthetic ones. This has some very important implications when it comes to dissenting. If those in the dissenting process are to respect this postmodern stance on communicating, then no one has the right to reject the dissenting views on so-called factual grounds. Instead, the value of the dissenting view(s) needs to be open to consideration on moral grounds and/or esthetic ones.

As a way of contemplating this proposal, consider my very own dissenting voice in this chapter. If you, the reader, are not willing to accept what I have to say about communicating but are willing to accept the postmodern stance when it comes to notions of truth, then you would need to make a judgment about the worth of my statements on non-factual grounds. For me, the most important grounds are practical and moral. I would want to ask: What can I do with such a dissenting view of communicating, where does it lead me in practice? And, then, I would want to ask: Does it lead me somewhere good, is it good for the human condition?

The final consideration is one of incompleteness, or open-endedness. If we are to engage in good communicating we must recognize its open-ended nature. In doing so, we acknowledge the unfinishability of the meanings generated in communicating. We recognize that there always can be a different interpretation, a different way of understanding, a different way of experiencing, as we proceed in open conversation with others.

Theories and practices of communicating that presume the possibility of perfect (and therefore only one way of) understanding illustrate bad communicating within the framework being developed here. In assuming that perfect understanding is possible, the ongoingness and unfinishability of the meaning generation process is denied. On the other hand, theories and practices of communicating that have no closure, when the practical exigencies of the world seem to call for it, could be classed as equally bad.

Although we might want to respect all opinions and theories, there may be very good practical reasons why we should not. The right to hold any opinion may be sustainable, but the implications for practice cannot always be supported morally. For example, while I might want to be open to, and respect, a range of understandings of the human condition, I cannot morally support a view that I believe has an impoverished representation of human experience and that, in practice, negates a range of possible actions for improving the human condition. As I've said earlier, the transmission view of communication illustrates an impoverished representation of human experience and, as such, can be classed as bad within my framework. Similarly, a reductionist model of human nature that views humans and societies within such narrow horizons and restricts opportunities for moral explorations and social growth can also be classed as bad.

When these four criteria are recognized as essential to this new worldview, then the place for dissent is opened. By respecting differences and by being continually open to alternative possibilities the practice of dissenting takes on value. Respecting these four criteria also ensures that the dissenting process is done well because it acts in good faith with the process of communicating. And, in the end, in our postmodern world, acting in good faith is acting truly.

WHAT DOES ALL THIS SAY ABOUT LEADING?

Leading from a Moral, Communicating Frame

In the postmodern worldview constructed here, leading is as much a communicating process as is dissenting. So, rather than see leadership as a technical or administrative act, we need to reconstrue it as a process of joint action with others, and when we make judgments about the process of leading we also need to rely on moral grounds, not so-called factual ones.

In the end, the whole argument in this chapter rests on a moral core. So here I want briefly to expound on what it is I'm really talking about when I use the world moral, because I am using it in a far broader and richer way than the understanding offered in the worldview of modernity.

The conventional understanding of morality has four main features. First, in everyday life, the concept of morality is relegated to an extraordinarily narrow domain and, most typically the domain of the religious – moral grounds are almost always taken to be religious ones only. Second, in philosophy, morality lies in the realm of reasoned principle – the moral order is based on a set of principles objectively derived and established. Third, the concept of morality has been instrumentalized as 'ethics' – a set of injunctions for professional behavior that is context-free and timeless (see Ciulla *et al.*, 2005). Fourth, our modern conventional understanding of morality is that it is unimportant – of no more than purely academic interest.

In contrast, here the moral domain is in the domain of everyday, practical experience. Hans-Georg Gadamer (1992) argued against a scientific, pure knowledge approach to morality and for the use of practical knowledge when it comes to understanding the human, social realm. For Gadamer, practical knowledge is moral knowledge and it has three important features. First, moral knowledge comes out of practice, from human activity itself; it is not something that is rationally discussed and derived. Second, moral knowledge is knowledge of particulars that help direct action in good ways, not to desirable ends. It is knowledge that emerges from particular practices in particular contexts to guide action in that particular situation. Third, moral knowledge is never knowable in advance, as is knowledge that can be taught. We do not possess moral knowledge in such a way that we already have it and can then apply it to specific situations. Rather it is in the doing of things that we bring about our moral knowing. A list of general ethical injunctions that are expected to be applicable across all situations does not reflect a moral knowing; moral knowing is always emergent in practice.

I think it is the last point that brings home how strikingly different this idea of moral knowing is from that inherent in the worldview of modernity. Moral knowing is a process that, in itself, is never-ending and always open to new developments – it is not something handed to us independent of ourselves. So, from this viewpoint, making moral judgments, or bringing about moral knowledge, has nothing to do with the independent application of a standard of good. Instead, making moral judgments is all about acting in good faith within the process of communicating; the aim being to bring about good ways of proceeding for all involved. This is where leading comes in.

Good leading is all about making contributions to the process of communicating that, in all good faith, enable those involved to move on and to do so in better ways. Good leading is about recognizing and fostering the importance of moral, practical knowing. Good leading makes a place for the practice of dissent. Good leading is about fostering and managing dissent.

Fostering Dissent and Asking Good Questions

The idea of dissenting and the idea of leading are related. Both take place within the process of communicating and for both to be done well there must be open respect for the inherent features of that process. And both in their different ways contribute to the process of morally knowing. So how do they differ?

Dissenting keeps on opening up new possibilities but does not necessarily provide the appropriate practical closure that I talked about above. It is here that the act of leading plays a critical role. While dissent helps to keep our options open, good leading helps us to maneuver through these options in ways that are best for us.

Richard Bernstein talked about one of the major challenges of living in this new constellation of postmodernity as follows: 'We have to learn to think and act in the in-between interstices of forced reconciliation and radical dispersion' (1992: 9). Good leading does this. Good leading helps to take us to where we can best act in the interstices. Good leading is working well in the practical moral domain and being open to continual revision of understandings and approaches to proceeding.

I find that I have come to a rather interesting position here and have something directly to say about the approach to dissent taken by John Howard, the former Australian Prime Minister in the new terrorism laws described at the beginning. Rather than suppressing all dissent as his laws intend, my argument here would suggest the need to consider ways to foster and manage dissent so that we can move forward in the 'interstices'. This does not mean that we must encourage terrorists. These terrorists no more engage in good dissenting practices than does the Prime Minister engage in good leadership practices. This approach is one of 'forced reconciliation' – and one forced to the Prime Minister's view alone – and neither the Prime Minister, nor the terrorists he has attempted to wage war on, show any respect for the process of communicating. Neither party is acting in good faith with the process.

On the other hand, we do need to consider ways in which good dissent can not only be allowed (and not suppressed) but encouraged. This is the task of leading in a postmodern world view. Central to this task of leading is the asking, and encouraging, of good questions. In the end, our way forward relies on the questions we ask – not necessarily the solutions we propose. It is in the very asking of good questions that we open up new pathways and generate new possibilities for going on. These good questions preserve an orientation to openness; they reflect genuine curiosity; they are concerned with practice; and, most important, they are asked in good faith, in the process of communicating.

Thus once again we return to the process of communicating and the practice of dissenting and leading within it. For both types of practices, participation is essential. And it is this 'methodical participation', to use John Ralston Saul's phrase (1992: 584), that is essential to supply the decent, democratic values on which advanced civilizations rest. Without continual, or methodical, participation in the public sphere, we simply cannot contribute to that sphere – as is the right and responsibility of all good citizens.

Dissenting well, and fostering and managing that dissent with good leading, are essential elements in a genuinely democratic society. In engaging in these practices, the essentially contestable nature of public life is brought to the fore and the open-endedness of that life encouraged. For Saul, the 'secret, then, is that we must alter our civilization from one answer to one which feels satisfaction, not anxiety, when doubt is established. To be comfortable with panic when it is appropriate. If ours is the advanced civilization we pretend it is, there should be no need to act as if all decisions were designed to establish certainties' (Saul, 1992: 584–5).

For us to alter our civilization, to one based on values – and important democratic ones at that – we need to enter the type of postmodern world I have been describing in this chapter. In this world, doubt through dissenting is encouraged and good leading brings about new and better questions through participating. Good leading and good dissenting, done in good faith, become two parts of a whole that point to the truth for the moment and ways forward into new ones.

REFERENCES

Bernstein, Richard (1992), *The New Constellation*, Cambridge, MA: MIT Press.
Campbell, Richard (1992), *Truth and Historicity*, Oxford: Clarendon Press.
Ciulla, J. B., T. Price and S. E. Murphy (eds) (2005), *The Quest for Moral Leaders: Essays in Leadership Ethics*, Cheltenham, UK and Northampton, MA, USA: Edward Elgar.
Davies, Tony (1987), 'The ark in flames: science, language and education in

seventeenth-century England', in Andrew Benjamin, G. Cantor and J. Christie (eds), *The Figural and the Literal: Problems of Language in the History of Science and Philosophy, 1630–1800*, Manchester: Manchester University Press, pp. 83–102.

Derrida, Jacques (1977), *Of Grammatology*, translated by G. C. Spivak, Baltimore, MD: Johns Hopkins University Press.

Dewey, John (1981), *The Philosophy of John Dewey*, edited by J. McDermott, Chicago, IL: University of Chicago Press.

Gadamer, Hans-Georg (1992), *Truth and Method*, 2nd revised edn, translated by J. Weinsheimer and D. G. Marshall, New York: Crossroads.

Hobbes, Thomas (1998 [1651]), *Leviathan*, New York: Oxford University Press.

Locke, John (1997 [1690]), *An Essay Concerning Human Understanding*, edited by Roger S. Woolhouse, London: Penguin Classics.

Pearce, W. B. (1995), 'A sailing guide for social constructionists', in Wendy Leeds-Hurwitz (ed.), *Social Approaches to Communication*, New York: Guilford, pp. 88–113.

Penman, Robyn (2000), *Reconstructing Communicating: Looking to a Future*, Mahwah, NJ: Lawrence Erlbaum Associates.

Rorty, Richard (1980), *Philosophy and the Mirror of Nature*, Oxford: Blackwell.

Saul, J. R. (1992), *Voltaire's Bastards: The Dictatorship of Reason in the West*, London: Sinclair Stevenson.

Scott, James C. (1998), *Seeing Like a State: How Certain Schemes to Improve the Human Condition Have Failed*, New Haven, CT: Yale University Press.

Shotter, John (1993), *Cultural Politics of Everyday Life*, Toronto, ON: University of Toronto Press.

Stewart, John (1995), 'Philosophical features of social approaches to interpersonal communication', in Wendy Leeds-Hurwitz (ed.), *Social Approaches to Communication*, New York: Guilford, pp. 23–45.

Toulmin, Stephen (1990), *Cosmopolis: The Hidden Agenda of Modernity*, Chicago, IL: University of Chicago Press.

Wittgenstein, Ludwig (1953), *Philosophical Investigations*, Oxford: Blackwell.

13. Afterword: the promise of dissent for leaders

Stephen P. Banks

INTRODUCTION

This volume began with a quote from Lee Iacocca about the absence of leaders in contemporary politics and corporations. His observation seconds Margaret Wheatley's question: 'Where have all the leaders gone?' (Wheatley, 2005: 164; Warren Bennis asked the same question over a quarter century ago – see Bennis, 1973; 2001: 11). Both Iacocca and Wheatley stress the urgent need for new leadership, but they see different routes to 'finding our way', as Wheatley characterizes the quest for more humane and effective group processes. Iacocca looks to greater citizen participation in public life, more accountability among legislators, improved character among leaders and less passivity among followers. Wheatley breaks away from traditional concepts of the individual leader and envisions new processes and forms of organizing that embrace connectivity, sharing, apprenticing and transforming aggression into creativity.

The dissent-focused essays in this volume may be thought to mark a midpoint between the ambitions of changing the motives and morals of leaders and followers, as Iacocca would have us do, and changing human nature and forms of sociation, as Wheatley advocates. As such, learning to embrace dissent might be a transitional step toward realizing the kind of world Wheatley envisions and observes being practiced in limited instances, a necessary phase of improved interacting that ultimately makes the current concepts of leadership and followership obsolete.

WHAT DISSENT BRINGS TO LEADERS

It might take many generations to overcome cultural resistance to Wheatley's ideas of flattened hierarchies and leading by community. She notes that the Dalai Lama cautioned it might take 700 years (2005: 198). In the meantime, today's position-leaders need to stop ignoring, subverting or quashing dissent, for their own good and for the good of their stakeholders. As demonstrated in earlier chapters of this volume, the good from welcoming dissent is multifaceted and multilayered.

It is multifaceted in that dissent delivers several strategic benefits for leading. It enriches leaders' surveillance of important issues and trends. Dissenters often carry news of impending challenges from constituents, trends that will require changes of course, perspectives on political and economic situations at odds with the norm or tradition. Second, dissent can point out flaws of internal procedures, inherent inconsistencies of policy and action, and unwarranted political hoarding of power in institutions. This benefit by extension can help institutions and leaders avoid criticism and even prosecution. Third, dissent can be a tool for judging the quality of established practices and policies, providing new metrics by feedback, instead of by measurement, for marking excellence or adaptability that more fully represent best new practices beyond the traditional or normal ones. Finally, dissent can generate creativity by injecting into deliberations and projects innovative perspectives, contrarian thinking and alternative values.

Dissent is multilayered in that it has social and ethical implications for leading. To be open to dissent is to embody and enact trust and courage. One of the most powerful forces in almost all cultures is the norm of reciprocity: to show trust and courage is to invite trust and courage in return. When welcoming dissent into deliberations, leaders actively discard fear and control as tools. Second, embracing dissent underwrites the shift from authoritarian rule to maintaining people's democratic rights. Assertively protecting dissent as a democratic birthright is, as Cass Sunstein (2003) has argued, the surest way to avoid tyranny. Third, as vividly portrayed in earlier chapters, the suppression of dissent has devastating personal effects. Allowing dissent protects people from psychological abuse, promotes self-respect and strengthens positive identities. More to the point, going beyond merely allowing the facilitation of dissent enables position-leaders to interact with fully functioning agents who advocate their own ideas, values and efforts without fear.

HOW LEADERS CAN BRING IN DISSENT

The practical question is one of procedure. How does a position-leader break through the pervasive cultural expectation that all dissent is risky; that opposition is, well, oppositional; that dissent is not just a challenge to the conventional thinking but is a repudiation of the power structure? At the risk of being overly formulaic, here are four avenues to use for bringing in dissent.

First, recognize the benefits to sharing power. Less an action than a narrative to be told to oneself, this avenue suggests that position-leaders gain influence by losing control. Although it sounds paradoxical, consider the gains research tells us are obtainable by sharing control with others involved in making change, responding to crises or solving problems. Group members exercise their initiative and creativity with greater enthusiasm when they are free to do so. When given accountability, people are more likely to buy-in to programs of institutional change. Participation in decisions leads almost inevitably to greater commitment to implementation. Shared power generates gratitude and empathy. When power is dispersed within groups, the members tend toward self-regulation, which means external control, rewards and punishments can be relaxed. For position-leaders, it takes only reminding oneself, as if with a mantra: recognize the benefits to sharing power.

Second, optimize information quality. Again I turn to Bennis for inspiration. His iconic essay on the doppelganger effect (Bennis, 1973) argued that leaders who shut themselves off from diverse viewpoints and information court disaster. The management of dissent by employing doppelgangers is a passive form of suppression, because the presumed leader surrounds her- or himself with like-thinking and -behaving colleagues. The problem is not one of having too little information; if anything, there is too much information available to any position-leader. The problem is one of having low quality information, and the way to improve the quality of inputs is to make sure it comes from diverse sources. Bennis advocated intentionally associating with people of diverse backgrounds, attitudes and beliefs; we would go further and say it is necessary to seek out persons whose ideas and beliefs are contrary to those of the institution's leadership and reward their participation. Where Bennis ruled out collaborating or staffing assistant positions with 'devil's advocates', we see a necessity for ruling in their participation, within an expansive community of diverse voices.

Third, challenge ideas instead of persons. 'Nothing personal' goes the conventional wisdom for organizational leadership; decisions are to be made based on rational, objective criteria. But exercising control *is* personal, and challenges to power are interpreted as challenges to the person. Until power and control are dampened down or removed altogether from deliberations, the threat to and from dissent will be as much about persons as about ideas. To dampen down the power dimension of relationships, consider techniques used by mediators to construct a power-neutral setting. Remove identifiers of position and authority; arrange seating in figures that facilitate desired forms of interaction, like those identified by Wheatley's phases of problem-solving (2005: 185–8); rotate facilitating and fact-finding roles among participants; require equal distribution of time and contributions; and invent local procedures for specific problems or issues.

Fourth, reward opposition. As a paradoxical form of prescribing the symptom, the simple step of rewarding persons for dissenting transforms dissent into legitimate, constructive participation. Elevating complaint and suggestion programs into fully rewarded problem-oriented forums can generate those expansive communities of diverse voices. Inclusion is one form of reward, but compensations can be more substantive, such as opportunities to influence decisions and change policies and practices, earning positive publicity and even direct financial payoffs.

Ultimately, the embrace of dissent will change what is now called leadership. The more readily opposition, resistance and dissent are reframed as legitimate differences that must be engaged and deliberated jointly and equally, the less dissent management will be required of position-leaders. Instituting procedures and values that welcome civil disputation from all perspectives, experiences and goals will necessarily disperse control and power-in-use. In this sense, the elevation of dissent to being a necessary and equal partner to the established way of thinking and acting not only restores and strengthens democratic principles in the public sphere, but it also points to the end of leadership as it has been known from its origins through modernity.

REFERENCES

Bennis, Warren (1973), 'The doppelganger effect', *Newsweek*, 17 September, p. 13.

Bennis, Warren (2001), 'The future has no shelf life', in Warren Bennis, Gretchen M. Spreitzer and Thomas G. Cummings (eds), *The Future of Leadership: Today's Top Thinkers Speak to Tomorrow's Leaders*, San Francisco, CA: Jossey-Bass, pp. 3–13.

Sunstein, Cass (2003), *Why Societies Need Dissent*, Cambridge, MA: Harvard University Press.

Wheatley, Margaret (2005), *Finding Our Way: Leadership for an Uncertain Time*, San Francisco, CA: Berrett-Koehler Publishers.

Index

accountability
  bureaucratic 10
  and leadership *see* leadership
Adams, Scott 79

Barry, Bruce 183
Berger, Bruce 102
Bread and Roses (film) 185
Brown, Michael, and Hurricane
  Katrina 2
Burke, Kenneth 7, 10
Bush, President George W.
  and Hurricane Katrina 82
  and Iraq War 108, 196, 197
  public perception of leadership 39
  and September 11th attacks 188, 195
  style of leadership 4–6, 76
  and use of secret information 43

Campbell, Richard 215–16
Carter, President James, and Iranian
  hostages 38–39
CIA, and plausible deniability 6
civil liberties 200, 209
Clegg, Stewart 103–4
communication
  actions in context 221–22
  and dissent 217–23
  interpretation of 222–23
  openness in conversation 218–19
  poor practice based on fixed beliefs
    221
  and understanding 217–19, 223
Conger, Jay 7, 9
constructive ambiguity (Kissinger) 6
The Contrarian's Guide to Leadership 8
Council on the Status of Women 132
crises
  artificially created 38
  and authoritarianism 37–38, 40–43,
    46
  catastrophic thinking 84

dissent suppressed during 37–41
disturb leaders 37
effect on considered decision-
  making 48–49
effective dissent during 38
fight-flight thinking 84
and human needs of followers 37,
  40, 45–47
and individual freedoms 41–42
intimidation of dissenters 40–41
Iranian hostages 38–39
and leadership 38–39
manipulation of public by leaders 46
9/11 terrorist attack 39, 43, 81
opportunities for potential leaders
  39
and policymaking 37–38, 47–49
and pragmatic needs 46–47
promoting instability 38
pseudospecies 83–84
and secrecy 42–43
strategies for effective dissent during
  49–51
suppression of media 43–44
Cronin, Thomas 3

de Zengotita, Thomas 196–97
The Dilbert Principle 79
dissent
  as acquired behaviour 26
  acting in good faith 220–23
  advantages to society 34
  against gender stereotypes 129, 131
  against management goals 138
  against pressure to conform 33
  against tokenism 129–30
  as anathema to reason 212
  and anti-think 37
  arenas for dissenting 31–32
  behavioral 28–29
  by women *see* leadership
  certainty over dissent 211–13